Routledge Revivals

International Bond Markets

First published in 1990, *International Bond Markets* analyses how the markets in public-sector debt have developed and how they operate in a number of countries, including those with chronic budget deficits. Alongside a detailed introduction to government borrowing, chapters consider the markets and debt management systems of the U.S.A., Japan, France, Italy and the U.K. With governments around the world struggling to manage their huge deficits, this is a particularly relevant title to students observing the current global economic situation, and those with a general interest in public debt management and bond markets.

International Bond Markets

Edited by

D. H. Gowland

Routledge
Taylor & Francis Group

First published in 1990
by Routledge

This edition first published in 2013 by Routledge
2 Park Square, Milton Park, Abingdon, Oxon, OX14 4RN

Simultaneously published in the USA and Canada
by Routledge
711 Third Avenue, New York, NY 10017
Routledge is an imprint of the Taylor & Francis Group, an informa business

Publisher's Note
The publisher has gone to great lengths to ensure the quality of this reprint but points out that some imperfections in the original copies may be apparent.

Disclaimer
The publisher has made every effort to trace copyright holders and welcomes correspondence from those they have been unable to contact.

A Library of Congress record exists under LC control number: 90044714

ISBN 13: 978-0-415-85484-9 (hbk)
ISBN 13: 978-0-203-74092-7 (ebk)
ISBN 13: 978-0-415-85487-0 (pbk)

International bond markets

Edited by

D.H. Gowland

ROUTLEDGE

London and New York

First published 1990
by Routledge
11 New Fetter Lane, London EC4P 4EE
29 West 35th Street, New York, NY10001

Typeset in English Times
by Pat and Anne Murphy, Highcliffe-on-Sea, Dorset
Printed and bound in Great Britain by
Biddles Ltd, Guildford and King's Lynn

British Library Cataloguing in Publication Data
International bond markets.
1. Bond markets.
I. Gowland, David
332.6323

ISBN 0–415–03504–X

Library of Congress Cataloging in Publication Data
International bond markets/edited by D.H. Gowland.
p. cm.
Includes bibliographical references and index.
ISBN 0–415–03504–X
1. Government securities. 2. Bonds. I. Gowland, David.
HG4715.I58 1990 90-44714
332.63′2044–dc20 CIP

Contents

Figures

Tables

Contributors

David Gowland worked at the Bank of England 1971–3 and 10 Downing Street 1975–9. He has been Director of In-Service Courses and Lecturer in Economics at York since 1973. He is author of various books on monetary and international economics, including *Monetary Control in Theory and Practice* (Routledge, 1990) and *The Regulation of Financial Markets in the 1990's* (Edward Elgar, 1990).

Barrie Craven is a senior lecturer in the Business School at Newcastle-upon-Tyne Polytechnic. He has been a visiting scholar at Davis University, California.

David Cobham is a lecturer in Economics at St Andrews. He has published numerous books and articles on monetary economics, including *Macroeconomic Analysis* (Longman 1987). With Jean-Marie Searre he is involved in a major research project comparing British and French financial institutions.

Professor Giuseppe Mauro is the Professor of Money and Credit at the Gabriele D'Annunzio University at Pescara. He has written many books and articles, including *Mutamenti nel Sistema Finanziario e Considerazioni di Politica Monetaria* (University of Pescara Press).

M. Okuda is a senior official in the Tokyo office of Nomura. Stephen James is a lecturer at Teeside Polytechnic. He is the author of several articles on various aspects of economics.

Mervyn Lewis is Professor of Money and Banking at the University of Nottingham and a member of the Nottingham Institute of Financial Studies. He has written numerous articles and books, and is co-author of *Monetary Control in the United Kingdom* (1981) and joint editor of *Personal Financial Markets* (1986), both published by Philip Allan.

Kevin Davis is Professor of Finance at the University of Melbourne. His special interest in monetary economics is reflected in many articles on the subject, as well as in his joint authorship with Professor Lewis of *Monetary Policy in Australia* (1981) and *Australian Monetary Economics* (1981).

1 Introduction: government borrowing, debt management and bond markets

David Gowland

Governments frequently choose to borrow. In this they are no different from other categories of economic agent, whether corporations, institutions or members of the personal sector. In many cases the borrower may regard borrowing as an act of necessity rather than choice. However, according to the criteria used in economic analysis, any act of borrowing represents a choice since there is always an alternative, however unpleasant. Like private-sector borrowing, government borrowing has a very long history. The earliest known examples of government borrowing were by the Egyptian Pharaohs from the temple of Amon. Once either a member of the private sector or a government has decided to borrow it faces a number of options both concerning its initial borrowing and the consequences thereafter. Economists assume that both categories of borrower will make these decisions so as to advance their own interest as much as possible, or more formally so as to maximize their utility. This process is known as *debt management*.

Despite similarities between sovereign government and private-sector borrowing referred to above, there are a number of important differences between these two types of borrowing. The most fundamental decision that a sovereign borrower must take is whether or not to pay back the loan. In the case of a private-sector borrower this option is not available. A private-sector borrower would be subject to various sorts of legal action if he were to decide not to pay back his loan. At the very least there is a formal default mechanism established and enforced by law, involving bankruptcy statutes etc. On the contrary, a sovereign borrower is largely immune from legal redress. Default is not entirely costless. The aggrieved creditors or their governments may take various sorts of retaliatory action. Nevertheless default is an option open to sovereign borrowers in a way that it is not to private-sector borrowers. Moreover governments can choose whether to default totally or merely to repudiate part of their obligations – for example, to continue to pay the interest on a debt but not the principal. Governments can also use the threat of default to persuade their creditors to accept a reduction in principal or interest or some other rearrangement of the terms of a loan in a way favourable to the debtor. Of course this option is open to private-sector borrowers as well. Similarly sovereign, para-statal and private-sector borrowers may be able to buy back their debt at a discount on a secondary market.[1]

It may seem strange to refer to these possibilities in the case of the industrialized nations that are the subject of this book, viz. the USA, Japan, France, Australia, the UK and Italy. However, at least one prominent commentator has argued that default by the USA is inevitable in some form. Moreover, defaults by several of these countries are matters of relatively recent history. For example, the US authorities issued various securities whose interest and principal were tied to the price of gold. In 1934 President Roosevelt increased the price of gold but persuaded Congress to pass an act depriving these security holders of the additional payments to which they were entitled. This action, later upheld by the Supreme Court, amounted to a partial default on US Treasury securities. Very recently, in 1986, the sovereign governments that had established the International Tin Council allowed it to default on its very considerable debts.

Nevertheless it is unlikely that any of the six countries which are the focus of this book will choose formally to default on their debt in the near future. However, sovereign governments may choose to reduce the burden of repaying debt by more subtle means than formal default. They may choose to pursue policies which increase the price level and so reduce the real burden of paying back money-denominated debt. Alternatively they may depreciate their currencies so as to reduce the foreign-exchange burden of repaying foreign creditors with assets denominated in the native currency. When the loan is denominated in a foreign currency then revaluation of the currency may decrease the real burden of the debt. Obviously private-sector borrowers are also affected by inflation and changes in the exchange rate. However, for private-sector agents these variables are beyond their control. The most that the private-sector debtor can do is lobby or use the political system in some other way to try to achieve inflation – a goal, for example, of agrarian groups in the USA in the 1890s. At least to some extent inflation and exchange rates can be influenced by government policy. There is therefore a complex inter-relationship between debt management policy on the one hand and broader macro-economic policy aiming at exchange rate and inflation objectives on the other.

The most basic decisions which a private-sector borrower faces concern the rate of interest which he pays and the duration of his loan. These decisions can be analysed using a relatively well-developed theory of private-sector debt management. It is assumed that, *ceteris paribus*, the private-sector borrower would like to minimize the cost of borrowing. However, it is also assumed that he would like to borrow for as long a period as possible, i.e. the borrower is assumed to have positive liquidity preference. However it may be more costly to borrow for a long period than a short period. This may arise because of an upward sloping yield curve. Alternatively, it may be that borrowing for a longer period leaves the borrower with surplus cash to reinvest for some part of the period for which he has borrowed. As most economic agents can only lend at a lower rate than that at which they borrow then whilst simultaneously having both financial assets and liabilities increases liquidity it would then impose a cost. In fact many if not all borrowers do choose this option at least in the UK. Dow and Saville (1988, pp. 202–6) have demonstrated that this is the case for most companies. Anecdotal and impressionistic evidence suggests that personal-sector borrowers do likewise, for example, when taking out a mortgage they borrow more than their immediate needs. The liquidity gain from simultaneous borrowing and lending reinforces the gain from borrowing for as long as possible. Accordingly the theory of private-sector debt management assumes that borrowers trade-off the advantages of borrowing for a longer period against the costs, if any, involved in so doing. This choice is analysed using the conventional apparatus of micro-economic theory, indifference curves, budget lines and the like. An important analytical tool in such analysis is the debt service charge. Debt service charges are the sum of capital repayment and interest due in any one year. Hence if someone borrowed £100 due to be repaid in five equal instalments at an interest rate of 15 per cent then the debt service charge in the first year would be £35, £20 repayment plus £15 interest. Debt service charges are frequently used by lenders to ascertain the risk of a loan and the maximum loan they will grant. Companies may face a maximum of debt service to cash flow or profits. Individuals are often constrained to keep debt service below some percentage of income or 'free income'. Similarly sovereign debt service changes are often monitored as a percentage of exports or GDP.

Such neo-classical analysis of debt management is not irrelevant to the problem of sovereign government debt management. However a number of additional considerations apply. In brief, these apply because the terms on which a private-sector agent can borrow are largely exogenous. On the other hand a sovereign government borrower is to a significant extent able to influence the terms on which it borrows. Governments can fix the rate of interest at which they borrow, at least in the short term on borrowing from domestic sources. However, this is not a costless operation and in some cases the costs can be so high that the government has very little choice about what interest rate to pay. Nevertheless, some governments have endeavoured to choose and peg the rate of interest at a specific level for many years; for example Italy. Moreover, sovereign governments by definition can borrow in the very special and peculiar form of issuing currency. Using the criteria of private-sector debt management such borrowing is optimal; it is both interest-free and need never be repaid, or at least be repaid only by issuing further currency. The gain by such borrowing is normally called seignorage. Indeed some economists have constructed models in which governments seek to maximize this.[2] Clearly very few governments in the modern world seek to minimize debt service charges let alone to finance all of their borrowing by printing currency and putting it into circulation. Instead, debt management is used as an instrument to achieve wider economic goals.

Indeed in the past debt management has often been used as a tool of government policy for objectives having nothing to do with economic management. For example in Eighteenth-century Britain allocation of government securities was used on occasion as a form of government patronage. On many other occasions governments and those lending to them have used the lengthy borrower-lender relationship as an important means of cementing already-established relationships. The most systematic use of debt management as an integral part of political management was by the Whigs in late-seventeenth-century England, especially with the establishment of the Bank of England in 1694. Indeed their Tory opponents believed that the National Debt was created and expanded as a political act. Investors in government debt would be a powerful (Whig) interest group with a significant role in politics. Certainly this proved to be the case.[3] Moreover, fundholders (government creditors) had a vested interest in the Protestant succession since Jacobite restoration would probably lead to default. In the Eighteenth century, favourable allocations of government bonds to city financiers was allegedly a patronage tool.[4] On other occasions lending to a government has been a penalty rather than a favour. At least in the six countries considered in this book such use of debt management is now relatively rare. Nevertheless it is not entirely absent.

The monetary authorities of the countries analysed here make various use of debt management as an instrument of economic policy. In virtually all countries management of public-sector debt is used as a means of controlling short-term interest rates. In general the authorities seek to create an active market in short-term public sector paper. They intervene heavily in this market so as to manipulate the level and structure of short-term interest rates on government securities. They then rely upon substitution between this and other financial markets as a means of increasing their control over other short-term interest rates. In none of the six countries considered here is this the only means of influencing short-term interest rates. Nevertheless it is one of the more important means of controlling short-term interest rates in all of the countries except the UK. It is also possible to use similar techniques to manage long-term interest rates. This is done in Japan, Italy, France and to a limited extent in Australia.

Instead of using debt management to control interest rates the monetary authorities in the USA use it as a means to control the money supply. Given the reserve base system of monetary control in force in the USA, this means that the crucial question is whether a security is a reserve asset or not. Considering the definition of reserve asset, this means that the sale of any conventional security, including Treasury bills, to the banking sector reduces the volume of reserves. The sales of any securities to the non-bank private sector reduces the volume of potential reserve assets in the system. Hence the emphasis within the US system is on what is sold.

By contrast in the UK the emphasis was on the identity of the purchaser. From the adoption of the monetary targets in 1976 until 1985 debt management was one of the principal means of controlling the money supply in the UK. Given the 'supply-side counterpart' method of monetary control this meant that the money supply would be reduced if debt were sold to the non-bank private sector but not if it were purchased by the banking or overseas sector.[5] Since 1985 the object of debt management has been the less ambitious goal of ensuring that the public-sector contribution to monetary growth is zero, usually called exact funding. This is usually phrased as being to ensure that neither over-funding nor under-funding occurs, i.e. that sales of public sector debt to the non-bank private sector should be equal to the PSBR adjusted for public-sector transactions with the overseas sector. In 1988–9 a combination of a budget surplus and a balance of payment deficit led to large-scale repurchases of government stock by the authorities.

The above emphasis implicitly took the size of the budget deficit as given, and so the total of outstanding debt. The role of debt management was then to manipulate this given total in such a way as to ensure the objectives of government policy were pursued in an optimal fashion. Obviously the size of the budget deficit itself can also be an instrument of economic policy but this lies beyond the ambit of this book. More relevant, however, is the possibility that poor prospects for the sale of public-sector debt might constrain the size of the budget deficit. In principle this is impossible since any budget deficit can always be financed by money-creation. In practice, however, the cost of this might be so great that the authorities felt that a budget deficit was acceptable only so long as it could be funded by debt sales.

Originally all government debt was in non-marketable form, that is the holder could not transfer his claim to a third party. However at a relatively early date governments realized that it was mutually convenient to permit the sale of government claims from one party to another. The growth of active market in government obligations soon followed. For example, in Britain this market originally took the form of trading in tallies, the pieces of wood which represented a government obligation to pay for goods and services at some future date. These and other claims on the government became an important part of the money transmission mechanism. This was one of a large number of ways in which the exigencies of government finance proved a spur to financial development: in particular the first organized capital markets were markets in which government securities were traded, renes in Paris and government stock of various kinds in London. These markets represented the first active bond markets. Indeed they were among the earliest markets on which securities of any kind were traded. In both countries as later in the USA, the stock exchange originally emerged as an offspring of these bond markets. Recently bond markets have once more assumed an important role in the process of financial innovation. This is very marked in France and Italy. However it can also be observed in the UK with the reforms introduced in the gilt-edged market in 1986.

This is one of a number of issues explored by the authors of this book: the nature and extent of financial innovation in the various markets in public-sector debt in different countries. Sometimes, as often in the USA, innovation originates in the private sector (see p. 36–8). More often its driving force has been the monetary authorities who have almost universally both encouraged and adopted innovative techniques and instruments. In large part this has been a response to necessity in the shape of large public-sector deficits and the internationalization of bond markets. The need to finance a large budget deficit (or PSBR) has been a problem in Italy, in the USA in the 1980s, and the UK in the 1970s. The authorities need to sell as many securities as possible. Hence, as for anyone faced with a marketing problem, new instruments and techniques may be the answer to the problem of increasing sales. However, a more interesting reason for innovation by the monetary authorities has been the growing internationalization of bond markets in the 1980s. The Eurobond market in particular has been the driving force behind the integration of capital markets. The British, French and Australian authorities have faced a consequent dilemma. They wish to retain an independent segregated bond market in which their securities are traded under their supervision. In part this is *amour propre* and a chance to preserve jobs in the private sector rather than see them move to Luxemburg. Largely, though, the authorities need to keep such a market so as to execute monetary policy. However, internationalization threatens such independence.

Nearly all transactions in German government bonds now take place in London or Luxemburg. The German bond market is now a part of the Eurobond market and not a separate entity. With weaker currencies and problems of inflation, other (smaller) countries feel that they cannot let this happen. Hence, especially in the UK, the authorities have introduced innovation so as to ensure that international traders prefer to deal in the UK government bonds in London under Bank of England auspices rather than those set in Luxemburg outside their regulatory ambit. In France such a strategy is part of a wider plan to maintain an independent French capital market (see p. 82). The greatest single force behind the internationalization of capital markets is now the enormous weight of Japanese funds. Japan is now the only major net exporter of long-term capital in the world. Hence the fascination of the Japanese bond market. Developments in London, Rome, Sydney, Paris and even (or especially) New York may be caused by the decisions of Japanese investment houses on where to invest.

In short the object of this book is to describe how the markets in public-sector debt have developed and how they operate in a number of countries. These were selected so as to include both the main capital exporter (Japan) and countries with chronic budget deficits (Italy and the USA).

On country (Australia) was included because it undoubtedly is a small open economy to provide contrast with the two large (Japan and the USA) and three medium-sized economies. However, the underlying aim is to see how internationalization and innovation have occurred, if at all, in the various countries. Hence the need for countries with a dirigiste tradition and little historical involvement with international capital markets (Japan, Italy and France) to balance the three Anglo-Saxon countries. Has any convergence occurred or is it likely to? The answer, according to the authors of this book, seems to be 'No'.

NOTES

1 See Shepherdson (1989).
2 See Blanchard and Fisher (1989) pp. 195 ff. and Cargill (1989).
3 For a modern discussion of the Bank's involvement in Whig policies see De Krey (1985).
4 See the discussion in Namier (1957) pp. 53 ff. and Christie (1958) p. 184.
5 See Gowland (1991).

REFERENCES

Blanchard, O.J. and Fischer (1989) *Lectures on Macroeconomics*, Cambridge, Mass.: MIT Press.

Cargill, T.F. (1989) *Central Bank Independence and Regulatory Responsibilities*, New York: Saloman Brothers Centre for the Study of Financial Institutions.

Christie, I.R. (1958) *The End of North's Ministry*, London: Macmillan.

De Krey, G.S. (1985) *A Fractured Society*, Oxford: Oxford University Press.

Dow, J.C.R. an Saville, I.D. (1989) *A Critique of Monetary Policy*, Oxford: Oxford University Press.

Gowland, D.H. (1991) *Monetary Control in Theory and Practice*, London: Routledge.

Namier, L.B. (1957) *The Structure of Politics at the Accession of George III* (2nd Edition), London: Macmillan.

Shepherdson, I.C. (1989) 'The Secondary Market in LDC Debt', *Quarterly Review*, National Westminster Bank (November).

2 Debt management in the United States of America

Barrie Craven

BACKGROUND

The whole issue of the federal debt has seldom been off the economics centre stage in the United States in recent years. Not only is the size of the debt perceived to be a major concern but so also is the seeming inability to curb its growth. President Reagan came to office in 1980 promising to 'balance the budget' but ended his eight-year term by presiding over the biggest increases in the federal budget deficit in the history of the United States. The intractable nature of the deficit was considered to be a contributory factor to the stockmarket crash in October 1987. Since then little of substance has changed in ways which will help reduce the deficit. The Gramm-Rudman-Hollings statutory requirements to eliminate the deficit over a period of five years seem unlikely, by themselves, to be successful in reducing the actual deficit.[1] The resolution of the crisis of bankrupt Saving and Loans institutions, the S&Ls, which is expected to add in excess of $150 billion to the federal debt, is a good example of how vulnerable the planned federal income and expenditure programmes are to the random shocks delivered to the economy. Furthermore there is much concern about the external trade deficit. The US economy is at virtual full employment and there are fears that interest rates will eventually rise significantly in order to maintain overseas financing of the federal deficit. While this would probably induce a recession and hence reduce the propensity to consume imported goods it would also put additional pressure on the Social Security budgets and provide further problems for the new administration in tackling the federal budget deficit.

HISTORY OF THE FEDERAL DEBT

The history of the federal debt in the United States is very similar to the history of national debt in most industrialized countries. In other words the debt would rise dramatically during times of war and this, for the United States, is especially so with respect to the Second World War. In addition debt has tended to increase in the post-Second World War period – the age of Keynesian debt management.

In the United States the federal debt did not assume any significant proportions until the slump of the 1930s and even at the start of the Second World War the debt had a value of only $50 billion. By the end of the war, however, the debt had increased five-fold to $250 billion. Despite the Korean War and several severe recessions in the 1950s the debt had reached a modest figure of $300 billion in 1962. Only after this point does the size of the debt and its rate of increase begin to change. By 1972 the debt had risen nearly 50 per cent to $432 billion. This ten-year period had been characterized by rising inflation and the war in Vietnam.

During the next eight years to 1980 the debt more than doubled to $914 billion. These were the years of the successive oil crises, in 1974 and 1978, and high commodity prices – both of which contributed to record post-Second World War peacetime inflation. Between 1980 and 1985 the debt doubled again to just over $1,800 billion and by 1988 had reached $2,614 billion, or about $10,000 per man, woman and child.

Whether such a size of debt is a burden or a problem has long been debated by economists. There will only be a 'burden' in the sense that tax or other revenues will be required to pay the interest charges to holders of the debt. The general view among economists is that there will only be a problem if the debt is held by foreigners or if the debt is increasing faster than the growth rate of the economy. The present debt is certainly relatively small if it is compared to the size of the US GNP. At the end of the Second World War the debt as a proportion of GNP was 100 per cent, while in 1987 the proportion was about 52 per cent. Much of the post-Second World War increase in the nominal federal debt can be explained by inflation, but it is quite possible for a rising nominal value of the debt to be accompanied by a falling real value. Since 1980, however, there has been concern because the debt has been rising rapidly in real terms at a time of relatively stable prices, and debt interest currently accounts for over 13 per cent of total federal budget expenditures. Furthermore, if the debt, in real terms, is growing faster than the economy a long-term problem will

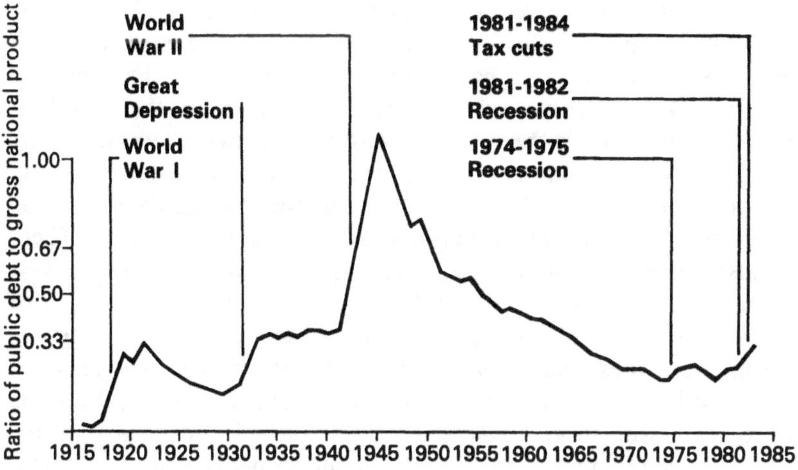

Figure 2.1 The ratio of public debt to Gross National Product
Source: Baumol and Blinder (1985)

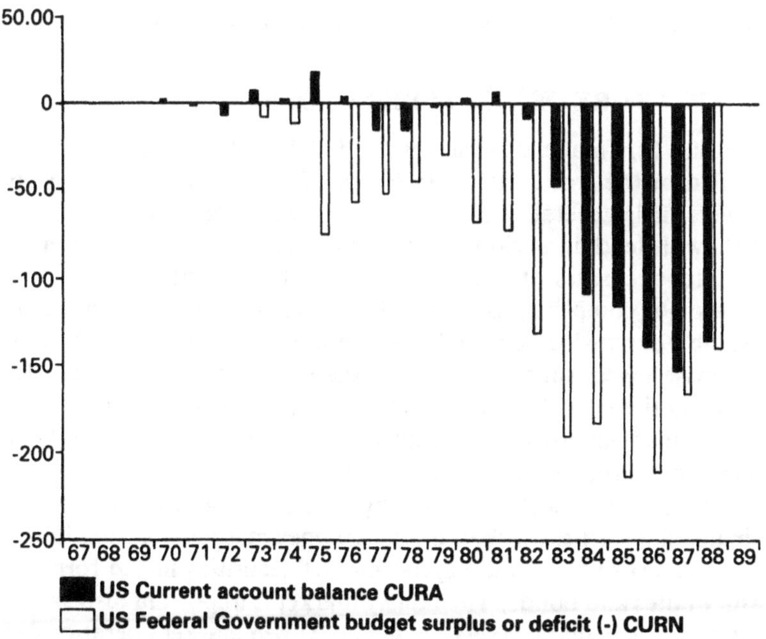

Figure 2.2 The federal and current-account deficits ($bn)
Source: Datastream

eventually emerge as the debt interest becomes a greater and greater consumer of federal revenues. In addition there are worries that the post-1980 increases in the debt will eventually have adverse effects on the general economy, especially concerning the trade balance and inflation. One of the most significant differences about the growth of the debt after 1980 is the proportion of it now owned overseas. The debt is no longer owed only to the people of the United States but also to foreign citizens. Much of the current increase in the debt has been financed by overseas investment and this will require servicing. There are also some 'off budget' items such as the eventual insurance pay-out to depositors in the bankrupt S&Ls. Fears about the strength of the commercial banks are growing too. Finally there are interest-bearing securities issued by non-government entities such as farm credit banks, the federal home loan banks and the Federal National Mortgage Association. Collectively these organizations have issued securities which amount in value to about 25 per cent of the federal debt. While these are not guaranteed by the government there would be immense political pressure for federal aid should financial difficulties arise. A good review of many of these issues is found in Buchanan (1987) and in the statement by Greenspan to the Deficit Commission, reprinted in the *Federal Reserve Bulletin* (January 1989).

THE STRUCTURE OF THE FEDERAL DEBT[2]

The market for financial securities in the US is the largest and most diversified in the world. It exists to transfer funds from lenders to borrowers. It is generally split into two broad categories: the capital market, with lending periods greater than one year; and the money market, for securities of less than one year to maturity. These categories are not completely separate. Borrowers can finance long-term projects by borrowing repeatedly in the money markets and lenders can likewise invest short term rather than buy long-term bonds. In recent years there has been a proliferation of innovations which have produced financial instruments which have some of the characteristics of both short-term and long-term securities.

The US Treasury is the largest single borrower and participant in the financial securities market. It issues money market securities in the form of Treasury bills, and capital market securities in the form of Treasury notes and bonds. The money market is important also as the medium for the Federal Reserve's (the Fed) open market operations – principally the buying and selling of government securities to determine the amount of reserves available to the banking system. The

Table 2.1 Summary of federal debt, 1988 ($bn)

			Total federal debt 2,614.6				
Agency securities 12.4	Public debt securities 2,602.2						
	Non-interest-bearing	2.3	Interest-bearing 2,599.9				
			Non-marketable 797.0 comprising:			Marketable 1,802.9 comprising:	
			US Savings Bonds	106.1		Treasury bills	398.4
			Government Foreign Series	6.3		Treasury notes	1,089.6
			Government Account Series	536.4		Treasury bonds	299.9
			State and Local Government	147.6		Other	15.0
			Other	0.4			

Source: Treasury Bulletin, December 1988

federal debt is '. . . overwhelmingly short-term in nature. In 1984 over 40 per cent of interest bearing public debt securities had only one year or less to maturity and during the mid-1970s this number was over 50 per cent (Hoelscher 1986). The debt is also overwhelmingly interest-bearing.

In 1988 out of a total federal debt of $2,614.6 billion (see Table 2.1), public debt securities amounted to $2,602.2 billion and $12.4 billion were Agency Securities. Until 1988 these were mainly issued by the Tennessee Valley Authority and the Government National Mortgage Association to the extent of about $4 billion. However, in 1988 the problems of the S&Ls had resulted in additional securities, of $10.6 billion being issued. Interest-bearing public debt amounted to $2,599.8 billion, of which $1,802.9 billion was marketable and $796.9 billion non-marketable. Non-interest bearing debt consists of notes and coin issued by the US Treasury Department. Marketable federal debt consists of Treasury bills, Treasury notes and Treasury bonds. Non-marketable debt consists of the government account series held almost entirely by US government agencies, state and local government series, savings notes and bonds, and foreign issues. It also includes securities issued to the Rural Electrification Administration: depository bonds, retirement plan bonds and individual retirement bonds. In recent years between 70 per cent and 80 per cent of gross federal debt has consisted of the marketable type although in the past it has been much lower – 59 per cent in 1951.[3]

Table 2.2 Proportions of federal debt securities held privately, Sept. 1988

	$bn	*%*
Total privately held	1819.0	—
Commercial banks	203.0	11.1
Individuals	179.8	9.9
Insurance companies	135.0	7.4
Money market funds	10.8	0.6
Corporations	86.6	4.2
State and local governments	287.0	15.8
Foreign and international	334.3	18.4
Other investors	583.1	32.0

Source: Treasury Bulletin, December 1988

Apart from the federal debt just described there is another source of borrowing, the government-sponsored entities, which are authorized to administer lending programmes to areas, social and economic, which, are deemed to attract insufficient funds from the market. These government-sponsored entities are not agencies of the federal government, nor are their securities guaranteed by the federal government. Many of the programmes they offer are directed by the federal government but they are owned by the private sector and their growth and borrowing directly in the financial markets is not subject to the control of Congress. In terms of interest bearing securities the most important of these agencies in 1987 were farm credit banks ($53.2 billion); federal home loan banks ($329.3 billion); the Federal National Mortgage Association ($223.1 billion) and the Student Loan Marketing Association ($13.6 billion).

These government-sponsored entities give help to the housebuilding and mortgage markets and in addition aid agriculture and farming. Although this debt is not guaranteed by the government the securities are viewed by the public 'as if' it is. Some observers have suggested that their securities are in effect an 'off budget' potential federal debt liability.

The debt instruments

As mentioned earlier marketable debt consists of bills, notes and bonds. Table 2.3 shows that the volume of Treasury bills outstanding has risen steadily over the period and until 1975 was an increasing proportion of the total marketable public debt. Since that date, however, this proportion has been decreasing because of a much faster growing Treasury deficit which has been funded more by the issue of marketable notes and bonds. Table 2.3 shows also the size of the Treasury bill market as a proportion of total interest-bearing marketable debt. The figures for the maturity structure of the marketable federal debt published by the Federal Reserve Bulletin were discontinued in 1982. It is possible, however, to show the maturity structure of marketable debt held privately. Private holdings of marketable debt accounted for 86 per cent of total marketable debt in 1988. Of this privately held marketable debt, 34 per cent was due to mature within one year.

The maturity structure of privately held marketable public debt has shown some change over the period since 1950. Until 1975 the life of marketable debt privately held was becoming shorter in structure, with a steady fall in the proportion of securities with lives of more than ten years. Since 1975 the average length of the debt has been increasing because of the increased prominence of Treasury notes in marketable debt. Changes in the maturity structure of the debt have implications for the operation of monetary policy. A shortening maturity structure implies that as more and more securities mature so the Treasury must become more and more active in the market as it

Table 2.3 Total marketable public debt

End of year	*Total marketable public debt $bn*	*Volume of bills outstanding*		*Volume of notes*		*Volume of bonds*		*Average length of marketable debt*[2] *(yrs)*
		$bn	*% MPD*	*$bn*	*% MPD*	*$bn*	*% MPD*	
1960	189.0[1]	32.4	20.8	51.3	27.0	79.8	42.2	4.8
1965	214.6	60.2	28.1	50.2	23.4	104.2	48.6	5.4
1970	247.7	87.9	35.5	101.2	40.9	58.6	23.4	3.5
1975	363.2	157.5	43.4	167.1	46.0	38.6	10.6	2.5
1980	623.2	216.1	34.7	321.6	51.6	85.4	13.7	3.8
1985	1437.7	399.9	27.8	812.5	56.5	211.1	14.7	5.0
1988	1802.9	398.4	22.1	1089.5	60.4	299.9	16.6	5.7

Sources: Federal Reserve Bulletin, various issues
Treasury Bulletin, December 1988

Notes: 1 In 1960 Certificates, of value $18.4bn were issued.
2 Held privately.

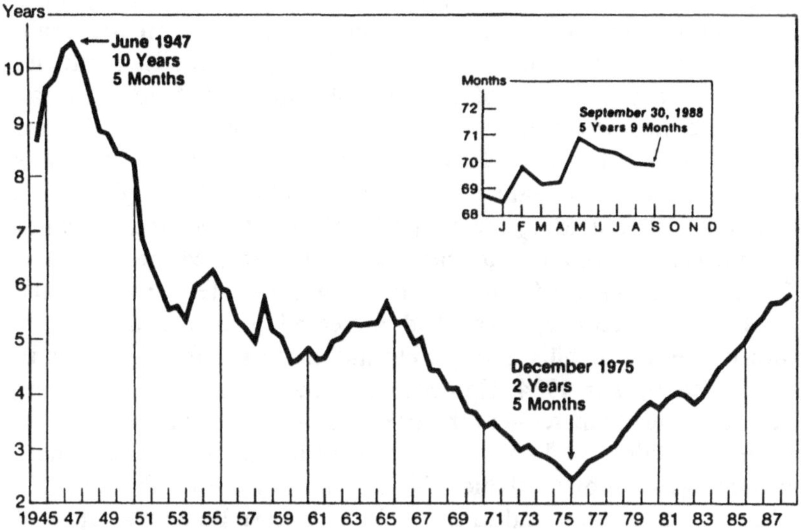

Figure 2.3 Average length of the marketable debt, privately held
Source: Treasury Bulletin, December 1988

redeems and issues new debt. If an objective of monetary policy is to attempt to restrict credit by the usual means of increasing the rate of interest, then the falling security prices that will accompany this strategy will make new security sales more difficult, or else limit the ability of the Fed to operate monetary policy – the standard 'debt management' problem. In addition if the debt is monetized then the reserves of the banking system are increased. This has given cause for concern to some economists who feel that it is not without significance that there is a recent correlation between a shortening debt structure and inflation.

The subsequent lengthening of the debt after 1975 may well have had its financing, in part, facilitated by an increase in demand for Treasury securities from overseas. These aspects of demand for US Treasury securities are delt with, in detail, later in the chapter.

Treasury bills

These were first issued in 1929 and are direct obligations of the US government. They have a maximum maturity of one year and are issued at a 360-day discount price without a coupon in minimum amounts of $10,000 and multiples of $5,000. The discount rate on a Treasury bill is not directly comparable with those of Treasury notes and bonds because of the 360-day discount price.[4] There are four main characteristics of Treasury bills which make them attractive to private investors. They are: lack of default risk, liquidity, favourable tax status (the income earned on Treasury bills is exempt from all state and local income taxes), and low minimum denomination. This last is certainly a distinctive feature of US Treasury bills. Although there is no default risk in holding Treasury bills, their riskiness would seem to have increased during recent years. Cox (1985) studied the behaviour of Treasury securities from 1942 through 1984. He found that the variability of security prices had increased greatly and that the maturity period of bills outstanding had increased from 45 days in 1942 to 109 days in 1984. He concluded that, over the period, there had been a steady increase in the riskiness of Treasury bills.

Treasury bills are held by a wide range of investors but specific data on holdings are not available. The closest estimate of Treasury bill holdings used to be found in the Federal Reserve Bulletin's 'Flow of Funds Accounts', which contained, until recently, information on the holdings of securities of less than one year maturity which are dominated by Treasury bills. The last estimate in 1979 suggested that the main holders of such securities were foreigners (14.5 per cent), the Fed (23.7 per cent), households (29.8 per cent), commercial banks (14.0 per cent), state and local governments (8.6 per cent), and private non-bank financial institutions (9.3 per cent). The information is no longer published in this form and unfortunately there is no alternative source of this data. The series was originally based on estimates made by the staff constructing the Flow of Funds tables in the Bulletin. The suspicion must be that these estimates were not accurate enough to justify continuing the series. The series did show, however, that individual holdings of Treasury bills became substantial especially after the mid-1960s. The extent to which these holdings have varied seems to be explained by the opportunity cost of holding alternative substitutable assets. Until the Depository Institutions Deregulation Act of 1980 (which included the phasing out deposit rates restrictions) federally insured institutions were subject to Regulation Q, which placed an interest rate ceiling on their deposits. Hence when yields on Treasury bills rose above this ceiling, private holdings increased. In the 1970s Regulation Q was changed to allow member institutions to issue six-month money market certificates tied to the prevailing equivalent Treasury bill rate. In addition the growth of money market mutual funds offered a similar investment opportunity (for small amounts $1,000–$5,000) which allowed investors to achieve current money market rates and hence bypass Regulation Q. (Throughout the 1970s Regulation Q gradually became unworkable and would now in practice be ineffective.)

The continued strength of household holdings seems to be explained by the tax advantages offered with Treasury bill ownership. An indication of the extent of individual activity in the Treasury bill market is usually the proportion of bills allocated to the non-competitive tender at the weekly auctions. The Fed holds around one-quarter of Treasury bills, which is about one-half of its holdings of Treasury securities, and by the buying and selling of bills either directly in the market or through a repurchase agreement is able to affect the reserve position of member banks.

Treasury notes

These have maturities of between one and ten years. They are default-free and exempt from state and local income tax. New issues of two-year notes are issued every two months, while three-, seven- and ten-year notes are issued every quarter. The price and coupon, which is fixed-interest and payable semi-annually, are usually determined at a competitive auction on a yield basis. The market participants are banks, dealers, institutions and, less significantly, individuals. Bids can be made directly to the Federal Reserve Bank or indirectly through a brokerage house or bank. Notes are issued in minimum denominations of $1,000 to $10,000. Kemp (1984) considers the daily trading volume for notes and bonds to be in the range of $40–50 billion. As with Treasury bills a twenty-four-hour secondary market exists.

Treasury bonds

The US government bond market is the largest fixed-rate market in the world. Bonds generally have issue maturities of more than ten years and can have a call option allowing Treasury redemption with four months notice. Ten- to thirty-year bonds are issued every quarter. The primary market participants are (as for notes) banks, dealers, institutions and some individuals. Bonds are issued in minimum denominations ranging $5,000 to $10,000 (although sometimes up to $50,000). The most common minimum denomination for both notes and bonds is $5,000.

Although both notes and bonds have a fixed-interest coupon payable semi-annually, the maximum rate payable on bonds is restricted under federal law to 4.25 per cent. This makes such bonds a more risky investment proposition because their long maturities subject them to considerable price fluctuations. It is therefore hardly surprising that over the period 1960–80, when general rates of interest were often in excess of 4.25 per cent and inflation rates were relatively high, that the proportion of bonds in total marketable debt fell steadily. During periods of relatively low inflation and interest rates – the mid-1980s for example – the attractiveness of bonds has increased. The 4.25 per cent restriction remains, but can be lifted with the dispensation of Congress. For example, during the 1988 August Quarterly Financing the Treasury announced that a thirty-year bond would not be offered. This resulted from the continued inaction by Congress on the Treasury's request to eliminate the $270 billion limitations on bonds with a coupon rate of more than 4.25 per cent that could be held by the public.

ISSUE PROCEDURES: MARKET MAKERS AND AUCTIONS

The purchase of a substantial proportion of new Treasury securities is by a group known as *primary* or 'recognized' dealers who then make a secondary market (although individuals may purchase by applying directly to the Fed). By the beginning of 1989 there were forty-four primary dealers. Of these about fourteen were departments of commercial banks and the rest were non-bank dealers. Thirteen of the dealers are overseas companies. In 1986 two Japanese firms, Nomura Securities Co. and Daiwa Securities, were awarded the status of primary dealer and during the first 1987 quarterly auction bought more than 10 per cent of the entire Treasury issue. Subsequently, in 1987, Nikko Securities International was awarded primary dealership. The primary dealers are approved by the Fed after conducting a range of financial tasks satisfactorily for a period of time. The status of primary dealer allows the possibility of regular contact with the dealing desk of the Fed and it is alleged to be favourable when attempting to attract new business because some institutions feel more comfortable dealing directly with the Fed. In 1987 the main point of interest concerned the future access of new overseas dealers and this was deemed to depend upon reciprocal access to other national financial markets.[5] However, following the stockmarket crash in October 1987, the market has been characterized by much reduced volume and it is now over-supplied. In addition, in November 1988, the New York Fed raised the minimum capital level required from primary dealers. As a consequence of both changes the alleged status from primary dealer membership seems to be much less valued. In January 1989 County Natwest and L.F. Rothschild withdrew as primary dealers. It has been rumoured that only half the primary dealers made a profit in 1988.

The primary dealers usually charge fees of between $25 and $40 per transaction although there would be no charge for transactions over $250,000. The narrow bid-asked spread, often as low as 2–4 basis points (hundredths of one per cent) or $50–100 per million dollars, of the most actively traded Treasury bills is indicative of a secondary market which is highly efficient. An 'efficient market' also refers to a market where there is either 'weak form' efficiency, whereby security prices fully reflect all historical relevant information, 'semi-strong form', where security prices fully reflect all publicly available relevant information, or 'strong form', where security prices reflect fully all that is knowable and relevant to the pricing of the securities (Allen 1983). It is generally considered that the large auction markets for US Treasury securities are, in both senses, as efficient as markets can be.

The government securities dealers provide three main types of service. As part of their market making function they provide information, analysis and advice to encourage consumer loyalty. They maintain stocks of government securities financed with loans but mainly with repurchase agreements (repos or RPs).[6] These are the acquisitions 'of immediately available funds through the sale of securities with a simultaneous commitment to repurchase the same securities on a date certain within one year at a specified price, which includes interest or its equivalent at an agreed upon rate' (Lumpkin 1986).

The Fed is a strong participant in the repo market, which it uses to implement open market operations. The dealers repo securities to the Fed when it wishes to inject reserves and reverse repo funds to the Fed when it wishes to absorb reserves. Generally it is the institution supplying the securities which makes a repurchase agreement. The institution receiving the securities makes a reverse repo.

The primary dealers also purchase bills for themselves and their clients, who are usually institutional investors, commercial banks, trust departments, foreign investors and individuals. The dealers trade actively (see Table 2.4) with each other through about a half-dozen interdealer brokers specializing in Treasury securities. These brokers post, on behalf of the dealers, anonymous bids and offers on issues they wish to trade. The market is decentralized, with most trading by telephone. The provision of electronic screen facilitates anonymity and the potential establishment of a twenty-four-hour world-wide market.

The daily trading volume in Treasury securities in October 1988 by the primary dealers was about $110 billion, of which about $30 billion was in Treasury bills. The main customers of the dealers are the US government securities brokers – about $65 billion of transactions in October 1988.

Table 2.4 Positions and sources of financing for US government security dealers

Averages of daily figures expressed in $m at par	*1982*	*1984*	*1986*	*1988 (Oct)*
Positions:				
US government securities				
Bills	4837	5504	12761	4064
Other securities				
within 1 year	(199)	63	3706	(5438)
1–5 year issues	3256	2159	9146	855
5–10	(318)	(1119)	(9505)	(11191)
over 10 years	2026	(1174)	(3197)	(13615)
Futures positions:				
Bills	(2507)	(4525)	(18059)	(4385)
Treasury coupons	(2303)	1794	3473	6532
Forward positions:				
US Treasury securities	(788)	(1643)	(2144)	(969)
Sources of dealer financing				
Reverse RPs:				
Overnight and continuing	26754	44078	98954	149450
Term	48247	68357	108693	193290
RPs:				
Overnight and continuing	49695	75717	141735	189508
Term	43410	57047	102640	145288

Source: Federal Reserve Bulletin, various issues

The dealers attempt to manage their affairs with a view to profiting from changes in interest rates and security prices. Meek (1982) states that profits are generally made by financing an outright position during recession when interest rates decline. Losses are incurred when interest rates move randomly or persistently upwards: 'it is difficult to maintain the effective markets customers expect with a sizeable net short position'. Government securities dealers take positions in the market where their liability as a ratio of equity may be as high as fifty for a non-bank dealer expecting a fall in interest rates. 'A one per cent rise in the price of securities held in such a situation would increase the dealer's capital by 50 per cent; a similar drop would wipe out half the present capital.' (Meek 1982) The positions of the government securities dealers in the market are significant and subject to substantial fluctuation. Table 2.4 shows net positions change rapidly.

It is noticeable how immediate positions in Treasury bills rose from 1984 to 1986 while at the same time dealers were taking increasingly short positions on five-ten-year issues. This seems to reflect the changing expectations of the participants concerning the state of the market in the future. If short-term interest rates are expected to fall, then a long position is called for in such securities enabling capital gains to be made. Alternatively, if long-term interest rates are expected to rise then a short position in long-term securities is appropriate. Table 2.4 also shows the sources of finance being repurchases, advances (from commercial banks) and the importance of futures and forward positions – obligations to supply securities in the future. Large corporations will use the dealer loan market to place short-term excess funds. Futures and forward positions are especially important when the Fed is pursuing a monetary policy which necessitates free movement of interest rates and security prices as occurred between October 1979 and autumn 1982.

The secondary market is organized and supervised by the primary dealers (who are in turn supervised by the Fed). It is not known exactly how many bank and non-bank 'secondary' dealers in government securities there are, but it is estimated to be between 350 and 450. In this market the dealing fees are included in the difference between the bid-offer prices. There are considerable risks involved in secondary market trading and the failure in 1982, for example, of Drysdale Government Securities raised the question of whether the level of dealer regulation is appropriate – an issue which is dealt with later in the chapter.

The auctions for Treasury securities

All new issues of Treasury bills, notes and bonds are auctioned. Bills of one-year maturity are generally auctioned monthly and three- and six-month bills are auctioned weekly. The amount of the weekly offerings, of three-and six-month bills, are announced on Tuesdays. The auction is held the following Monday and delivery and payment required the following Thursday. The monthly auctions, for one-year bills, are held every fourth Thursday for issue one week later. In addition there are irregular issues of 'cash management' bills with the purpose of smoothing seasonal Treasury flows especially between Federal tax dates.

In general the bid-asked spread on Treasury bills is greater when there is increased interest rate volatility. Prior to 1979 and after 1982 the spread was only about 2 basis points, but between that date and 1982, when greater emphasis was placed by the Fed on rationing reserves by price the spread increased to about ten basis points. For example the details of the 15 September 1988 auction for the three-month Treasury bills are given in Table 2.5. Applications for the securities are initially made to the Federal Reserve Banks. The Treasury first allocates bills to foreign official institutions and rolls over the maturing issues of the Fed. Auction bids may be non-competitive or competitive. The noncompetitive bids are first removed from the total on offer and the remainder are auctioned.

Table 2.5 Details of 15 September 1988 auction for three-month Treasury bills

Offering of bills (91-day maturity issue)	
Amount of bids tendered	$29.50bn
Amounts of bids accepted	$7.04bn
competitive basis	$5.96bn
noncompetitive basis	$1.08bn
Average price per hundred	98.177
Average discount rate	7.21%
On competitive bids accepted:	
(High discount rate 7.22%)	Price per hundred 98.175
(Low discount rate 7.20%)	Price per hundred 98.180

Source: US Treasury Bulletin, December 1988

A competitive tender occurs when a subscriber applies at a specific price for a specific allotment of bills. Each bidder may make multiple applications at different prices. Competitive bidding is dominated by institutional investors and the bidding is very aggressive. The bids are arranged in decreasing price order and are then allocated at the bidded prices to the bidders with the highest price and the remainder to the bidders with the second highest price and so on until either all bills are allotted or the 'stop-out price', which represents the lowest price the Treasury is prepared to accept, is reached.

A noncompetitive bid is one made, generally, by a small investor who agrees to accept the average issuing price set in the auction. The investor pays the par price with the tender and then on issue day receives a refund from the Treasury representing the average discount established at the auction. Noncompetitive tenders are usually for amounts less than $500,000 and allow the small investor to partake in the market while minimizing risk. The Treasury does attempt to accommodate all noncompetitive tenders, which have accounted in recent years for a range of 10–25 per cent of the total auction. The noncompetitive bids seem to increase when interest rates are relatively high (Cook & Rowe 1986).

The prices of Treasury notes and their coupons, which are fixed interest and payable semi-annually, are usually determined at a competitive auction on a yield basis. Such 'yield auctions' differ from the 'price auction' method used occasionally for the sale of notes and bonds (whereby the Treasury sets in advance the amount on offer, the coupon rate and the minimum price it will accept). At a yield auction the Treasury does not set either the price or the coupon of the security but merely announces the amount available. Those bidding for the notes (and bonds) express offers on an annual percentage yield basis accurate to two decimal places. The securities are first allocated to the noncompetitive bidders and then to the competitive bidders from the lowest yield (highest price) upwards until the issue is exhausted. As with the competitive auctions for Treasury bills the successful applicants pay the bidded price. The process is described fully in Rose (1986). The minimum denomination for both notes and bonds is $5,000.

Treasury bonds are auctioned by yield, as with notes, and occasionally a 'uniform price' or 'Dutch auction' is adopted. In this case, after the noncompetitive bids have been allocated the Treasury deals with the competitive bids by allocating the stock first to the highest bidder and then on down until the issue is exhausted. The price paid, however, by all investors is the lowest accepted competitive bid.

Like the UK system, where the Treasury bill issue is underwritten by discount houses 'covering the tender', new Treasury bond issues in the US are also underwritten by the primary dealers. However there is pre-issue consultation between the officials of the Treasury, Federal Reserve and government securities dealers to judge the market strength at the auctions. Unlike the UK system, where bonds can be issued 'on tap', new US Treasury issues are issued discretely and directly to the investing public.

TREASURY SECURITIES MARKETS AND REGULATION

An issue of concern during the 1980s has been whether there should be a greater degree of regulation in the market. The problem arises because the regulations of the Fed and the Federal Deposit Insurance Corporation (FDIC) apply to institutions identified as banks (King 1985). The dealers trading in Treasury securities are not classified as banks, so while they do not come under the general Fed and FDIC regulations they do come under the jurisdiction of the Securities Exchange Commission (SEC). The SEC is a semi-government agency with legal powers. It 'regulates' by attempting to prevent insider trading and the conflicts of interest within firms (who both advise customers and trade their securities) which can lead to breaches of 'Chinese walls' where people in various parts of the same firm are forbidden to talk to one another. The SEC does not concern itself with, for example, whether a firm is under-capitalized.[7] Furthermore, the problems of regulation are complicated by legal uncertainties.

During the 1980s there were several failures of firms dealing in government securities. Lombard-wall Inc. and Drysdale Securities failed in 1982, RTD Securities and Lion Capital Group failed in 1984 and ESM Government Securities and Bevill, Bresler & Schulman Asset Management Corporation failed in 1985.

The failure of Drysdale Government Securities in 1982 symbolizes the problem. Drysdale was capitalized at $20 million and was unregulated and unaffected by the SEC's capital requirement which limits the extent to which brokerage houses, for example, can take speculative positions. The trading of Drysdale Government Securities, as with all dealers in government securities, was based on repurchase agreements. With such agreements there was uncertainty regarding the legal identification of principal and agent. This may have helped trade to continue for a longer time than would have been prudent had the legal uncertainty not existed.

What differentiated Drysdale's approach was its tactics. When government notes and bonds are used in repos they were priced 'flat', that is, without any accrued interest from the date of the last semi-annual coupon payment. This is a practice which originated with the Fed in its repo dealings when interest rates were much lower and the calculation of the accrued interest did not seem worthwhile. Securities which had five months accrued interest would be bought 'flat' by Drysdale (they were eventually known as 'Drysdale issues') in a repo deal and then sold outright in order to realize the accrued interest. Drysdale's bids at auctions were so large that they occasionally forced out the primary dealers. It was estimated that a bid from them of, say, $400 million at an issue of $4 billion gave the company the whole of the issue after account is taken of the Fed, foreigners, individuals and others who did not lend securities. 'To unwind his reverses when they became due, to forward interest when it was paid to the ultimate owners of securities in reverses when they became due, to forward interest when it was paid to the ultimate owners of the securities in reverses that remained open, as he was required to do, and to cover his growing losses, he kept having to arrange an even larger series of reverses and short sales to generate new infusions of artificial capital' (Welles 1982). The practice was not regarded by most traders as being financially respectable!

Eventually matters came to a head. Chase Manhattan Bank had borrowed Treasury securities on behalf of Drysdale from leading government bond dealers. Drysdale had subsequently financed a long position of $2.4 billion by selling the securities to Chase of cash while agreeing to buy them back at a later date. Drysdale was nonetheless, obliged to pay accruing interest to the government bond dealers in the meantime. On 17 May 1982 Drysdale announced that it could not pay $160 million in accrued interest. The resoluton of ownership of the securities became a pressing issue. Chase eventually conceded that it was liable to the government bond dealers and announced a $135 million write-off in the second quarter. Repos were subsequently priced with accrued interest included in full in the purchase price.

Examples of bond trading malpractices are not limited to small traders such as Drysdale. On 29 April 1987 Merrill Lynch announced a loss of $250 million – double its quarterly net profits – from unauthorized positions in the mortgage-backed securities market just before the collapse of bond prices. Merrill Lynch disclosed two days later that another trader had taken unauthorized positions in Texaco bonds just before the company filed for Chapter 11 bankruptcy.

The Drysdale affair raised the issue of the perennial banking conflict that arises between macro-economic stability and micro-economic efficiency in a fully competitive minimally restricted banking system when substantial spillover costs result from failure (Hirsch 1977). It is important to remember that the global market is also unregulated and many different kinds of security have appeared which might have been brought to the attention of the authorities in a domestic market.[8]

If an insurance system is offered, such as FDIC, then the problems of 'moral hazard' and 'adverse selection' arise.[9] Without insurance the costs of regulating effectively the non-bank security dealers may be prohibitive. The evidence of the rises in share prices in the US prior to the announcement of a take-over bid and the revelations concerning Ivan Boesky, the Wall Street financier, and Nahum Vaskevitch of Merril Lynch, accused by the SEC of insider trading, demonstrate the difficulty of the latter approach.

TREASURY SECURITIES AND THE FEDERAL RESERVE SYSTEM

The central bank of the USA is the Federal Reserve System. Its responsibilities include the maintenance of a stable, secure and efficient banking system, and the implementation of monetary policy consistent with the desired macro-economic objectives.

In order to discharge these responsibilities the Fed is required to intervene substantially in the market for Treasury securities. The Fed relies, in the main, upon the work of the Federal Open Market Committee (FOMC). This committee consists of twelve voting members, five reserve bank presidents and the seven Fed governors appointed by the President. The committee, which meets eight times a year, instructs the Federal Reserve Bank of New York how to conduct the most frequently used instrument of monetary policy-open market operations. These refer to the sale and purchase by the Fed of Treasury and Agency securities. All new purchases must be made on the secondary market – the trading desk cannot bid for new Treasury issues that are sold for cash. Such transactions alter the reserves of the banking system and therefore ease or tighten the availability of credit. An excellent comprehensive picture of open market operations is contained in Meek (1982).

There are two main types of open market operation. The first, outright transactions, is used by the Fed when it wishes to provide or absorb reserves over relatively long time spans. The second, temporary transactions, is used when changes in reserves are required for relatively short periods of, usually, less than two weeks. An indication of the relative dominance of temporary transactions is shown in Table 2.6.

The Federal Reserve Bulletin publishes figures monthly which demonstrate the importance of Treasury bills in open market operations. 'Most of the System's outright transactions, whether in the dealer market or directly with foreign official accounts, take place in Treasury bills. From time to time the system extends its purchases beyond Treasury bills to include intermediate- and long-term US government securities and Federal Agency issues, but in recent years it has not had occasion to sell such issues' (Board of Governors of the Federal Reserve System 1984a). In 1985, of $26.45 billion gross outright Fed open market purchases, $22.21 billion (84 per cent) were Treasury bills. Of $4.22 billion of outright sales, $4.12 billion (98 per cent) were Treasury bills. Most of the temporary transactions are also conducted in Treasury bills.

Table 2.6 Volume of open market operations ($bn)

	1978	*1979*	*1980*	*1981*	*1982*	*1983*	*1984*	*1985*
Outright transactions								
Purchases								
in market	15.0	7.1	8.5	8.8	10.5	10.7	14.1	17.1
foreign account	9.9	14.1	4.4	8.4	9.4	11.8	9.7	9.4
Sales								
in market	0.2	2.3	2.8	2.6	1.5	0	1.1	1.5
foreign accounts	13.7	5.6	4.5	4.1	7.1	3.4	7.6	2.7
Redemptions	2.3	3.0	3.5	1.9	3.2	2.8	8.0	3.7
Total outright	41.1	32.1	23.7	25.8	31.7	28.7	40.5	34.4
Temporary transactions								
Repurchase agreements								
System	221.5	185.8	167.2	110.9	179.1	124.0	144.8	156.4
Customer-related	47.3	53.0	64.3	79.5	89.1	159.9	126.7	116.7
Matched sale/purchases in market	140.2	194.6	138.6	78.4	42.0	11.9	55.0	36.6
Total temporary	409.0	433.1	370.1	268.8	310.2	295.8	326.5	309.7

Source: Roth, 1986

The Treasury bill rate itself has only been a target for the Fed between 1942 and 1947, when the Fed converted Treasury securities into reserves at a fixed price and this was the reserve adjustment mechanism adopted by the banks. The principal target of Fed reserve policy is the terms it makes nonborrowed and borrowed reserves available to the banking system. Borrowed reserves are those that member banks have obtained from the Fed discount window. (The discount window is the name given to the borrowing of funds from the Fed by the member banks). The discount rate is the rate of interest charged by the Fed on the borrowed funds. Nonborrowed reserves are those obtained elsewhere, for example, from the Federal funds market or from the result of open market purchases. The Federal funds market is a market for unsecured loans between banks in immediately available funds. These funds are, essentially, excess reserves held at Federal Reserve Banks.[10] Federal funds borrowed are exempt from reserve requirements[11] and as such are used to discourage borrowing at the discount window which might attract closer Fed scrutiny of the borrowing company.[12] The majority of reserve funds consist of nonborrowed funds and the majority of these are Treasury bills.[13]

The Fed has direct control only over the volume of nonborrowed reserves since it must supply funds (borrowed reserves) to those member banks requesting them from the discount window.

Frequent changes in the deposit reserve requirement do not occur because, although a potentially very powerful tool, such changes would introduce considerable uncertainty and insecurity into the banking system.

The convential way for the Fed to influence the reserves of the banking system is through open market operations which are designed to change the level of reserves rather than the level of interest rates. Should the intention of the Fed be to change the direction of monetary policy then a change in the discount rate and the accompanying 'announcement' effect is the usual approach. This is considered in more detail below. If the Fed wishes that the supply of reserves to the banking system be increased it will buy securities, primarily Treasury bills, from the primary dealers or other official agencies, such as foreign central banks. The Fed will pay for such securities by crediting their accounts with the Fed. In other words, federal funds with depository institutions (member banks) increase.

The most frequent form of open market operation (see Table 2.6) is through repos which affect the level of reserves and are generally used when temporary factors, such as holiday periods, result in a shortfall of reserves. A temporary sale of securities to a bank is a reverse repo (from the bank's point of view) and such sales occur when, again for temporary periods, the banks have excess reserves.[14] Federal funds of one bank can be lent to another for satisfying reserve requirements and this generates the federal funds market, which resembles the British inter-bank market except that in the United States the market is for a specific asset rather than a market for loans. These additional funds from the open market purchase provide the potential for increasing loans and deposits – with a similar process in reverse taking place with security sales.

Federal funds rate targeting was the objective during the 1970s while from October 1979 to the autumn of 1982 nonborrowed reserve targeting was the objective. Since 1982 the policy has been, broadly speaking, one of borrowed reserve targeting. It should be stressed, however, that there is doubt concerning the ability of the Fed to eliminate the effects of 'noise', seasonal factors and lags in deciding weekly open market strategy in order to control one specific target (Meek 1975).

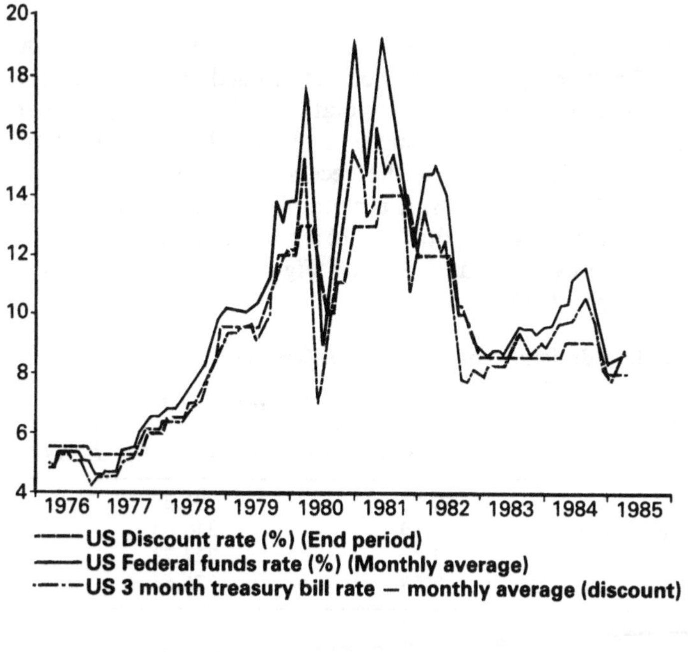

Figure 2.4 The discount, federal funds and Treasury bill rates
Source: Datastream

The objective of the policy adopted during the 1970s was to keep the federal funds rate within a narrow band – often 50 basis points. If the member banks found themselves short of reserves there would be upward pressure on the federal funds rate. The Fed relieved this pressure by supplying whatever reserves are required to keep the rate from rising. This policy has implications for Treasury securities because the purchase of them by the Fed to relieve the pressure on the federal funds market will tend to drive up their price.

Alternatively, a rise in the discount rate – 'the announcement effect' – will lead to a switch from borrowed to nonborrowed reserves and the Fed would be forced to buy more Treasure securities to prevent the federal funds rate from rising. With a policy of federal funds targeting a change in the discount rate was, sometimes, used to indicate a preference for a higher funds rate in the future.

Nonborrowed reserve targeting was the policy between October 1979 and fall 1982. The objective was to control the level of nonborrowed reserves and discount window borrowing in periods when demand for the funds increased. This 'monetarist' policy was introduced in an attempt to break the expectations of accelerating inflation.

There is some agreement between economists that the policy was unsuccessful. Friedman (1982), a monetarist, argued that a monetarist policy had not been tried because volatility of monetary growth increased during the period. By contrast Kaldor (1982), a Keynesian, argued that the policy worsened the recession caused by the substantial hike of oil prices in 1978. It is certainly the case that the costs of controlling a monetary magnitude were a greater variability of both the federal funds rate (see Table 2.7 and Figure 2.4) and the money growth rate (Rasche 1985).

Table 2.7 Standard deviations of interest rates (weekly)

Interest rate[1]	*Sample period*[2]	
	1978 (41)–1979 (40)	*1979 (41)–1980 (40)*
Federal funds	60.90	291.54
3-month Treasury bills	55.59	240.03
6-month Treasury bills	38.47	227.73
20-year US Government bonds	17.08	276.64

Source: Walsh, 1982

Notes: 1 Measured in basis points.

2 The sample period runs from the 41st week of 1978 to the 40th week of 1979 which is equal to the year immediately prior to the week of 6 October 1979.

In examining the period between 1979 and 1982 it can be concluded that given the intention of the Fed to target nonborrowed reserves and its willingness to allow the federal funds rate to vary much more it was quite consistent to observe the decline in temporary transactions which occurred between 1980 and 1981 (see Table 2.6). In addition the rate of inflation did fall from about 13 per cent in 1980 to 3 per cent in 1983, although the causal link with monetary policy is disputed.

The policy since 1982, until spring 1987, can be described as borrowed reserve targeting together with a federal funds policy. This involves supplying nonborrowed reserves in response to changes in demand. The effect will be similar to federal funds rate targeting in that for a given discount rate the federal funds rate will be constant on the assumption that a steady federal funds rate is necessary for a steady demand for borrowed funds. In this case if there is also an interest rate consideration, then as Table 2.6 shows, 'the use of temporary transactions might be expected to be more frequent than under the nonborrowed reserves procedure used from late 1979 to late 1982 but less frequent than under the federal funds rate procedure used until late 1979' (Roth 1986).

Fed policy seems to have changed, in spring 1987, towards increased use of monetary policy in an attempt to stem the falling value of the dollar (see Figure 2.5). In addition, on 30 April, the then Chairman Volcker told a congressional hearing that the Fed had raised short-term interest rates in an effort to make dollar-denominated investments more attractive to foreign investors (see Figure 2.5). On 4 September 1987 the discount rate was raised one half point to 6.0 per cent – the first increase since April 1984 – and in August 1988 was raised again to 6.5 per cent and to 7 per cent in February 1989. These more frequent changes in the discount rate give clear signals (announcement effects) to the market of an increased emphasis on a tight money policy. The main reason for this change is that the problem of financing the budget and trade deficits has rendered the US much more dependent upon foreign capital. Subsequent to the collapse of stock prices in 1987, monetary policy eased (see Figure 2.5) as the Fed supplied the financial system with liquidity in order not to repeat the errors of 1929. Gradually however, throughout 1988, concern reverted back towards the perceived problems posed by the twin deficits and monetary policy has become more restrictive.

DEREGULATION AND INTERNATIONALIZATION

Two of the most significant developments in money and capital markets over the past decade have been the deregulation of those markets and the growth of 'internationalization' or 'globalization' – disintermediation on a world-wide scale. It is difficult to examine one without considering the other. Internationalization has been accommodated by the technological revolution in computers, the gradual removal of exchange controls, international trends towards deregulation in financial markets and the growth of international banking. And to a large degree internationalization, together with the new technology, has forced deregulation.[15] The USA has been at the centre of much of this change, in the 1980s, and internationalization has made New York the capital of the world bond markets. These developments, by moving towards the creation of a global merger of markets from many national financial centres, have introduced new problems for the Treasury and the Fed in their attempts to control the quantity and price of securities and credit.

The US 'Big Bang' occurred on 1 May 1975 when Wall Street ended fixed commissions. As was to be the case in the UK eleven years later, 'off-floor screens' (epitomized by NASDAQ, the computerized system introduced in 1971 for dealing with unlisted securities) facilitated 'off-floor' trading. Such changes in technology have also facilitated 'off-floor' trading on a world scale and can be used for dealing in all kinds of financial instruments.

Deregulation has also taken the form of removal of the 'withholding tax' – the tax owed by non-residents on their holdings of certain types of securities being deducted at source. This was dismantled in the USA in 1984 and subsequently by Germany with the likelihood that Japan will eventually follow.[16] Another, anachronistic, regulation which has been relaxed was the 4.25 per cent coupon limit on Treasury bonds.

The USA abolished exchange controls early in the 1970s and this was followed by most of Europe, including Britain in 1979, Japan at the beginning of the 1980s and France and Italy in 1989–90. In addition, the growth and US exporting of financial futures and options markets has also facilitated the futures market in Treasury bills.

As Table 2.3 shows, the amount of marketable public debt has increased substantially in recent years (and this was matched by bond brokers' profits until the crash in 1987). To finance this increasing debt – 'the deficit' – the USA has had to compete in world markets by influencing international interest rates – with charges of 'global crowding out'. The financing of the deficit has also required frequent auctions of notes and bonds and has had a significant impact on foreign holdings of USA securities. Foreign holdings of USA Treasury securities have increased seven-fold since 1981. During some recent years it would appear that there has been a large reduction in the amount of private foreign finance to support the trade deficit. To take the place of this it would appear that there has been enormous official intervention from Japan and Europe (see Table 2.8). In recent years the Japanese have emerged as large investors in US capital markets and the reason is found in Japan's continuing current account and trade surplus – an estimated $93.76 billion and $101.43 billion in 1986. 'Japan's export of capital has been huge, as great as Britain's in the Nineteenth century and the USA's just after the war. But, unlike those two experiences, Japanese capital is an export that has so far gone largely into short-term dollar instruments' (Hamilton 1986).

Table 2.8 Net foreign purchases of marketable Treasury notes and bonds ($mn)

	Total	*Official institutions*	*Other foreigners*	*International and regional*
1984	21,499	507	15,989	5,003
1985	29,208	8,135	20,633	440
1986	19,388	14,214	6,278	(1,103)
1987	25,587	31,064	(176)	(5,302)
1988*	37,664	21,672	16,087	(95)

Source: Treasury Bulletin, December 1988

* Jan.–Sept.

The Japanese involvement in the Treasury securities market has also introduced uncertainty; first because the Japanese are big investors, second because their trading habits are not yet understood by US dealers and traders and third, because their future commitment is not known. An indication of the size of the Japanese involvement is that they have bought, on several occasions, one-third of the Treasury bills on auction and at the end of 1985 were estimated to hold more than 20 per cent of USA debt with the remainder being held by other countries, most notably Switzerland and Germany. The uncertainty surrounding their trading strategies was demonstrated during the May 1986 auctions of Treasury debt, when they were deemed to have 'outsmarted' the US bidders. During May 1986 some banks and securities firms made large losses after being caught short of the 9.25 per cent bond issue which was auctioned in February and for which there was strong Japanese demand. The expected switch from that bond to the 7.25 per cent bond issued in May did not occur and this caused a short squeeze of unprecedented magnitude. After the Treasury's refunding the bond market dropped sharply and Pardee (1987) estimated that the collective losses to the buyers of securities from the Treasury exceeded $1.5 billion and that a large part of the loss was borne by government securities dealers. The third area of uncertainty is concerned with the longer term willingness of the Japanese investors to continue lending to the USA in the face of potential exchange rate losses. Further uncertainty arises from the exchange risks associated with Japanese purchases of US bonds. These rather uncertain trading conditions continued and were not helped by the 1987 crash. The scale of the problem was an influence on President Bush abandoning his 'read my lips' tax pledge in 1990.

The extent to which the USA now relies on overseas demand for securities (see Figure 2.6) has caused nervousness in the markets because the Fed's credit policy may now have to take into account the external value of the dollar. It was feared that a declining dollar – it declined from being worth 251 yen in May 1985 to 126 yen in January 1988 – could reduce the foreign demand for Treasury securities. There would then be consequences for the domestic economy of financing the deficit through high interest rates see Figure 2.5.

The potential losses made as a result of a declining dollar since February 1985 have been counterbalanced on occasions by the capital gains made by bond holders – bond yields fell from 10.97 per cent in 1985 to 7.28 per cent in August 1986. However bond rates have fluctuated substantially in recent years. They rose almost 3 per cent to nearly 10 per cent in the nine months up to the October 1987 crash – indeed it was a not uncommon view that this contributed to the crash. The bond yield then fell back to about 8.3 per cent in February 1988 and has been fairly stable since. It is of little surprise that official purchases of Treasury notes and bonds have been very substantial since 1985.

Trends and innovations

There has been very considerable innovation in financial markets in recent years, mainly facilitated by deregulation, technical and structural change. Many types of new financial instruments have been developed. They have helped improve the efficiency of financial markets by transferring risks, enhancing liquidity and generating

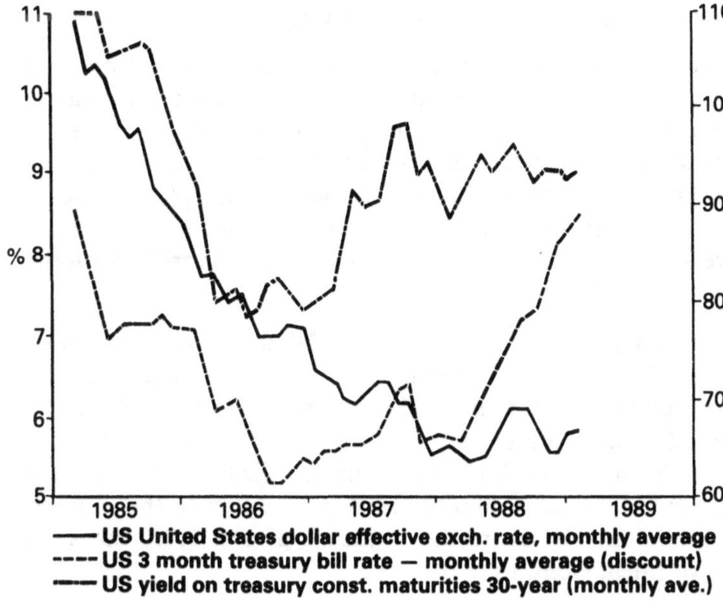

Figure 2.5 Interest rates and exchange rates, 1985–9
Source: Datastream

credit and equity. An excellent survey of the area and the issues raised by these developments is found in BIS (1986).

Innovation has also occurred in Treasury securities. The first significant development in the note and bond market was the 'stripped-coupon' security. In 1982 Merril Lynch introduced the 'Treasury Investment Growth Receipts' (TIGRs) and Salomon Brothers the 'Certificate of Accrual on Treasury Certificates' (CATs). These are similar to ZEBRAs and STAGs (the 'in house' colloquialisms for zero-rated bonds and security Treasury accrual) in the UK. Essentially they are Treasury securities bought by the dealer, whereupon the security is placed in a custodian bank, the maturity par value is discounted to the present and sold (stripped) without the coupon whilst the coupon payments themselves are discounted to a present value and sold. A good review of these developments is contained in Becketti (1988).

In order to compete more effectively with the private sector a similar device, the STRIPS programme, (Separate Trading of Registered Interest and Principal of Securities) was offered by the

Treasury on its own securities in 1985 and this, too, enabled the interest and principal to be separately owned and traded. Such securities have several attractive features for buyers:

1 there is a large potential for capital gain when the TIGR matures since the further away the maturity date the lower the present value;
2 the low present cost of, for example, a twenty-year TIGR enables the creation of an income upon retirement – a type of annuity;
3 TIGRs, being based on Treasury securities, are completely safe;
4 a large number of different maturities is available and
5 they are attractive to those foreigners whose tax authorities treat the income as capital gain.

Those countries with tax treaties with the US do not hold 'stripped-coupon' securities liable to withholding tax. They have attractions, too, for speculators. 'An investor who bought a long-term TIGR at a price of say $3,500 would be able in theory to borrow about $90,000. The margin requirements for some securities, financial futures, for example, would then allow him to invest in securities to the value of about $2.5 million. This represents a gearing of over 7,000 times the original investment (Kemp 1984).

Government securities, futures markets

Financial futures markets were developed in October 1975 for trading in the securities of the Government National Mortgage Association – 'Ginnie Maes'. In January 1976 futures contracts on three-month Treasury bills were available and by 1978 they were offered in twelve-month Treasury bills. Futures are now available for Treasury notes and bonds.

A futures contract is an obligation to buy or sell a given amount of the security at a specific time and price. It differs, therefore, from an option contract which gives a right but not an obligation to buy (call) or sell (put) a given amount at a specific price and time. The only obligation under an option contract is the premium. Options are taken out on futures. In a futures market the vast majority of trades take place without delivery of any securities – only 0.2 per cent of all Treasury bonds were settled this way on the Chicago Board of Trade (CBoT) in 1983.

Futures and options markets are dominated, as shown in Table 2.9, by the CBoT and the Chicago Mercantile Exchange (CME). Treasury bond futures are the world's most actively traded futures' contract dealt at the CBoT. 'In 1984 the volume of bond contracts on the CBoT

Table 2.9 Futures and options volume, Jan.–March 1986

	Thousand contracts (number of contracts)		
	Futures	*Options*	*Total*
United States			
Chicago BoT	16,065 (7)	5,495 (2)	21,560 (9)
Merc.	12,774 (14)	1,672 (6)	14,446 (20)
MidAm	153 (7)	—	153 (7)
NY Futures Exchange	824 (1)	57 (1)	881 (2)
NY Cotton Exchange	72 (2)	—	72 (2)
Coffee, Sugar Exchange	339 (2)	—	339 (2)
Total	30,235 (34)	7,225 (9)	37,460 (43)
Other			
Liffe	1,434 (11)	88 (5)	1,522 (16)
Tokyo	1,125 (1)	—	1,125 (1)
Sydney	579 (4)	40 (4)	619 (8)
Montreal	—	191 (5)	191 (5)
Toronto	31 (4)	15 (2)	46 (6)
Singapore	176 (4)	—	176 (4)
Total	3,346 (24)	333 (16)	3,680 (40)

Source: US Futures Ind. Assn.

exceeded the total volume of all commodity futures contracts traded a decade earlier' (Hamilton 1986). The daily volume of the Treasury bonds traded on the CBoT has been as high as eight times the value of trading in the bonds themselves. Volume in US Treasury bond futures is the world's largest contract, with 70 million lots traded in 1988. The importance of the futures markets was recognized as long ago as 1982 when just before Christmas the US Treasury postponed an auction of securities in an unprecedented and highly unusual action. The reason was that the CBoT was scheduled to close early for the holiday and this meant that government securities dealers had no place to hedge the risk associated with bidding on bonds (CBoT handbook).

A proposed extension of the market, which was announced in February 1987, was a link between the CBoT and the London International Financial Futures Exchange (LIFFE). Under the arrangements traders in US Treasury bond futures would be able to open a position in London, close it in Chicago later in the day and pay only one set of transaction costs. However, this link has not yet been completed. Likewise, approval has been given by the Ministry of Finance in Japan to allow domestic financial institutions to deal in financial futures and options markets from June 1987, but again no formal link has been established. These proposals together with the LIFFE link with Treasury bond futures at the Sydney futures exchange, have the potential to create a virtual global market. Futures and options in Treasury bills are offered by the CME and by the MidAmerica Commodity Exchange. Contracts are of units of $1 million and exchanges are quoted in multiples of 0.01 points; prices are allowed to fluctuate between 0.01 points (minimum) and 0.05 points (maximum) above or below the previous day's price. In addition they are quoted at an annualized discount rather than the approximate quarter of this in the cash markets – see the auction prices earlier. Futures in twelve-month bills are traded in minimum contracts of $25,000.

A futures market for Treasury notes began in 1979 at the CBoT for notes of up to six years maturity. Presently the basic unit is a Treasury bond with a face value of $100,000, a coupon rate of 8 per cent and a maturity of fifteen years or more. Futures prices are quoted as a percentage of par, with a minimum price fluctuation of 1/32 of a point – $31.25 per contract. Prices can fluctuate by up to 96/32nds or $3,000 per contract above or below the previous day's settlement price.

As can be seen from Table 2.3 the market for Treasury bonds has tended to be the smallest of the three main types of Treasury securities issued. The prices of bonds have been relatively volatile as a result of their long maturities and, until recently, the 4.25 per cent interest ceiling. As a result they have been an uncertain investment proposition. Hence a futures market for bonds is particularly appropriate.

The economic purpose served by these markets is primarily the means by which risks such as interest rate and exchange rate changes can be transferred from firms and individuals less willing to bear them to those more willing to do so. In addition, the Board of Governors of the Federal Reserve System (1984b) concluded that financial futures and options markets appear to have enhanced the liquidity in some of the underlying cash markets on which they are based.

Regulation of the futures markets

The exchanges are self-regulatory organizations. Their activities are monitored by the Commodity Futures Trading Commission (CFTC) and the SEC. Until recently this was felt to be adequate. The Board of Governors of the Federal Reserve System (1984b) concluded that no additional legislation was required other than the monitoring by the CFTC (which is empowered to assess up to $100,000 in penalties for each violation of the commodity Exchange Act or Commission regulations) and the SEC. While there have been fears that the futures and option markets destabilize prices in cash markets there has been virtually no evidence to support these concerns.[17] Following the sharp falls in the world's stock markets in October 1987 a study published by NYSE recommended fundamental changes in the regulation and trading of financial futures. The study recommended that the control of stocks, currently regulated by the SEC, and futures markets, regulated by CFTC, be brought under one agency. The report suggested that the large trading volumes and liquidity claims of the futures markets may have encouraged institutional investors to use them in their attempts to leave the traditional equity markets and thus 'may have contributed to the quick fall in prices'. The Brady Commission report issued in January 1988 suggested first that the margins of the futures markets should be increased to bring them closer to those of the stock market. Second that stock and futures exchanges should co-ordinate emergency circuit breakers or trading halts and third that the Fed should be given an overall supervisory role. The SEC report issued in February 1988 concluded that futures trading and strategies were not the sole causes of the market fall. Specific but piecemeal action followed in 1988–90.

Since the 1987 crash there have continued to be severe doubts about the adequacy of the existing arrangements. For example the head of the SEC, David Ruder, has repeated the Brady Commission's call for higher margins. In addition there have been examples of malpractice. In January 1987 the CFTC filed a total of thirteen administrative complaints against the CME for allegedly failing to report violations of federal rules by member firms, or properly to audit firms. A much more serious situation arose at the beginning of 1989 when the FBI began an investigation into futures trading on the Chicago exchanges. For two years FBI agents had been infiltrating the CBoT and the CME by acting as traders. When the news broke in January it was accompanied by the issuing of 300 subpoenas on individuals and firms for activities dating back to 1983. The trade practice most at issue was that of dual trading where traders can take customer orders as well as trade for their own accounts. This gives rise to the possibility of conflicts of interest. It is also alleged that the customers have been paying for dealers' trading errors by having a few points clipped off each transaction order. The eventual introduction of electronic screen systems such as the CME's 'Globex' should eventually provide an audit trail which will assist in improving the efficacy of investor protection.

THE DEFICIT CONTROVERSY IN THE 1980s

As the decade of the 1980s has come to a close it can be seen that the dominant features of debt management were the twin deficits, the problems associated with supervision in a deregulated global market and the appropriate role of futures markets. However, discussions about the federal deficit, its financing and management are likely to dominate the other issues in the future not least because in assessing its significance economists are divided into two quite distinctive opposing camps.

The first, and the conventional wisdom, is that the deficit has a real and detrimental impact on the economy. The borrowing of funds by the public sector either raises rates of interest or, if interest rates do not rise and the debt is monetized, increases inflationary pressures. Alternatively public borrowing 'crowds out' funds that would otherwise be available to the private sector for spending on either consumers or capital goods. Furthermore, if deficits are financed by borrowing from abroad, by attracting foreign capital with higher domestic interest rates, the capital inflow supports the exchange rate. The deficit in this case can 'crowd out' exports rather than domestic investment and consumption. The extent to which foreign countries have been net purchasers of long-term US securities is shown below in Figure 2.6. A further consideration is whether the net import of capital is used to finance consumption or investment type government expenditure. A good review of these issues can be found in Buiter (1986). Another concern is that an increasing public debt will lead to a loss of confidence among investors, requiring the payment of a risk premium. The ultimate fear is that the attempt to finance persistent deficits by borrowing leads to a spiral where interest payments to overseas holders form an increasing proportion of the debt and the ultimate consequence of such an unfortunate position is Treasury bankruptcy and repudiation of the debt.

The second, and minority, view – the equivalence theorem – states that increases in government debt, regardless of how financed, will have no real impact on the economy and to the extent that reserves in the system are monetized prices will rise. This view assumes that economic agents are rational market participants who will view an increase in the debt as implying future tax liabilities, properly discounted. Market participants will react therefore by saving more. As a consequence an increase in government spending resulting from the deficit is exactly offset by a decline in non-government spending.[18] The reason why governments run deficits according to those who hold

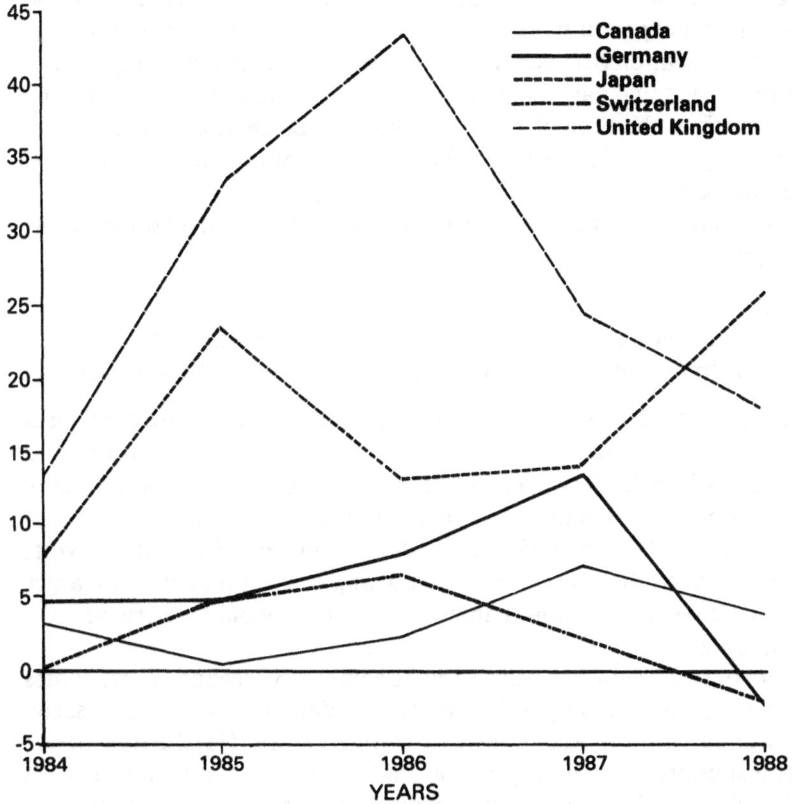

Figure 2.6 Net purchases of long-term domestic securities by selected countries ($bn)
Source: Treasury Bulletin, December 1988

this view is that it provides a mechanism for minimizing tax collection costs and smoothing tax collections (Barro 1979, Seater 1985).

The recent academic evidence concerning the extent of the impact of the federal deficit in the US is equivocal. One of the problems of attempting to resolve the issue is the appropriate measure of the deficit. Much of the discussion uses the par value of the public debt. Seater (1985) states that 'these values are subject to measurement errors arising from the impact of inflation on real values, of interest rate changes on market values, and of state and local deficits on the total deficit' (see Cox 1985 op.cit.). Seater also considers that studies of debt and deficits often overlook important modelling issues. For example, deficits are often used as an explanatory variable while government expenditure is omitted. This is puzzling given that there is a high correlation between the two. Finally he states that many studies assume that some part, at least, of government debt is perceived to be net wealth at the time of issue and that this perception lasts for ever. Another problem identified by Hoelscher (1986) is the assessment of federal loan guarantees on the credit markets.

In general terms there is evidence to support the conventional, first, category that

(a) the debt affects real variables;
(b) that deficits are monetized only to a small extent and
(c) that long-term debt 'crowds out' more than short-term debt.

In addition Hoelscher (1986) found that 'deficits cause long-term interest rates to rise . . . and the . . . connection is strong, robust and very significant'. Hervey (1986) found an effect on the real economy in the opposite direction. He found that because the economy was growing rapidly during 1983 and 1984 the increase in foreign investment 'reduced the incidence of "crowding out" and facilitated larger private investment at lower interest rates than would otherwise have been the case'.

By contrast, evidence supporting the minority, second, view, comes from Canto and Rapp (1982), who found 'deficits were not necessarily associated with increasing interest rates'. Plosser (1982), too, found 'little support for the proposition that increases in government debt drive yields up'. Huang (1986) examined whether monetization had any significant impact on the markets for debt including government long-term and short-term debt. He found results compatible with the equivalence theorem.

At a practical level the twin debt problems need not be of great concern if there is continued overseas demand for US treasuries – to finance the budget deficit, and/or US corporate stocks and bonds – to finance the trade deficit. Such overseas support is already substantiated as shown above in Figure 2.6. However, it does imply that ownership of the United States economic activity is increasingly transferred overseas. Whether this is politically acceptable as a long-term strategy is doubtful. During 1987 and 1988 there was only slight evidence from the trade figures that the position is improving and indeed the perception is growing that only a recession is likely to improve matters. It was widely believed that similar thinking was one of the underlying reasons for the financial crash in October 1987.

Since the crash there has been little change of substance. The trade and federal budget deficits have remained. In addition there is evidence that a new problem, an acceleration in the rate of inflation, will add to the likelihood that monetary policy will remain restrictive in the immediate future.

NOTES

1 The Gramm-Rudman-Hollings (G-R-H) statutory targets relate to the budget deficit forecast rather than outcomes. For example the G-R-H target for 1989 was $94.7 billion, but the outcome was $170.2 billion.

2 For further reading I suggest Cook and Rowe (1986), Rose (1986) and Kemp (1981, 1984). All are excellent and are principal sources for parts of this chapter. Rose provides a comprehensive treatment of the US banking and financial markets and Kemp a concise survey of all money and capital market instruments.

3 The figures for Treasury debt in this chapter are par values from a variety of sources principally the Treasury Bulletin and the Federal Reserve Bulletin. Market values have been calculated by Seater (1981), Cox and Hirschhorn (1983), and Cox (1985). These estimates were obtained by multiplying the par value of federal debt by a security price index. The index was calculated as a simple ratio (indexed to 100) of market value to par value for each marketable debt aggregate.

4 Take, for example, a ninety-one-day Treasury bill issued at an auction at an average price of $97.479 per $100 face value. The annual rate of return on a discount basis is:

$$\frac{100 - 97.479}{100} \times \frac{360}{91} = 9.973\%$$

However to compare yields on other securities with the true yield on Treasury bills the discount must be divided by the price and a 365 day year used. With the above example the true yield is:

$$\frac{100 - 97.479}{97.479} \times \frac{365}{91} = 10.373\%$$

This simple example shows that the yield calculated on a discount basis understates the true yield. Clearly the difference is greater the longer the maturity of the bill and the higher the level of discount (which is closely related to general levels of interest rates). A full account of yields and discounting can be found in Rose (1986).

5 The Federal Reserve Bank of New York has reviewed the progress of Japan in opening its financial markets to foreign financial institutions and concluded that progress has been 'constructive and mutually beneficial'. In particular the agreement on capital adequacy policies for international banks is welcomed as is the growing foreign access to the Japanese government bond market.

6 A comprehensive treatment of all aspects of repurchase is to be found in Lumpkin (1986).

7 On 8 January 1987 The Bank of England and The Federal Reserve announced a bilateral banking regulation agreement on common capital requirements and common ways of measuring credit risk. There is speculation that business will be subsequently removed from the (controlled) banking system to the (uncontrolled) securities market – a variant of Goodhart's law. The longer term aspirations will presumably be directed to the problem of capital inadequacy in the securities markets.

8 Examples include American Depository Receipts (ADRs) – receipts for holdings of US corporate stock held by foreigners; FRNs – securities with 'floating rates' generally related to the Federal funds rate – floating-rate CDs, bonds, notes; junk bonds – bonds of low-rate companies often considered to be high risk.

9 'Moral hazard' is the name given to the change in the behaviour of an insured person after obtaining insurance and the change in behaviour causes a change in the insurable risk. 'Adverse selection' occurs where an insurance company has to offer the same insurance premium against a given event to a group even though it is aware that within the group the riskiness of individuals differs. The difficulty arises because the individuals know their own risk characteristics better than the insuring firms.

10 In the 1960s the federal funds market began to change, from being simply a means of altering reserve positions, to a method by which the banks could use the funds to avoid the reserve requirement tax and the interest prohibition on demand deposits (Goodfriend and Hargraves 1983).

11 Reserve assets are those that, by statute, can be used to satisfy reserve requirements. There are only two such assets: vault cash and reserve balances. Vault cash is the currency and coin held by depository institutions. Reserve balances with Federal Reserve Banks are accounts (other than required clearing balances) of depository institutions with their Reserve Banks. No other asset may count as reserves (The Federal Reserve System 1984a).

12 It is the convention that discount window borrowing should be temporary. It is a 'privilege, not a right' – continuous borrowing at the window is interpreted as indicating that a bank has permanent reserve difficulties. It should be noted that it is generally the case that the federal funds rate is above the discount rate but less than 10 per cent of depository institutions borrow regularly from the window.

13 *Table 2.10* Reserves of depository institutions ($bn)

	76	*77*	*78*	*79*	*80*	*81*	*82*	*83*	*84*	*85*	*86*
Total	34.9	36.1	41.3	30.7	32.5	33.8	34.2	361	39.5	45.6	50.5
Non-borrowed	34.8	35.5	40.4	29.2	30.8	33.1	33.7	35.4	36.3	44.3	49.8
Req'd	34.6	36.0	41.0	30.4	31.9	33.4	33.8	35.6	38.7	44.6	49.6
Monetary base	118.4	127.8	142.3	139.3	151.1	158.8	170.4	185.4	199.2	216.7	228.3

Source: Federal Reserve Bulletin, various issues

14 Another type of 'open market operation' is the 'run-off' whereby the Fed deals directly with the Treasury in securities' dealing.

15 Early internationalization, especially of the Eurobond and currency markets, was stimulated by attempts to avoid regulation not least Regulation Q, which put a ceiling on interest rates paid by banks in the USA, and the 1963 Interest Equalization Tax (IET), which limited the amount of foreign loans which could be made by USA banks. The IET was removed, in effect, in 1974 following the rise in oil prices which required all western countries to seek much larger quantities of capital.

16 The removal of this tax in the USA may have been connected with the need to finance the 'deficit'.

17 A review of these issues can be found in Kwast (1986).

18 The theoretical origins of this position are contained in Modigliani and Miller (1958) and more recently developed with reference to the government sector by Barro (1974).

REFERENCES

Allen, D.E. (1983) *Finance: A Theoretical Introduction*, Oxford: Martin Robertson.

Bank of International Settlements (1986) *Recent Innovations in International Banking*, Prepared by a Study Group established by the Central Banks of the Group of Ten Countries.

Barro, R.J. (1974) 'Are government bonds net wealth?', *Journal of Political Economy* 82 November/December: 1095–117.

—— (1979) 'On the determination of the government debt', *Journal of Political Economy* 87: 940–71.

Baumol, W.J. and Blinder, A.S. (1985) *Economics: Principles and Policy* (3rd edn), New York: Harcourt Brace Jovanovich.

Becketti, S. (1988) 'The role of stripped securities in portfolio management', *Economic Review* of Federal Reserve Bank of Kansas City, May.

Board of Governors of the Federal Reserve System (1984a) *The Federal Reserve System Purposes and Functions*, Washington, D.C.

—— (1984b) *A Study of the Effects on the Economy of Trading in Futures Options*.

Buchanan, J.M., Rowley, C.K., Tollison, R.D. (1987) *Deficits*, Oxford: Basil Blackwell.

Buiter, W.H. (1986) 'A guide to public sector debt and deficits', *Economic Policy*, November: 14–79.

Canto, V.A. and Rapp, D. (1982) 'The crowding-out controversy: arguments and evidence', *Economic Review* of Federal Reserve Bank of Atlanta, August.

Cook, T.Q. and Rowe, T.D. (eds) (1986) *Instruments of the Money Market* (6th edn), Federal Reserve Bank of Richmond.

Cox, W.M. (1985) 'The behavior of Treasury Securities: monthly, 1942–84', *Journal of Monetary Economics* 16, 227–40.

Cox, W.M. and Hirschhorn, E. (1983) 'The market value of outstanding government debt: monthly 1942–80', *Journal of Monetary Economics* 11, March: 261–72.

Friedman, M. (1982) 'Monetary policy: theory and practice', *Journal of Money Credit and Banking* 14 Part 2, November: 20–23.

Goodfriend, M. and Hargraves, M. (1983) 'A historical assessment of the rationales and functions of reserve requirements', Federal Reserve Bank of Richmond, *Economic Review* 69, March/April: 3–21.

Hamilton, A. (1986) *The Financial Revolution*, New York: Viking.

Hervey, J.L. (1986) 'The internationalization of Uncle Sam', *Chicago Economic Perspectives*, Federal Reserve Bank of Chicago, May/June 1986.

Hirsch, F. (1977) 'The Bagehot Problem', *The Manchester School* Vol. 45 No 3: 241–57.

Hoelscher, G. (1986) 'New evidence on deficits and interest rates', *Journal of Money Credit and Banking* Vol. 18 No 1, February.

Huang, R.D. (1986) 'Does Monetization of Federal Debt Matter?', *Journal of Money Credit and Banking* Vol. 18 No 3, August: 275–89.

Kaldor, N. (1982) *The Scourge of Monetarism*, Oxford University Press.

Kemp, L.J. (1981) *A Guide to World Money and Capital Markets*, New York: McGraw-Hill.

—— (1984) *World Money and Securities Markets*, London: Euromoney Publications.

King, B.F. (1985) 'Nonbank banks: what next?', *Economic Review*, Federal Reserve Bank of Atlanta, May: 40–43.

Kwast, M.L. (1986) *Financial Futures and Options in the US Economy*, Washington: A Study by the Staff of the Federal Reserve System.

Lumpkin, S.A. (1986) 'Repurchase and reverse repurchase agreements', *Instruments of the Money Market*, Federal Reserve Bank of Richmond: 65–81.

Meek, P. (1975) 'Nonborrowed reserves or the federal funds rate as desk targets – is there a difference?'. *New England Economic Review*, March/April: 31–47.

—— (1982) *US Monetary Policy and Financial Markets*, Federal Reserve Bank of New York.

Mingo, J.J. (1978) 'The effects of deposit rate ceilings on bank risk', *Journal of Banking and Finance* Vol. 2: 367–78.

Modigliani, F. and Miller, M.M. (1958) 'The cost of capital, corporation finance, and the theory of investment', *American Economic Review* 48, June: 261–97.

Pardee, S.E. (1987) 'Internationalization of financial markets', *Economic Review*, Federal Reserve Bank of Kansas City, February: 3–8.

Plosser, C.I. (1982) 'Government financing decisions and asset returns', *Journal of Monetary Economic* 9: 325–52.

Rasche, R. (1985) 'Interest rate stability and alternative monetary control procedures', *Economic Review* of Federal Reserve Bank of San Francisco, summer: 46–63.

Roth, H.L. (1986) 'Federal reserve open market techniques', *Economic Review* of Federal Reserve Bank of Kansas City, March: 3–16.

Rose, P.S. (1986) *Money and Capital Markets*, Texas: Business Publications.

Seater, J.J. (1981) 'The market value of outstanding government debt, 1919–1975', *Journal of Monetary Economics* 8: 85–101.

—— (1985) 'Does government debt matter? – a review', *Journal of Monetary Economics*, Vol. 16: 121–31.

Walsh, C. (1982) 'The federal reserve's operating procedures and interest rate fluctuations', *Economic Review* of Federal Reserve Bank of Kansas City, May: 8–19.
Welles, C. (1982) 'Drysdale: the untold story', *Institutional Investor*, September: 454–68.

3 The Japanese bond market

M. Okuda and Stephen James

In recent years the Japanese bond market has grown at a substantial pace and now stands, after the United States, as the second largest market in the world. By the end of the financial year 1986–87, outstanding yen bond issues amounted to 281 trillion yen, with total trading during that year in excess of 3,700 trillion yen. Given its size and the enduring strength of the Japanese economy, it is likely that the Japanese bond market will be of increasing international importance. This process has been aided by a number of steps towards deregulation and internationalization which, although relatively limited, may well gather momentum as the yen takes on a greater role as an international currency.

This chapter sets out to explain the operation of the Japanese bond market and its evolution. It is divided into five parts. The first section sets out a brief history of the Japanese economy since 1945 and the second relates the developments in the economy to bond market developments up to the early 1980s. A detailed description of the bond market is provided in section three, followed by an analysis of the most recent steps that have been taken towards liberalization in the next section. The final part offers a brief conclusion.

HISTORICAL BACKGROUND

The devastated state of the Japanese economy at the end of the Second World War is amply illustrated by the collapse in output in 1946 to its 1917–18 level and the fall in per capita income to no more than the level it had been forty years previously. Yet by 1953, with US aid and military expenditure during the Korean war, output had regained its pre-war peak, rising by an average of over 10 per cent p.a. between 1946 and 1953. Furthermore, by the end of the occupation in 1952, two important developments that were to contribute to later growth had occurred: the pre-war industrial groupings had re-formed and the unions became more moderate as political attitudes shifted to the right. This early progress was not achieved without some strife. Industrial unrest was not uncommon as unions became more militant in the most immediate post-war years. In 1949, the US authorities intervened to squeeze the economy as a rapidly expanding money supply and rising budget deficit boosted demand too far in excess of supply, producing a rapid inflation. Prices rose by a factor of 30 between 1945 and 1949, and on average by 58 per cent p.a. in the eight years up to 1953.

It was during the twenty years after 1953 that Japan achieved a growth rate of impressive proportions: averaging 9.3 per cent p.a., GDP grew far faster than that of any other country. Even in the worst downturn, growth was never below 4.5 per cent. Numerous reasons have been advanced to explain this performance, the most cogent of which rest on both the quantity and quality of investment. In quantitative terms, fixed investment rose dramatically from 15 per cent of GDP to 35 per cent between the early 1950s and the early 1980s; the comparable figures for the UK were 19 per cent and 20 per cent. Operating through ministries such as MITI, the government encouraged and directed investment into selected growth sectors ensuring that its quality was growth enhancing. The incentive to invest was also great as the intense competition between Japan's oligopolistic industrial giants meant that they had to innovate rapidly to maintain market shares.

Indeed, the whole ambience of economic policy was to create a climate in which business expectations were high and investment and growth encouraged. This is also true of the stance of macroeconomic policy; rather than concentrating on short-term economic management, the prime objective was long run growth. Restrictive policies were required from time to time to cope with inflation and a weak current balance but these were invariably short-lived and in the most severe recession in 1965 the government quickly responded with expansionary fiscal measures. In general, fiscal policy was designed to stimulate investment: tax concessions were granted on fixed investment and government infrastructure spending favoured industry. On the monetary side, the central bank had considerable control over the banks, which were the main source of funds for investment. These funds were made available at pegged interest rates.

A sharp deterioration in economic performance came in 1973–74 as the first oil price shock hit the world economy. Inflation accelerated to peak at over 24 per cent in 1974, the current account moved into serious deficit and output fell by 1 per cent, a very sharp slowing for an economy used to such high growth. Despite the initial seriousness of the situation, the economy showed great resilience and soon returned to growth rates in excess of 4 per cent, double that of other major economies at the time. The policy response played an important part in the adjustment. An initial monetary squeeze, operating mainly through quantitative restrictions on bank lending, brought inflation under control by 1975, after which the policy switched to one of stimulating expansion by raising public expenditure. In fact fiscal policy remained loose right into the 1980s, with the budget deficit averaging 4 per cent of GDP between 1975 and 1982. Financed by bond issues, this policy did not cause excessive rises in interest rates because of the ability of the government to sell bonds to a strictly regulated financial sector, and as a result of the lack of demand for funds from the corporate sector.

During the 1980s Japan's growth continued at internationally high levels, averaging 4 per cent between 1980 and 1988. There has been some faltering at times, as in the early part of the decade when the world economy went into recession after the second oil price shock. The appreciation of the yen in 1986 also brought a significant slowdown in activity; growth fell to 2.5 per cent notwithstanding the contemporaneous fall in oil prices. However, it has been the massive current account surpluses and the pressure for international policy co-ordination that have been the distinguishing features of this period. In spite of an expansionary policy, with low interest rates, the current account surplus has continued to mount. Some problems have been created for Japanese firms by the substantial appreciation of the yen – it rose by approximately 50 per cent against the dollar from 1985 to 1988 – but rationalization and high productivity growth has helped maintain their competitiveness. On the other hand, the appreciation has contributed to an exceptionally low inflation rate; consumer prices barely rose in 1986, fell in 1987 and increased by only 1 per cent in 1988.

Fuelled by domestic consumption, which has been stimulated by rising real personal incomes due to tax cuts and subsiding inflation, and by rising investment in both the private and public sectors, economic growth continued apace in 1987 and 1988. In the latter year GNP grew by 5.8 per cent. The Stock Market crash had comparatively little effect; it was a relatively minor downturn by international standards and in any case it was quickly reversed. By 1988–9, however, it had become apparent that demand was expanding too fast and there was a serious prospect of accelerating inflation. This was compounded by a fall in the yen against the dollar, pushing up import prices, and the introduction of a 3 per cent value added tax. Mid-June 1989 saw consumer prices 3 per cent higher than they had been a year previously, and there was evidence of an increasingly tight labour market. In response, the authorities pushed up the official discount rate from 2.5 per cent to 3.25 per cent – the first rise in nine years. Other rates have followed suit.

Some uncertainty surrounds the future course of Japan's economy, especially after the recent setbacks for the conservative Liberal Democratic government and the electoral success of the Socialist Party. At the time of writing it is the view of some commentators that on current trends the economy will return to its long-run growth rate of around 4.5 per cent with stable prices and further, if less marked, appreciation of the yen.

THE DEVELOPMENT OF THE BOND MARKET

During the 1960s and 1970s there were a number of important steps that can be identified in the development of the bond market in Japan. The first came in 1965, when the government pursued an expansionary economic policy at a time of a severe cyclical recession. Facing a significant shortfall in revenue and a need for greater public expenditure to stimulate the economy, the government financed part of the resulting deficit by issuing bonds for the first time since the end of the War. To do this a special resolution had to be passed in the legislature since the issue of bonds to cover expenditure in the national budget is unconstitutional by Article 4 of the Financial Law. Since that time the government bond issue has grown significantly (see Table 3.1) as the government has frequently used bond finance to cover its deficit.

A second major economic development that affected the bond market was the oil price rises of 1973–4. As the economy stagnated (in the wake of the first price shock), the Japanese government actively pursued expansionary policies once the inflation rate had subsided. This required substantial increases in the bond issue both to finance the additional expenditure and to cover lost tax revenue resulting from poor corporate profits and stagnant personal incomes. In 1975 the government bond issue was raised by 3.3 trillion yen above the planned total of around 2 trillion yen, increasing the proportion of the government budget financed by bonds to 26.3 per cent in the process. This ushered in the period of 'the massive government bond issue', during which the proportion of the budget financed by bonds rose to

Table 3.1 Historical development of the Japanese bond market (billion yen)

	Issuing amount		*Outstanding amount*[b]		*Trading amount*			*Total bond*	
	Total bonds	*Government bonds*	*Total bonds*	*Government bonds*	*Total bonds*	*Government bonds*	*Gensaki trading*	*GNP*	*Outstanding/ GNP (%)*
1965[a]	—	.3	—	.6	—	—	—	33.6	—
1966	—	.8	—	1.4	2.9	.0	—	39.5	—
1967	—	.8	—	2.2	3.4	.2	—	46.2	—
1968	4.7	.6	15.9	2.7	5.1	.2	—	54.8	29.0
1969	5.0	.5	18.3	3.1	6.3	.3	—	64.9	28.2
1970	6.3	.7	21.1	3.6	9.2	.4	—	75.2	28.1
1971	9.0	1.3	25.9	4.7	12.2	.3	—	82.8	31.3
1972	11.0	2.1	32.0	6.5	17.7	.5	—	96.5	33.2
1973	13.0	2.5	38.4	8.3	23.5	1.1	—	116.7	32.9
1974	15.3	3.1	46.2	10.5	38.6	1.7	22.6	138.2	33.4
1975	20.9	5.9	59.0	15.8	57.3	1.3	31.6	152.2	38.8
1976	24.3	7.5	72.8	22.1	73.7	3.3	40.8	171.1	42.5
1977	29.1	10.2	90.8	31.9	138.1	21.7	70.7	190.0	47.8
1978	32.6	11.4	109.7	42.6	206.3	68.5	111.4	208.8	52.5
1979	34.9	13.6	131.2	56.3	229.7	112.2	125.8	225.4	58.2
1980	36.1	14.6	152.7	70.5	289.9	166.8	160.1	245.2	62.3
1981	38.5	13.9	173.3	82.3	312.3	197.9	134.2	259.7	66.7
1982	45.0	18.1	195.7	96.5	350.1	237.2	136.1	272.4	71.8
1983	47.9	18.4	218.0	109.7	462.1	329.0	137.4	284.1	76.7
1984	50.4	18.2	239.9	121.7	878.1	804.9	150.9	303.2	79.1
1985	61.8	23.0	261.5	133.4	2672.1	2497.7	283.8	320.8	81.5
1986	68.8	25.9	281.1	145.1	3737.4	3483.4	754.2	334.0	84.2

Source: Ministry of Finance, Japanese Bond Dealers Association, Economic Planning Agency.
Notes: Trading counts both buy and sell.
[a] Fiscal year (April to March, next year) [b] at the end of fiscal year.

over 30 per cent as the government attempted to maintain a growth rate between 3 per cent and 5 per cent.

Prior to the 1970s there had been little competition for funds between the public and private sectors. The highly segmented and regulated financial system had been designed, at least in part, to channel the relatively scarce savings of households through the banking system to the corporate sector for investment in expanding productive capacity. The rising government bond issue introduced an element of competition for funds that made for further developments in the operation of the bond market. This coincided with two further changes that added to the competitive pressure, making progress and some deregulation inevitable. The first was that the business sector, as well as reducing their overall demand for funds, began to look for finance from sources other than bank loans. They turned to the more efficient domestic capital market and also to overseas markets. The second was on the investment side where there was a new dynamism in investment behaviour: it is what is known as 'zia-tech financial technology'. Facing reduced profit margins and a need for nationalization, business sought a higher return on their short-term investment rather than holding cash and waiting to invest in plant and equipment. Individual investors also began to look to the riskier capital market for higher returns while leaving only their basic savings in the traditional low-yielding bank deposits. It could be argued, however, that this change in investor behaviour was a response to the developments in the capital markets as opposed to a cause of it. None the less, it is likely that the increasing discernment of investors was a factor that speeded up the process of financial evolution.

The changes in the bond market towards the end of the 1970s were steps towards the liberalization of the market and the introduction of a wider variety of instruments. In order to ensure stable sales of bonds to cover the budget deficits of the period the issuing conditions – coupon rate and subscribing yield – became more flexible and were revised to match yields in the secondary market. Bonds of a greater variety and range of maturities were introduced such as the five-year discount bond (1975) and the three-year medium-term bond (1978). In addition, to ensure that there would be sufficient investors, a number of restrictions were removed; these included the lifting of the prohibition on the open market sale of bonds by financial institutions (1977). In sum, the main changes in the bond market at this time were concerned with financing a large and rising debt.

THE BOND MARKET: INSTRUMENTS AND DEALING

By mid-1988 the national debt in Japan exceeded 200 trillion yen, a substantial rise both in total and proportionate terms since the early 1970s (see Figures 3.1 and 3.2). Public bonds comprised the lion's share of this debt, and at the end of 1986–7 the value of outstanding government bonds stood at almost 43 per cent of GNP. Indeed, as Table 3.1 shows, since 1980 over half the outstanding value of Japanese bonds consisted of government bonds and, taking the public sector bonds as a whole, the figure is around three-quarters (see Table 3.2). Government bonds are also the most actively traded.

Type of yen bond

Classified according to issuer, there are six types of bond in the Japanese market: government bonds, municipal bonds, government agency bonds, bank debentures, corporate bonds and yen-denominated foreign bonds. Tables 3.2, 3.3 and 3.4 provide an indication of the importance of the various types in the market.

Table 3.2 Outstanding amount of Japanese bonds (as of March 1987)

	Trillion yen	*%*
Public bonds	170.6	60.8
Government bonds	145.1	51.7
Municipal bonds (public offering)	6.4	2.3
Government agency bonds (public offering)	18.1	6.5
Special bonds (public offering)	1.0	.4
Corporate bonds	16.4	5.8
Bank debentures	46.9	16.7
Private placement	41.3	14.7
Municipal bonds	14.1	5.0
Special bonds	26.8	9.6
Corporate bonds	.4	.1
Foreign yen bonds	5.3	1.9
Total	280.5	100.0

Source: Ministry of Finance, Japanese Bond Dealers Association

Government bonds

Depending on the use to which the proceeds of a bond issue is put the government will issue one of two types of bond – a construction bond or deficit covering bond. Although there is no difference in the nature

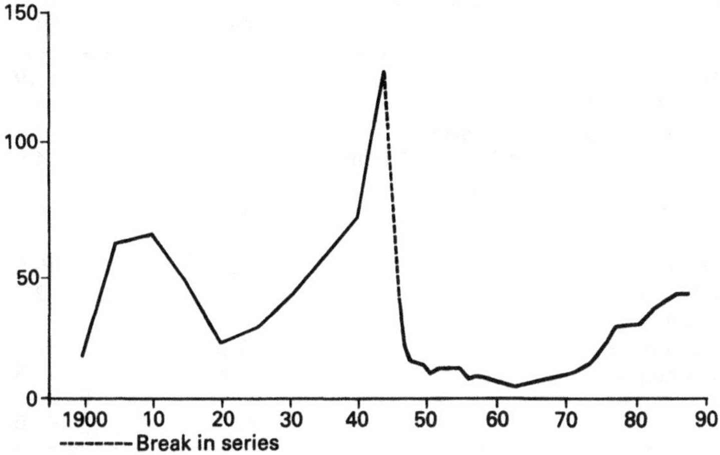

Figure 3.1 National debt as a percentage of GDP
Source: Ministry of Finance

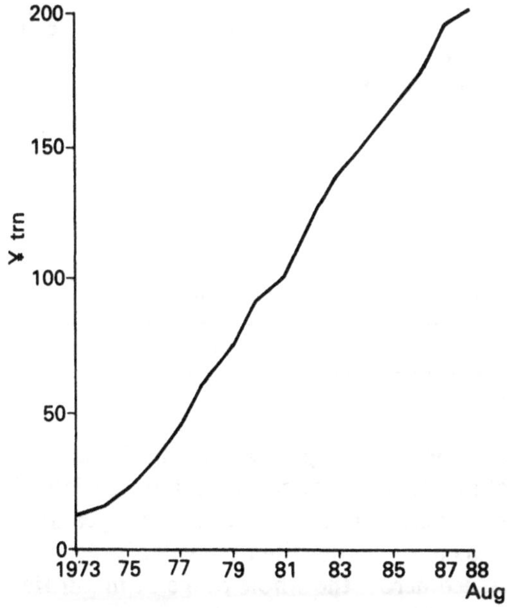

Figure 3.2 Total national debt
Source: Ministry of Finance

Table 3.3 Issuing amount in FY 1986

	Trillion yen	%
Public bonds	29.6	41.9
Government bonds	25.9	36.6
Municipal bonds (public offering)	.9	1.3
Government agency bonds (public offering)	2.8	4.0
Special bonds (public offering)	.0	.0
Corporate bonds	4.6	6.5
Bank debentures	28.6	40.5
Private placement	7.5	10.6
Municipal bonds	1.6	2.3
Special bonds	3.9	5.5
Corporate bonds	2.0	2.8
Foreign yen bonds	.4	.6
Total	70.7	100.0

Source: Ministry of Finance, Japanese Bond Dealers Association.

Table 3.4 Trading volume in FY 1986

	Trillion yen	%
Public bonds	3532.3	94.2
Government bonds	3483.3	92.9
Municipal bonds (public offering)	11.7	.3
Government agency bonds (public offering)	37.5	1.0
Special bonds (public offering)	.0	.0
Corporate sector bonds	146.8	3.9
Bank debentures	36.2	1.0
Private placement	25.6	.7
Municipal bonds		
Special bonds		
Corporate bonds		
Yen-denominated foreign bonds	7.6	.2
Total	3748.7	100.0

Source: Japanese Bond Dealers Association

of these bonds, as their name suggests the proceeds of the former are allocated to the financing of public works whereas the latter are issued to cover the financing of the government budget. Generally speaking, construction bonds are an exception rather than the rule.

Government bonds are issued across the whole range of maturities from the six-month short-term bills to the super long-term government bonds of over ten years. The most important are the long-term bonds.

Long-term bonds The long-term bond has a life of ten years, though this was initially only seven when they were first issued in 1966. They pay interest semi-annually. These bonds account for about 85 per cent of all outstanding types of government bond and they are also the most actively traded. It is because of their pre-eminent position that the conditions on which they are issued affect the issuing conditions of other government bonds as well as bank debentures and corporate bonds.

The bonds are issued through an underwriting syndication and is explained below. It takes place monthly, although the issue may be suspended if the state of the market is not considered satisfactory. When the issuing conditions are the same over a significant period of time consecutive issues over three months are eventually bound into one issue having the same series number. Redemption of the bonds is at final maturity. These bonds are traded on the Tokyo Stock Exchange and two other exchanges; however, most trading takes place in the over-the-counter market. The date of listing is the first business day of the month following the month in which the first interest payment is made.

Medium-term bonds Medium-term bonds, on which interest is paid semi-annually, are issued for two-, three- and four-year terms, and in 1987 they accounted for 5.5 trillion yen. Since their introduction in 1978, the issue has grown rapidly, with the expansion being helped by the establishment of medium-term bond funds in 1980 for the specific purpose of investing in medium-term government bonds.

As with long-term bonds, medium-term bonds are issued monthly but through public auction. Each issue in 1987 amounted to about 300 billion yen.

Discount government bonds These 'zero coupon bonds' carry no interest entitlement but are offered at a higher discount to other government bonds in a similar way to the deep discount stock in the USA; this confers tax advantages on individual investors at whom they are aimed. The objective of their introduction in 1976 was to cultivate a stable take-up and holding of government debt. They have a maturity of five years.

In 1986–87 the bi-monthly issue amounted to around 125 billion yen, the method of issue being through an underwriting syndicate.

Super long-term government bonds First issued in 1983, super long-term bonds have a maturity in excess of ten years. They are of limited marketability, with restrictions on resale usually for a fixed period or in some cases until maturity. The reason for their introduction was to tap the plentiful supply of long-term stable funds in the Japanese capital market that exist in loan trust funds, pension funds and life insurance reserves. The issue is by private placement, although recently an auction system has been introduced.

Short-term government bills Short-term bills are issued to cover temporary shortages of funds – mainly to purchase rice crops and to intervene in the foreign exchange market. The three kinds currently available are Treasury bills, Food bills and Foreign exchange bills. They have a term to maturity of six months, with the discount rate being set at around ⅛ per cent below the official discount rate. Apart from their liquidity, a benefit of the bills to investors is that they are free of Securities Transfer Tax. The method of issue is by public auction. However, most of the bills are taken up by the Bank of Japan.

A recent development (since May 1987) has been the extensive trading of the bills in the money markets. This has included sales by the Bank of Japan of its bill holdings at the prevailing discount rate in order to influence market candidates. Non-residents have been particularly active traders in the market; for example, in 1983, 52 per cent of the total trading value of the bills was by investors in this category. (Further developments in the Treasury bill market are considered in pp. 71–2.)

Municipal bills

These are bonds that are issued by the municipalities (prefectives, cities, towns) to finance local projects. Public issues are restricted to thirteen of the forty-seven governments, including Tokyo and Osaka, the rest being privately placed with a small number of financial institutions.

Government agency bonds

A number of government agencies, such as the Japan Railway Corporation and Japan Highway Public Corporation – the number was twenty-three in 1987 – are authorized to issue bonds. A full list is given in Appendix 3.1. These may or may not be guaranteed by the government.

Bank debentures

Bank debentures come in two forms: three- and five-year coupon debentures and one-year discount debentures. While the latter are purchased by individual investors, the coupon debentures are taken up by financial institutions and business corporations. Foreign investors are also major purchasers of these debentures. The coupon debentures are traded actively in the secondary market as medium- and short-term bonds although the trading volume (13.2 trillion yen in 1986/7) is low relative to the outstanding value of the debentures (16.4 trillion yen). In terms of new issues of bonds, however, they constituted some 40 per cent of the total in 1986–7.

Only six banks are authorized to issue debentures.[1] The Bank of Tokyo uses debentures as the main source of funds for its foreign exchange business and the three long-term credit banks, the Industrial Bank of Japan, Japan Long Term Credit Bank and Nippon Credit Bank, use them to finance long-term loans to industry. Bank debentures also constitute a main source of funds for the Central Co-operative Bank for Commerce and Industry to finance loans to small businesses, and for the Central Co-operative Bank for Agriculture and Forestry for its loans to members.

Corporate bonds

Corporate bonds in Japan are of three types; straight bonds, convertible bonds and bonds with warrant. The outstanding amount in issue at the end of March 1987 was 16.4 trillion yen, almost 6 per cent of the total value of bonds. A distinctive feature of Japanese corporate bonds is that they are all issued with collateral; they are generally secured by mortgage although the Electric Power Company bonds are secured by lien. It is because of this security that investors in these bonds tend to regard the yield as the most important factor when assessing an investment.

The total value of bonds issued by business corporations is restricted by the Commercial Code of Japan. The total amount is twice the sum of capital and legal reserves or shareholders equity, whichever is the smaller.

Foreign yen bonds

These are yen-denominated bonds issued in the Tokyo capital market by foreign borrowers such as governments, government agencies, local governments, business corporations and international institutions such as the World Bank. They are also known as Samurai Bonds, although strictly speaking this term refers only to these bonds that are publicly issued, not those issued by private placement.

Foreign yen bonds issues have risen markedly since the first issue in 1970, and they now account for almost 2 per cent of the outstanding value of bonds (5.3 trillion yen). The investors tend to be non-residents. There are two reasons for this; first, the bonds confer tax advantages, like Eurobonds and second, the investors tend to be attracted by the fact that the issuers are leading foreign governments or international institutions. Further, opportunities for trading Samurai bonds exist in London providing another advantage for non-resident investors. The recent rapid development of the Euroyen bond market, however, has made the market relatively inactive.

New issues: the primary market for government bonds

Table 3.3 gives details of the volume of bonds issued in the financial year 1986/87. It indicates clearly that the new issues are dominated by public bonds, especially government bonds, and bank debentures. The following discussion concentrates solely on the issue of government bonds.

Currently there are three major ways of issuing government bonds: underwriting by a syndicate, underwriting by the Trust Bond Bureau and by public auction. In addition some bonds are issued by private placement. The underwriting of government bonds by the central bank – the Bank of Japan – is in principle forbidden, but as a special case the Bank underwrites the refunding bonds issued for the purpose of redeeming the bonds the bank itself holds.

Underwriting by syndicate is used for long-term government bonds and discount bonds. Under this method syndicate members, consisting of various financial institutions including banks and securities companies, agree terms with the government to underwrite the whole of the bond issue. Thus any bonds syndicate members are unable to sell to the public during the subscription period are taken up by the underwriters.[2] Apart from the securities companies, who are exempt, the underwriting institutions cannot resell any unsold bonds for a period of about 100 days after the issue date.

Syndicate members number more than 700 and in the process of underwriting it is the proportion taken up by the securities companies that is determined first, around 16 per cent to 26 per cent of the total. The issuing procedure is described below.

First, the issuing authority, the Ministry of Finance, discusses possible issuing terms with the lead manager, who is a representative from one of the city banks. The role of lead manager is on a rotation basis. Second the lead manager sets up a managers' meeting to agree on the issuing terms among the syndicates' members. Finally the syndicate managers meet with the Ministry of Finance and the Bank of Japan to decide officially on the terms of the bond issue.

Issues under the public auction method are of medium-term bonds. The Ministry of Finance, having announced the planned amount, life and coupon rate of the bonds, invites the participants in the public auction to tender for the bonds. The tender includes the price and quantity they are willing to purchase. The participants in the auction are the various financial institutions and securities companies that are included in the underwriting syndicate for long-term bonds. However, as the financial institutions other than the securities companies had not been authorized to retail bonds to public investors until September 1983, their main reason for acquiring the bonds was to hold them in their own portfolio. Securities companies, on the other hand, took up the bonds both to resell as well as to hold in medium-term bond funds. Until the relaxation of the regulations, therefore, most of the bonds were initially subscribed by the securities companies.

A complement to the syndicate underwriting is the underwriting by the Trust Fund Bureau. The Trust Fund Bureau is a public institution which manages funds from personal-sector savings, mainly in the form of postal savings and post office life insurances. It uses these funds to underwrite a sizeable part of the government bond issue. In principle government bonds should be issued to the private sector not the public sector, however, since the Trust Bureau's funds are derived from the private sector it is argued that the principle is upheld even though the funds are publicly managed.

A private placement or direct issue of bonds is made when there is direct negotiation of issuing conditions and procedures between the government and individual investors. In a sense Trust Fund Bureau underwriting is a form of private placement.

Since 1982 super long-term bonds have been issued regularly using this method with the main subscribers being from the institutions with surplus long-term funds such as the trust banks, the life insurance companies and the Central Co-operative Bank for Agriculture and Finance. The main reason for the introduction of private placement was to relieve the pressure on the public offer market especially at times of excess supply of bonds. The result has been effective and the public offer market has worked rather more smoothly since the commencement of private placements.

Dealing in Japanese bonds – the secondary market

At the centre of the market are the bond dealers, confined exclusively to the twenty-three companies until 1984 when a number of banks were authorized as dealers. In addition to their brokerage function, securities companies also purchase bonds, which they hold on their books in anticipation of investors' requirements. Thus they ensure prompt trading in the market. In order to adjust their holdings of bonds, securities companies also trade with each other; this is known as inter-broker-dealer trading. It is conducted through the Japan Bond Trading Company, which was established in 1973 to facilitate such trading. In 1986–87 the value of transactions reached 750 trillion yen.

Since June 1984 thirty-four banks[3] have been authorized bond dealers – their trading as dealers is known as bank dealings. These banks, therefore, operate in the bond market on two levels – as intermediaries and as investors. Their dealing accounts, however, have to be distinguished from their investment accounts as do the dealing and banking organization. However, it is impossible from the outside to determine the category into which their bond trading falls.

The traditional picture of the Japanese bond market is one in which the city and regional banks, the main subscribers to government bonds issued through the underwriting syndicate, are the major suppliers of bonds to the investors. The main investors include the agricultural financial institutions, investment trusts, that bank as well as foreign investors. Table 3.5 shows the importance of each of the institutions as holders of government bonds and the significance of bond holdings in their total assets.

In 1986, however, there was a reversal in traditional position of the banks and some of the other financial institutions as banks became net purchasers of bonds. This is illustrated in Table 3.6, which shows gross and net dealing for all Japan's financial institutions. The reason for the change in the bank market position is due mainly to the depressed demand for loans from business corporations – their main borrowers – as the economy's growth rate slowed. Banks, therefore, switched to good quality government bonds as an alternative asset. It is thought that in the future the lower growth prospects for the economy will make this change a permanent one.

The trust banks, of which there are seven as well as one city bank engaged in the same business, are the largest holders of government bonds among Japan's financial institutions. They accounted for 25 per cent of government bond holdings in March 1987. Their main role

Table 3.5 Financial institutions as of March 1987 (trillion yen)

	Financial source (deposit etc.)	*Total asset*	*Total securities holdings (government bonds)*	*Government bonds as a percentage of total securities*	*Government bonds as a percentage of total assets*
City banks	154.0	238.9	27.5 (7.2)	12.4	3.1
Regional banks	103.6	122.8	22.5 (7.2)	12.4	5.9
Long-term credit banks	39.5	50.5	10.3 (3.0)	5.2	5.9
Trust banks	82.7	160.6	49.2 (14.7)	25.4	9.2
Agricultural financial institutions	50.4	59.0	24.7 (9.5)	16.4	16.1
Mutual saving banks	42.3	48.9	7.4 (1.8)	3.1	3.7
Credit associations	54.6	73.6	11.9 (3.1)	5.4	4.2
Other financial institutions	19.1	19.1	4.3 (0.4)	0.7	2.1
Life and non-life insurance companies	77.4	80.4	33.9 (4.9)	8.5	6.1
Investment trusts	35.3	—	26.8 (6.1)	10.3	—
Mutual aid associations	12.1	—	29.4 —	—	—
Postal savings trust fund bureau	108.9	—	53.7 —	—	—
Total	779.9	—	301.6 (57.9)	—	—

Source: Bank of Japan

Table 3.6 Secondary market of Japanese bond market (trillion yen)

	Bond transaction (in FY 1986)				*Share in net sale (%)*	*Share in gross trading (excluding dealing) (%)*	
	Buy	*Sell*	*Net*	*Gross*			
City banks	31.5	28.8	2.7	60.3	−57.4	2.8	11.8
Regional banks	10.7	10.1	.6	20.8	−12.8	1.0	4.1
Long-term credit banks	11.9	12.3	−.4	24.2	8.5	1.1	4.7
Trust banks	64.6	64.7	−.1	129.3	2.1	6.0	25.3
Agricultural financial institutions	15.1	14.8	.3	29.9	−6.4	1.4	5.9
Mutal saving banks	6.0	5.7	.3	11.7	−6.4	.5	2.3
Credit associations	5.9	6.1	−.2	12.0	4.3	.6	2.4
Other financial institutions	9.5	6.8	2.7	16.3	−57.4	.8	3.2
Life and non-life insurance companies	10.5	8.5	2.0	19.0	−42.6	.9	3.7
Investment trusts	13.2	7.9	5.3	21.1	−112.8	1.0	4.1
Mutal aid associations	2.3	1.9	.4	4.2	−8.5	.2	.8
Business corporations	27.4	29.5	−2.1	56.9	44.7	2.6	11.1
Non-resident	36.0	37.1	−1.1	73.1	23.4	3.4	14.3
Individuals	4.5	5.6	−1.1	10.1	23.4	.5	2.0
Others	8.9	12.6	−3.7	21.5	78.7	1.0	4.2
Bond dealers	822.1	832.4	−10.3	1654.5	219.1	76.4	
Total	1080.1	1084.8	−4.7	2164.9	100.0	100.0	
Total excluding dealing				510.4			100.0

Source: Japan Bond Dealers Association

Note: Trading excludes Gensaki transactions.

has been to supply long-term capital to the industrial sector but, in the same way that the city and regional banks have had to adapt to the falling loan demand, the trust banks have also adjusted by investing heavily in securities, especially bonds. By the end of the financial year 1986–87 only 40 per cent of their assets were in the form of loans while security holdings were over 30 per cent of assets, with bonds accounting for 9 per cent.

Investment trusts have also become major purchasers of bonds in recent years as their business has flourished. Standing at only 4.1 trillion yen in 1976, their funds have grown rapidly at a rate of over 20 per cent and now exceed 35 trillion yen (March 1987). Their portfolios are made up of 58 per cent domestic bonds, 21 per cent equity, 10 per cent foreign securities and the balance held in the money market.

Agriculture in Japan operates its own financial system through the 4,523 Agriculture Co-operatives (Nokyo), the Prefectural Credit Federation of Agricultural Co-operatives (Kenshinren) and the Central Co-operative Bank for Agriculture and Forestry (Norinchukin). With significant funds available, derived mainly from the sale of rice to the government, these agricultural institutions are major investors in bonds. They account for around 16 per cent of the government bond holdings of all Japanese financial institutions. At the end of March 1987, total securities holdings were 42 per cent of their total assets, almost 40 per cent of which were government bonds.

The agricultural financial system operates in the following way: Kenshinren accept deposits from the Agricultural Co-operatives which they use for lending within the agricultural sector. Of their surplus funds, approximately half are deposited with Norinchukin. It, in turn, relends within the agricultural sector, but it also invests its surplus funds in the money and bond markets. In recent years, as the growth in lending to agriculture has slowed down, both Norinchukin and the Kenshinren have invested more heavily in the financial markets, with the former becoming a major supplier of funds in the money market.

A final major category of investor in the bond market is the non-resident. Historically there has been a high correlation between the yen/dollar exchange rate and yen bond investment by foreign investors; whenever the yen appreciated, foreign investments in bonds increased. An example occurred in 1982 when net bond investments by foreigners amounted to 1.6 trillion yen, a record total, at a time when the yen appreciated sharply against the dollar. In principle, non-residents investments in Japanese bonds will be determined by expected exchange rate changes and expectations of the market trend; they may well be operating in opposite directions. This appeared to happen in 1986 when, despite an appreciating yen, foreign investors became net sellers of bonds. Indications are that, in their judgement, the bond market had reached a peak when long-term bond yields dipped as low as 2.5 per cent during August at that year.

Trading in bonds takes place in both the stock exchange market and in the over-the-counter market. However, it is the over-the-counter transactions that account for by far the greater part of bond trading; in 1988 the volume of over-the-counter trading was 3,490 trillion yen, whereas that of exchange trading was 247 trillion yen. For government bond trading the volumes are 2,475 trillion yen and 139 trillion yen respectively. The main reasons for the dominance of over-the-counter trading are twofold; first is the fact that there are so many issues of bonds (around 60,000) that it is technically impossible to list them all on the exchanges. Second, the complex bond trading methods are not suitable for exchange trading. An example of this is in the case of switching when some issues are sold and others purchased concurrently. It is difficult to conduct such trading at the desired prices and quantities on an exchange where investors buy or sell through securities companies.

One difficulty that arises from the domination of over-the-counter trading is that it is not possible for non-participants to observe actual trading prices. Exchange trading, in which trading prices are disclosed publicly, therefore, plays a particularly useful role since it gives investors a good indication of the prices at which bonds are being bought and sold. In recent years, as the volume of bond trading on the Tokyo Stock Exchange has increased, the Exchange prices have been increasingly used as a reference point for over-the-counter transactions.

Table 3.4 indicates that trading volume is heavily concentrated on government bonds. In fact most of the trading that takes place is in a single issue of the government bonds known as the benchmark issue. In 1986–87 this was issue number 89. As a result the benchmark issue offers good liquidity compared to other bonds of similar maturity and coupon. Furthermore, a particular characteristic of the Japanese market has been the yield gap that has opened up between the benchmark and other issues.

One particularly important form of bond dealing is known as Gensaki (or repo) trading. In the absence of a well-developed money market, bond traders have traded bonds under a form of sale and repurchase agreement in which the seller contracts to buy the bonds after an agreed period at a given price. In effect bonds bought and sold under the Gensaki trading became a form of short-term money

Table 3.7 Maturity distribution of Japanese bond market (trillion yen)

	Maturity										
	less than 1-yr	*2-yr*	*3-yr*	*4-yr*	*5-yr*	*6-yr*	*7-yr*	*8-yr*	*9-yr*	*longer*	*Total*
All bonds	25.3	23.1	22.2	19.2	19.7	13.3	14.4	16.7	14.9	13.1	189.9
Government bonds	13.7	12.3	9.3	5.7	7.3	5.5	6.4	7.0	7.9	8.9	87.7

Source: Nomura Research Institute

Notes: 1 Excluding discount bonds, convertibles, warrant and private placement.
2 as of November 1987.

market instrument and their liquidity is greatly enhanced. When Gensaki trading was first introduced in the mid-1970s it accounted for around 55 per cent to 60 per cent of total bond trading. By the mid-1980s however, as the bond market became more active, Gensaki trading fell in proportionate terms to between 10 per cent and 20 per cent of total transactions (see Table 3.1).

As regards maturity distribution, Table 3.7 shows that this is reasonably evenly spread although there is a rather greater proportion of bonds with shorter maturities. Compared with other bond markets, such as that in the US, bonds of more than ten years maturity were relatively scarce in 1987, with most of these being government bonds.

STEP-BY-STEP DEREGULATION

Unlike in the United Kingdom, there has been no Big Bang in the Japanese financial markets in the last five years. On the other hand there has been a steady, albeit slow, evolution towards a more open and deregulated system in which financial institutions, previously kept in their separate markets by law, have been permitted to compete on more even terms in a wider number of settings. Furthermore, there has been a burgeoning growth in the variety of financial instruments. One possible explanation for the comparatively slow pace of liberalization in Japanese finance has been the resistance from the financial institutions eager to protect their business. This is especially true of the securities companies. The government's traditionally protectionist and regulatory philosophy has bolstered this resistance as may have the 'Japanese way of doing things', namely that of seeking a consensus before proceeding with major reform. Another possibility is that since Japan has been an exporter of capital it has not had to dismantle its restrictive financial system as fast as it would have done if it had had to attract overseas funds. Naturally, the abolition of exchange controls has worked in the opposite direction.

The pressure for the recent changes in the bond market have come from a number of sources. These include: the continuing need to finance the budget and re-finance outstanding debt; pressure from the banking sector to expand their business beyond deposit taking and lending; and from overseas, as other countries, who have removed some of their controls, have sought reciprocal arrangements in Japan.

As in the 1970s, much of the change in the bond market has been in the form of an increased variety of instruments, but there has also been some relaxation of the constraints on the participants in the market. An example of the former is the introduction (in 1983) of super long-term bonds, which were designed to tap long-term investment funds and thereby ease any problems that might arise in funding a budget deficit. Attempts to increase competitiveness in the primary market has resulted in the use of an auction system for some bond issues rather than private placement or syndicate underwriting. Thus in 1987, super long-term bonds were issued by auction, and from 1989 some 20 per cent of each month's issues of long-term bonds will be auctioned. In the secondary markets the dominant position of the securities houses has been undermined first in 1983, other financial institutions were permitted to retail bonds and then, in 1984, a number of banks were able to act as dealers in the bond market.

The legal separation of the banking and securities business is enshrined in Article 65 of Japan's Securities and Exchange law. This has given the securities companies a virtual monopoly of an especially lucrative business, in which their commissions are both high and fixed. They are also the sole underwriters of corporate bonds, another very profitable activity. It is into these areas that the large city banks would like to move, especially as their traditional business has been squeezed. On one side, corporate customers have been obtaining finance from alternative sources – bonds and equities – in preference to bank loans. On the other, the deregulation of deposit interest rates have pushed up banks' costs of attracting funds. As a result there has been pressure from the banks for a change in the law to allow them to compete more freely with the securities companies. At the time of writing no firm decision had been taken at the Ministry of Finance, although a number of possibilities had been considered ranging from wholesale deregulation to limited entry into each other's markets through subsidiaries.[4] Whatever the form of the changes, the result will be an increase in competitive pressure across the financial markets including the bond market; this will help iron out some of the structural rigidities.

Evidence of the rigidities that exist in the bond market is shown by the concentration of trading in the benchmark issue. Nomura Research Institute estimated that the general yield level in mid-1987 represented by the par yield of government bonds of ten-year maturity was around 4 per cent. Heavy trading in the benchmark issue (number 89) produced a yield of 2.55 per cent.[5]

Another area in which important changes are occurring is in the issue of Treasury bills, and in the money markets as a whole. Deregulation of some interest rates has meant that the Bank of Japan has had less leverage on the general level of rates than previously, as there are now fewer tied to the official discount rate. This is particularly significant as the size of the money market is small – it is only 4 per cent of the size of the US market. Steps that have been taken so far to expand the market, and hence the Bank's influence on short-term interest rates, include a doubling in the size of the planned bill issue in 1989–90 to 4 trillion yen and, from October 1989, the issue of three-month bills in addition to the current six-month bills. In the operation of the market there has been an expansion in the scope of permitted dealings. Dealing is now allowed in bills of less than one-month maturity, and the Bank of Japan's intentions are that its own market operations will be in the one to three week range. In an attempt to link movements in short- and long-term interest rates more closely the Bank has also relaxed the regulations on commercial banks' ability to arbitrage between long- and short-term rates; specifically, raising the limit on funds that can be borrowed from the unsecured call market and the ceilings on the holdings of certificates of deposit.

Besides the requirements of more effective implementation of monetary policy, there are a number of other possible explanations for the encouragement of the bill market. One is that, with current short-term rates lower than long rates, the government will be able to reduce the costs of financing its debt; in the future it will be able to hedge its interest rate exposure. Another factor is that the booming economy of the late 1980s, with the consequent rising tax revenues, meant that the government has been able to retire long-term debt.

It has, therefore, been able to consider replacing long-term with short-term debt, a particularly important development given the intention of ceasing to issue new deficit covering bonds in 1990–91. It is the view of some commentators that the Japanese government believes that the savings surplus in the economy is so ingrained that it is possible to change the structure of the debt without any undesirable side effects.[6]

The recent scarcity of long-term government debt has resulted in pressure from another direction. Public financial institutions, which have hitherto held a substantial proportion of their assets in bonds and a very restricted proportion in equity and other instruments, have successfully pressed for an easing of the legal constraints. It is likely the equity investment will rise as they look for profitable outlets for their funds. In the case of Norinchukin, agriculture's central bank, since 1986 its legal status has been transformed from a non-profit making institution into a bank; in principle it can now offer the same range of services as the city banks. It has also moved into the trustee business and lately has been able to invest in foreign equity markets.

Just as there has been a slow liberalization of the bond market, so too has there been a movement towards internationalization, with the abolition of exchange controls in 1980 being one of the most significant deregulatory measures. Japanese corporations have increasingly turned towards foreign bonds issued as a means of raising finance: the foreign bond issue rose from only 300 billion yen to 400 billion yen between 1965 and 1975, but expanded ten-fold up to 1986, reaching 4.37 trillion yen. Deregulation in the Euroyen market allowing the issue of new instruments such as zero coupons, debt and equity warrants and floating rate notes produced a rapid growth in the market, the pace of which has been increased by the lifting of exchange controls and the abolition of withholding taxes for Euroyen issues by Japanese companies.

Pressure from abroad, especially from the USA but also from the European Community, has led to the gradual opening up of some of Japanese financial sectors to overseas firms. This pressure has come particularly in response to entry by Japanese financial institutions in foreign markets. European banks, for example, can set up 50 per cent-owned securities subsidiaries in Japan; this is preferential treatment when compared to the 5 per cent ownership limit imposed on Japanese banks. Non-resident members of the underwriting syndicate for long-term government bonds have also seen their allocation raised, and in future the increasing use of auctions will permit greater participation by foreign investors in the bond markets.

One final important development has been the establishment of the bond futures market. Bond futures were introduced in 1985 to provide a hedging mechanism for institutional investors and, although it had a troubled opening period because of an unexpected rise in money market interest rates, the market has developed quickly. In 1987 the size of the future contract exceeded that of the US Treasury contract in Chicago.

CONCLUDING REMARKS

Japan's financial markets have developed steadily over the past twenty-five years. Once highly regulated and compartmentalized markets in which the different types of financial institution were kept in their separate businesses by rigid legislation, they have gradually become freer and more competitive. To some extent they have had to adapt to the changing demands of a highly developed economy. In the early years the principle objective was to channel the relatively scarce savings into funds for investment: this was done through the banks. As the economy has developed, not only have businesses looked elsewhere for finance, investors also have not been satisfied with the low returns obtained from banks. In a similar way, the development of the bond market reflects a shifting preoccupation, from financing the government debt to improving the way in which the market works and meeting the requirements of investors.

Further steps towards liberalization are likely but its progress will probably be piecemeal. Not only is it dependent on the external pressures of the increasing internationalization of financial markets, it is also dependent on internal pressures from the institutions, the government and investors. As a recent survey in *The Economist* noted:

> Change in Japan's financial system usually evolves through competitive horse-trading among the existing institutions, under the guidance of the Ministry of Finance, which nudge negotiations in the direction it wants by changing the ground rules.[7]

Appendices to chapter three

APPENDIX 3.1

Table 3A.1 Government agency bonds

The following government agencies are now allowed to issue this type of bond:

Japan Railway Construction Corporation
Japan Highway Public Corporation
Tokyo Expressway Public Corporation
Housing and Urban Development Corporation
Water Resources Development Corporation
Housing Loan Corporation
Hanshin Super-Highway Corporation
Finance Corporation of Local Public Enterprise
Small Business Finance Corporation
Honshou-Shikoku Bridge Authority
Hokkaido & Tohoku Development Corporation
New Tokyo International Airport Corporation
Maritime Credit Corporation
Small Business Promotion Corporation
Keihin Port Development Authority
Hanshin Port Development Authority
Japan Regional Development Corporation
Japan National Oil Corporation
Oversea Economic Corporation Fund
Employment Promotion Project Corporation
Osaka International Airport Environmental Development Organisation
Fukuoka International Airport Environmental Development Organisation
Tohoku District Development Company

Note: Japan National Railways and Nippon Telegraph and Telephone Public Corporation had been major issuers in this category, but both were privatized in 1987.

APPENDIX 3.2

Table 3A.2 Main economic indicators in Japan, 1979–88

	Growth (% change in GNP)	*Inflation (% change in consumer prices)*	*Unemployment (% of total labour force)*	*Current balance (US$ billions)*
1979	4.4	5.5	2.1	−9
1980	4.3	8.1	2.0	−11
1981	3.7	4.9	2.2	5
1982	3.1	2.7	2.4	8
1983	3.3	1.9	2.7	21
1984	5.1	2.3	2.7	34
1985	4.5	2.0	2.6	50
1986	2.5	0.4	2.8	86
1987	4.5	0.0	2.9	87
1988	5.8	1.0	2.5	80

Source: *National Institute Economic Review*, various issues

APPENDIX 3.3

Figure 3A.1 Japanese government bond yield
Source: Nomura Research Institute

NOTES

1 The maximum amount authorized to twenty times the sum of paid-up capital and legal reserves with the exception of the Bank of Tokyo, for which it is five times.
2 The subscription period lasts from the 25th of the month prior to the month of issue to the 15th of the month of issue.
3 The 34 include the 13 city banks, seven trust banks, three long-term credit banks, the Central Co-operative Bank for Agriculture and Finance and ten regional banks.
4 See *The Economist*, 18 March 1989: 125–6.
5 In the Japanese bond market the yield is quoted on a simple yield base rather than a compound yield base. The calculation is as follows:

$$\text{Simple yield} = \frac{100 \cdot \text{Coupon}}{\text{price}} + \frac{100}{\text{years to maturity}} \cdot \left(\frac{100}{\text{price}} - 1\right)$$

6 See *The Economist*, 1 April 1989: 91–2.
7 See *The Economist*, 10 December 1988, ‘A survey of Japanese Finance’: 4–9.

4 The French bond market: state-led innovation

Jean-Marie Serre and David Cobham

I

The French bond market has traditionally been distinguished by three characteristics, each of which is now in the process of disappearing: it was a narrow market, like the French capital market as a whole; it was a market separated from the rest of the French capital market (e.g. the money market, the mortgage market) by a profound segmentation; and there was no substantial market in government bonds that could serve as a fulcrum for an active debt management policy or for monetary policy in general. These three characteristics have been gradually becoming less marked since 1978, as the structure and size of the French capital market have been moving closer to those of other capital markets.

The word 'explosion' is commonly used to describe the rapid development of the bond market since the start of the 1980s, which has occurred under the impact of the growing importance of government bond issues in particular. Table 4.1 shows the rise in gross bond issues since 1976. In the ten years to 1986 gross bond issues increased by a factor of 8.2 and government bond issues by a factor of 56.5. The fall in government bond issues in 1987 was offset at the wider level by the large sales of equity involved in the privatizations undertaken by the Chirac government.

There are several reasons for this explosion. The first is the rapid rise in the government borrowing requirement, which had previously been very small in France. The budget surpluses of the mid-1960s and the early 1970s were followed by budget deficits of varying sizes, and there has been a significant structural budget deficit since 1981 (see Table 4.2). While the budget deficit was a conjunctural or cyclical deficit only, it could be financed by short-term debt instruments or even by 'sight' debt instruments if use was made of the 'monetary

Table 4.1 Gross bond issues (FFr bn), 1976–87

	1976	*1977*	*1978*	*1979*	*1980*	*1981*	*1982*	*1983*	*1984*	*1985*	*1986*	*1987*
Total	42.2	51.4	57.8	65.5	111.6	106.9	154.7	193.6	242.1	307.0	347.2	294.6
Government bond issues*	2.5	8.0	13.5	15.0	31.0	25.0	40.0	51.0	84.9	97.6	141.3	81.0
Share of government in total (%)	5.9	15.6	23.4	22.9	27.8	23.4	25.9	26.3	35.1	31.8	40.7	27.51

Source: *Rapports Annuels* de la Commission des operations de Bourse, 1976–87

* Conventional, ORT and OAT bonds

Table 4.2 General government borrowing requirement (−) as percentage of GDP

Year													
1976	*1977*	*1978*	*1979*	*1980*	*1981*	*1982*	*1983*	*1984*	*1985*	*1986*	*1987*	*1988**	*1989**
−0.5	−1.0	−2.1	−0.8	+0.2	−1.8	−2.7	−3.1	−2.8	−2.6	−2.9	−2.4	−1.6	−1.6

Source: *Comptes de la Nation*

* Forecasts

circuit' of the Treasury (see p. 83). But the change in the nature of the deficit, together with the concern of all governments since 1977 to develop long-term saving, led to a major increase in the issue of government bonds to prevent the excessive monetization of the national debt.

The second reason for the explosion of the bond market was the rapid development of the *organismes de placement collectif en valeurs mobilières* (OPCVM), financial intermediaries which collect personal savings and other small-scale funds for investment in financial assets.[1] Within this category the short-term *sociétés d'investissement à capital variable* (SICAV) and the short-term *fonds communs de placement* (FCP) have grown several times over since 1981. Like that of the US money market funds which they resemble, the growth of these institutions was encouraged by the official regulation of the interest payable on term deposits in banks as part of a policy to encourage the growth of saving in less liquid forms.

The third reason relates to the qualitative development of the market. On the one hand there have been numerous financial innovations, mostly initiated by the state; on the other hand there has been a process of deregulation as in other markets (discussed later in this chapter). In so far as the state has been behind nearly all of these innovations, they can be described as 'policy innovations': new financial products; new placing techniques; variable, adjustable or floating interest rates; new redemption arrangements. These innovations have then been taken up by the private sector so that 'policy innovations' have been followed by 'system innovations', which in turn stimulate new policy innovations, and so on.[2] These changes in the nature of financial transactions in the markets were a necessary condition for the expansion of their volume, for they provided better protection against interest rate rises (through more attractive investments and less risky loans) and a *ceteris paribus* reduction in the cost of finance (through new forms of borrowing).

The French bond market is also becoming more integrated into a unified capital market. Before 1985 there was no single capital market in France. Instead there was a number of segmented markets which had almost no communication with each other. Each of the three primary markets (money, stocks and shares, and mortgages) was regulated by a different supervisory authority (the Banque de France, the Treasury and the Commission des opérations de Bourse, and the Crédit Foncier de France respectively). Access to the various markets was restricted to certain categories of financial agent. For example, the banks and certain other specified institutions only[3] had access to the money market but it was closed to companies and individuals. On the other hand the banks hardly ever operated in the bond market and never operated there as buyers of bonds. Finally some maturities were not covered by the variety of financial instruments which existed at that time.

These markets were also highly regulated. In the bond market, for example, the Treasury controlled the timing of new issues, prior authorization to issue was necessary in some cases, commissions and brokerage fees were fixed administratively, and so on. Moreover, the functioning of the various financial intermediaries was regulated either by administrative requirements or by cartel agreements. Thus there was relatively little competition. Whatever the original rationale for these arrangements, the natural result was that the financial system became increasingly unable to satisfy the demands of economic agents, to withstand international competition or to play a useful role in economic policy.

These basic features of the system have been gradually modified, particularly while Pierre Bérégovoy was Minister of Finance in 1985 and 1986, with the aim of creating a unified market covering all sorts of transaction from the overnight to the very long term and accessible to all economic agents. The origin of the measures undertaken – that is, the various reports commissioned by the authorities from groups of experts – and their contents are discussed in sections II and V below.

Until recently budget deficits were financed mainly through the 'Treasury circuit' rather than in the capital market. The Treasury circuit consists of its 'correspondents', that is the institutions which place deposits with it – mainly *chèques postaux* (the equivalent of the National Girobank), local authorities and the Caisse des Dépôts et Consignations (which itself acts as banker to a large number of savings associations (Caisses d'épargne)): this network is so large that a substantial part of the funds injected into the economy by budget deficits is automatically recovered by the Treasury because the institutions concerned provide finance to the Treasury, either directly through their deposits with it or indirectly through purchases of bills. The system was developed in response to the financial crises experienced by the Treasury in the inter-war period, when there was no real capital market in France, so that the state had to turn in emergency to the Banque de France. Thus the marketable national debt was relatively small; it was also undiversified, and mainly long-term. Moreover, the earlier national debt had been significantly reduced by the higher inflation and the more nearly balanced budgets in France than in other countries. Thus government borrowing was only intermittent

Table 4.3 The national debt (FFr bn)

Year	Medium- and long-term debt			Short-term debt			Sight debt	
	Capital market borrowing							
	Bonds outstanding	Revaluation[1]	Various government liabilities[2]	Treasury bills	Short-term borrowing[3]	Credit from Banque de France	Deposits of correspondents[4]	Treasury account at Banque de France, etc[5]
1964	16.59	—	7.15	49.45	—	9.00	49.01	1.98
1965	16.28	—	6.84	49.68	—	7.13	51.67	1.91
1966	16.59	—	6.54	43.01	—	8.88	57.31	2.14
1967	16.88	—	5.88	54.58	—	8.60	53.31	2.24
1968	15.86	—	4.70	61.05	—	8.82	60.12	2.02
1969	15.27	—	3.90	65.65	—	8.35	61.45	2.85
1970	13.66	—	3.57	64.72	—	7.10	63.55	2.17
1971	12.57	—	3.30	64.82	—	6.54	75.29	2.80
1972	11.93	—	3.02	55.88	—	7.02	85.19	0.20
1973	28.28	—	1.83	40.68	—	6.92	95.62	−2.15
1974	42.21	—	1.69	36.78	—	6.70	105.03	0.76
1975	34.48	—	1.54	77.61	—	9.65	104.32	0.06
1976	28.96	—	1.39	91.44	0.65	11.50	109.76	4.73
1977	35.52	9.16	1.27	101.14	1.73	10.05	124.71	2.08
1978	46.56	11.50	1.74	125.86	1.83	12.11	137.79	−20.58
1979	66.57	29.90	4.18	136.59	1.83	13.81	146.66	−12.21

1980	111.03	50.05	5.99	181.60	1.82	15.46	159.28	−25.47
1981	134.49	40.39	9.66	186.47	0.76	—	173.79	−22.05
1982	154.12	53.71	48.41[6]	269.75	0.27	—	194.97	−71.06
1983	200.17	57.40	46.15	307.95	13.64	5.76	208.01	−36.48
1984	278.18	55.09	42.74	353.87	14.20	11.54	251.59	−55.23
1985	365.91	43.50	44.81	373.32	14.33	23.58	274.53	−65.52
1986	480.02	44.70	39.98	436.70	0.91	25.28	261.16	−49.63
1987	526.39	26.04	35.28	501.86	0.72	36.50	293.75	−112.98

Source: Situation résumée des opérations du Trésor (SROT) *Journal Officiel* de la République Française et *Bulletin trimestriel de la Banque de France* no 69, décembre 1988–janvier 1989, p. A-63.

Notes:

1 The additional liability resulting from the indexation on the gold price of the 1973 7% stock. The revaluation for other indexed stocks is included in the figures for bond issues.

2 Mainly securities issued in compensation for nationalization and war damage.

3 The semi-compulsory and compulsory loans levied in 1976 and 1983.

4 Mainly *chèques postaux*, Caisse des dépôts et Consignations and local authorities. There is a break in the series in 1975.

5 Including coin issued by the Treasury.

6 Including FFr 38.12 bn resulting from the industrial and banking nationalizations of 1981–82.

(for example, the Treasury issued no debt at all on the capital market between 1958 and 1963).

Table 4.3 shows the evolution of the national debt from 1964 to 1987, differentiating between medium- and long-term debt, short-term debt, and 'sight debt' (as in 'sight deposits'). Medium- and long-term debt has been the most important category only since 1980. Apart from the development of bond issues for reasons already given, attention should be drawn to the increase due to the (over-generous) indexation of the 7 per cent loan of 1973 on the price of gold (column 2), and to the increase in the 'various liabilities' associated with the nationalizations of 1981–82. All these factors combined to raise the long-term debt twenty times over between 1976 and 1987.

At the same time the average maturity of this debt has been shortened. The perpetuities once issued (which now account for only FFr500 million) were succeeded by bonds with maturities of over thirty years, and then by bonds with maturities of less than thirty years (the latter including all the bonds issued since 1970. Moreover, conventional bonds have been replaced by variable rate bonds, by renewable bonds and by *assimilable* bonds (that is, bonds issued in successive tranches but with the same terms and conditions: see section IV).

Short-term debt, defined to cover all debt with a maturity of less than five years which is paid a return comparable to that on the money market, is a more heterogeneous category which includes both monetary and non-monetary financing of the budget deficit. Treasury bills *sur formules*[4] (non-negotiable bills reserved for individuals, amounting to a little under 7 per cent of this category of debt at the end of 1987), Treasury bills *en comptes courants* held by the Caisse des Dépôts et Consignations (33.5 per cent of the total) and 'short-term borrowings'[5] constitute non-monetary financing. Treasury bills *en comptes courants* held by banks (the category which has risen most) and credit from the Banque de France (which is subject to a ceiling agreed between the Treasury and the Banque) constitute monetary financing.

Finally the 'sight debt' is the finance provided by the funds collected directly through the Treasury's circuit, the most important element being the obligatory deposits of the Treasury's 'correspondents' – *chèques postaux*, local authorities, the Caisse des Dépôts et Consignations, etc. These funds still provide some of the financing of the budget deficit, but they no longer seem absolutely necessary. In so far as the cost of collecting these deposits through the Treasury's own network has been rising relatively to the cost of funds on the capital market, there is a tendency for the Treasury to withdraw from the collecting of deposits and the associated operating of mechanisms of payment and to make greater use of the capital market. Such a change will make possible a genuine debt management policy.

The structure of the debt will therefore continue to alter, with the share of long-term debt – only 9 per cent in 1972 but 44 per cent in 1987 – rising further, and that of sight debt – 55 per cent in 1974 but 14 per cent in 1987 – falling; short-term debt shows no clear trend and may well retain or even increase its share in the light of the recent development of an active market in Treasury bills, which are likely to become the key intervention instrument of the Banque de France.

At the same time as the structure of the national debt has been changing, a higher proportion of it has come to be marketable. Up to 1985, only medium- and long-term government securities were negotiable on the Bourse. Treasury bills *sur formules* could be redeemed prematurely, on the basis of a predetermined interest rate schedule, but could not be transferred. Treasury bills *en comptes courants* could be traded on an active secondary market, but were reserved for financial agents.[6]

Since June 1983 the issue of renewable bonds (*obligations renouvelables du Trésor* – ORT), which will gradually replace the Treasury bills *sur formules*, has increased the marketability of the national debt, for ORT bonds can be traded on the Bourse. Moreover in December 1985 the restrictions on non-financial agents holding current account Treasury bills were lifted and all fixed-rate current account bills became negotiable. The secondary market in Treasury bills has developed significantly since then, and the outstanding total of marketable debt has also increased (see Table 4.4).

Thus the French national debt is becoming closer in terms of its maturity structure and its marketability to the national debts of the other major countries. At the same time its size relative to GDP has risen appreciably, from 14.8 per cent of GDP in 1976 to 24.9 per cent in 1987 (see Figure 4.2).

The last kind of change which is occurring relates to the techniques by which loans are issued and placed. The new techniques are discussed in Sections IV and V, but two basic characteristics of the earlier methods should be noted here. First, since 1946 the Minister of Finance has had a general power to authorize new issues, which was used to suspend the issue of private-sector securities during the issue of a government loan or when the authorities wished to regulate interest rates. In a normal period, that is when there is no rationing of issues, it is up to the Issues Committee to fix the timetable of new

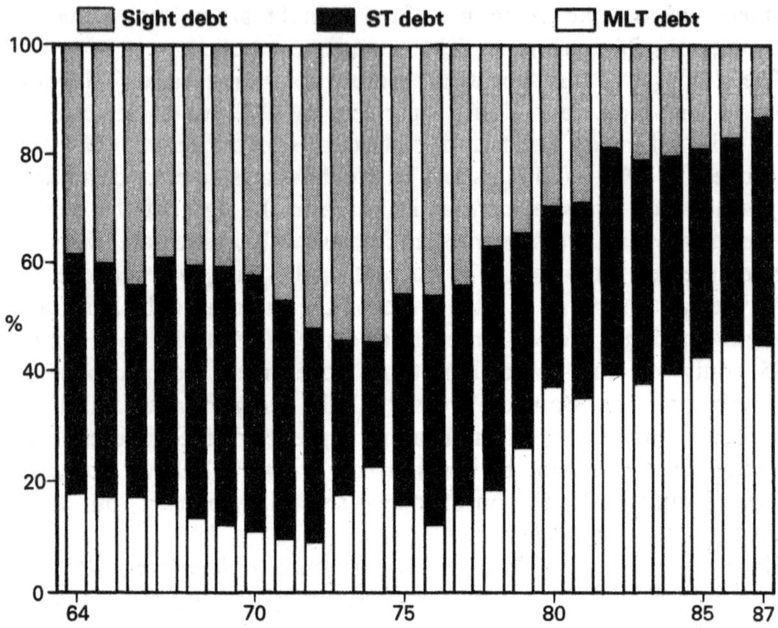

Figure 4.1 The structure of the national debt, 1964–87

issues. This committee, which includes the main banks of the primary markets and the Caisse des Dépôts et Consignations as well as the Treasury, intervenes two or three times a month, or even more often if necessary; and until recently the timetable was determined around the needs of the public sector (including semi-public institutions such as Crédit Foncier, Crédit National, the nationalized electricity and railway industries, etc.). Thus the bond market was the 'prisoner' of the public sector, which contributed the bulk of new issues.

The trend towards more continuous and less discrete public drawings on the capital market, together with the growth and development of the latter, should lead in the future to a gradual elimination of the timetable constraints, at least in normal periods. Moreover, since November 1984 the Treasury has exempted issues of less than FFr500 million partly or entirely from the timetable, thus creating the so-called *petit marché*; and the maximum size of issue for this market was raised to FFr1 billion at the beginning of 1986.

Second, the techniques by which securities are placed remained

Table 4.4 The marketable national debt

	FFr bn		*Percentage of total national debt*	
Year	*Narrow*[1]	*Broad*[2]	*Narrow*[1]	*Broad*[2]
1980	168.14	244.06	37.38	54.26
1981	186.23	314.60	35.57	60.08
1982	257.76	433.24	39.65	66.63
1983	305.76	524.32	38.10	65.32
1984	379.03	648.68	39.81	68.14
1985	464.70	746.49	43.24	69.46
1986	(588.76)[3]	895.06	(47.51)[3]	72.23
1987	(677.90)	986.86	(51.84)	75.47

Sources: Table 3 and SROT, *Journal Officiel*.

Notes:

1 Narrow definition: bonds outstanding, revaluation, and Treasury bills in current accounts held by non-financial agents and OPCVM.

2 Broad definition: as 1, plus bills in current accounts which are negotiable only between the financial intermediaries allowed access to the money market.

3 From 1986 Treasury bills in current accounts have been freely transferable between all agents: the 'broad' definition therefore remains the only one which is relevant.

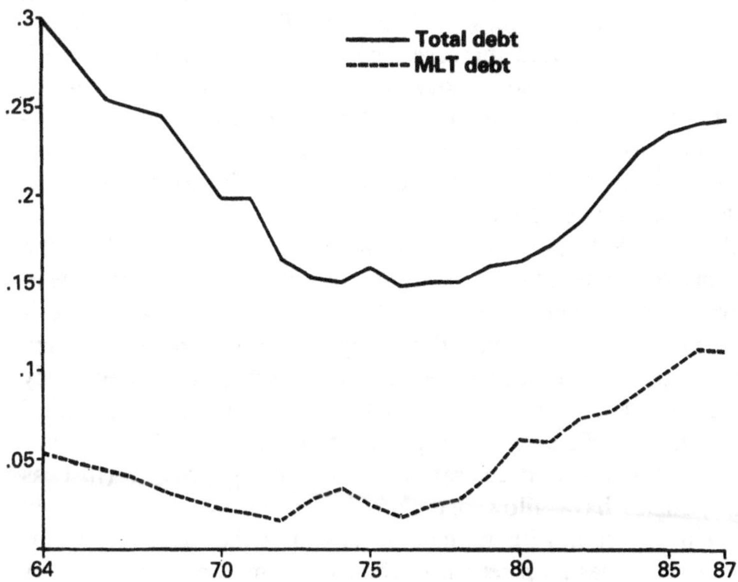

Figure 4.2 The ratio of national debt to GDP, 1964–87

unchanged from 1968 to 1985 (i.e. from the Leca Report to the implementation of the recommendations of the Tricot Report – see Sections II and V). These techniques involve the banks being responsible for placing new issues, after consultation with the authorities, in such a way as to equilibrate the supply of and demand for capital.

The banks get together in 'syndicates' led by a 'leader' (sometimes assisted by 'co-leaders'). The leader takes charge of relations with the issuer, the organization of the operation and the contractual details. Even for private securities the leader negotiates the conditions with the Treasury, with reference to current yields on the secondary market. The leader also has to 'police' the secondary market, that is to maintain the price for a period after the security has been issued on the Bourse. In practice the Caisse des Dépôts et Consignations participates in nearly all new issues, either to absorb securities (if the placing is difficult) or to supply the leader with extra securities (in the opposite case). Some banks act as underwriters, while others merely place securities without assuming the underwriting risk, although in practice they also hold on to unbought securities. In both cases the banks receive commissions, which are not supposed to benefit the subscribers. However there exists a 'grey market' on which the holders of securities (banks and issuing houses) relinquish part of their commission in order to facilitate the placing of the securities and to avoid being left with large holdings of their own. This makes the primary market more flexible and increases the turnover of securities. With government issues, all the various financial networks participate in placing the securities. The high street banks place them with individuals, while other financial institutions (at least in recent years) channel a large part of their supplies towards institutional investors, particularly insurance companies.

Finally it should be noted that the bond market, and particularly the market for government bonds, has not so far played any direct role in the operation of monetary policy: the banks hold hardly any negotiable government securities and the Banque de France does not carry out conventional open market operations. Nevertheless indirectly, by shifting the financing of the economy from bank credit to the capital market, official policies on saving and the demand for money have greatly facilitated the deceleration of monetary growth (just as incomes policies have allowed companies to increase their internal funds). This concern with monetary growth is the most important reason for the Treasury's return to the capital market since 1977. A secondary reason is that the cost of funds on the market has become more competitive because of the problems of profitability encountered in the Treasury circuit. However the desirable side-effect of these problems is that a modern monetary policy based on open market operations and an active debt management policy will now be able to develop.

II

The reforms of the French bond market in the 1960s and 1970s were designed to reorganize and enlarge it. They were undertaken in response to a perceived need, and did not evoke major criticism other than the complaint that they were overdue. They were also the result of extensive consultation with professional circles by means of numerous reports of expert committees. Even at a time when it hardly ventured on to the market (it had kept out of the market in eleven years out of the period 1959–77), the Treasury was concerned to get the best out of this source of finance and to improve its operation. Nevertheless towards the end of the period the criticism that the system inherited from the 1960s was unsuited to the new economic and financial context became louder and more frequent.

In 1963 the government returned to the bond market after five years of absence and the Lorain Committee produced its report on the financing of investments. This report detailed the weaknesses of the market – the crowding out of private issuers due to the inadequate absorptive capacity of the market, negative real interest rates, the predominance at issue of purchases by individuals (institutional investors bought securities only after their price on the Bourse had declined sufficiently). A first, limited, result of this critique was the more favourable tax regime for bonds introduced in 1965.

However the main reform came in 1968 in the wake of the recommendations of the Leca Commission; the bulk of the new arrangements remained in force until 1985. The Commission's contribution was most important in the matter of the techniques by which public and private securities are placed. The rules it proposed were designed to restore the unity of the primary market and to induce the banks to assume more responsibility, both *vis-à-vis* the issuers (through the practice of underwriting instead of merely placing on a commission basis) and *vis-à-vis* the market (so as to avoid excessive discounts or premia). It was the state borrowing of January 1973 (the Treasury had made no call on the market since 1967) that provided the first occasion for a contract between the state and the leaders of a placing syndicate under which the latter undertook to settle the whole issue in no more than fifteen days. The payment to the syndicate was the difference between the price it paid to the state and the price it received from subscribers: in return for the underwriting of the issue the Treasury paid a guarantee commission of 0.15 per cent and a placing commission of 0.50 per cent.

The difference in terms of the tax regime and interest rates between conventional (non-indexed) government securities and private securities has also been gradually reduced. Most specific tax exemptions[7] have been eliminated and interest rates on government securities have moved closer to those of the money market, as recommended by the Leca Report. In addition coupon rates now correspond to actuarial interest rates, for public as well as private securities, as recommended by the Committee for the financing of the Sixth Plan (the Chatillon Report of 1971).

Finally the administration of securities and the redemption procedures have been modified. Since 1973 the administration of securities has been undertaken not by the Treasury but (as with other issuers) by SICOVAM.[8] The system by which the redemption price increased with the delay in redemption was abandoned in 1967, and the January 1973 loan inaugurated the procedure of redemption *in fine* (at term) whereby the full issue is redeemed at a given date, as opposed to redemption by annual drawings in which portions of an issue chosen by lot are redeemed at specified intervals: the new procedure is simpler for both issuers and subscribers.

In practice, however, although the system guaranteed to the Treasury the placing of its securities, it turned out to have a number of defects. On the one hand the predetermination of yields and the fixing of a single price over a longish period (usually three months) thanks to the supervision of the syndicate leaders caused problems when the volatility of interest rates increased. This was the main reason for the development of the 'grey market' (Section I above), which enables yields to be adjusted during the period when the debt is being placed. On the other hand, savers suffered serious capital losses from conventional securities, particularly after 1979. Finally it is not clear if this method of placing securities provided the cheapest finance for the Treasury given current conditions. The commissions paid to the banks were obviously higher than if there were no underwriting risk assumed by the syndicate; and the size of the placing commission is less obviously justified than in the past since the institutional investors now dispose of more and more funds so that large amounts of securities can be placed easily and cheaply. The relative cost is a question of the size of the risk premium offered to the syndicate compared to the additional cost involved in fixing the interest rate at a level which would itself guarantee the entire placing of the loan.

More generally public borrowing policies have been accused (e.g. Eck 1982: part 3) of causing subscribers important capital losses and excessive gains. The latter have occurred in the case of indexed securities such as the 7 per cent stock of January 1973, the so-called Giscard loan, the notional redemption value of which was indexed on the price of gold and rose from FFr6.5 billion in 1973 to FFr46.1 billion in 1981, while important capital losses have occurred in the case of conventional loans.

In view of these defects, a reorganization and modernization of the way loans are placed as well as of the various kinds of loan seemed desirable. Such changes have undoubtedly been hastened by the growing international (particularly European) interdependence of capital markets, which implies a convergence of the rules and practices by which they function.[9]

III

Until the beginning of the 1980s there was a growing divergence between the financial system in France, stuck in its traditional mould, and those in other countries, particularly the USA and the UK. This was emphasized by the Plescoff Report of 1980 (foreword):

> When prices are decontrolled and there is full international competition, above all in the Common Market, it is inconsistent to preserve segmented financial structures unchanged and to maintain administrative procedures and punctilious regulations designed to protect more and more important categories (of agent) from the rigours of the capital market.

The immediate risk was that the financial marketplace of Paris would be deserted by French investors while French companies moved their operations to other markets which offered instruments better suited to their needs. Ultimately the risk was that Paris would be deprived of any international role.[10]

A series of reforms of the capital markets as a whole were therefore set in motion by the socialist government of 1981–86 (particularly by Minister of Finance Pierre Bérégovoy), starting with the instruments of the national debt. Thus it was essentially the state that initiated the deregulation, innovation and reintroduction of competition into the French financial system.

IV

Section I mentioned the favourable conditions attending the explosion of the French bond market: increased budget deficits, the growth of financial institutions such as the SICAV, and financial innovation. The latter made possible the rapid growth of new issues without excessive interest rates, by making available to both issuers and subscribers a much wider range of instruments. Thus the 'qualitative' development of new issues was complementary to their quantitative development.

Bondholders had been badly affected by the sharp rises in interest rates in 1980–1 which reduced substantially the value of conventional fixed-interest rate stocks. The problem was particularly serious for institutional investors which were obliged to employ part of the funds they were managing in the capital market whatever the conditions of the market. Issuers on the other hand – and particularly the state – found the annual cost of fixed-rate issues becoming prohibitive and were concerned as to how to obtain the benefit of the likely relaxation of interest rates in the future. Hence the period 1980–5 saw the creation of three main types of innovation. Two of these, related to conventional fixed-rate stocks and the new variable rate stocks, were soon taken up outside the public sector which had introduced them, while the third referred specifically to the debt instruments of the state.[11]

Fixed-rate stocks

Fixed-interest rate stocks have developed in three directions since 1980–1. First the traditional method of redemption, by which a certain proportion of an issue, chosen by lot, was redeemed each year, has been largely replaced by redemption *in fine*, that is where the entire issue is redeemed at the end of a fixed term of eight, ten or even twelve years. The latter puts all holders on an equal footing and reduces the administrative burden on the issuer. For the investor it avoids the risk of redemption at par when the market price of a stock is above par (if interest rates have fallen since the date of issue). Some companies have gone even further, for example the nationalized Gaz de France from December 1984, in capitalizing the interest and paying it too in one lump at the term of the loan; while in January 1986 the Treasury issued the first tranche of a zero coupon bond (FELIN – *fonds d'état libres d'intérêt nominal*). The disadvantage of redemption *in fine* is that it may be poorly suited to the needs of the issuer, who may find himself 'overfinanced' for part of the life of the loan; it also runs counter to the general tendency for a reduction in the duration of loans.

The second innovation relating to fixed-interest rate stocks is the introduction of stocks with 'windows' or optional exits, the first of which was issued by a subsidiary of the nationalized Electricité de France in 1982. These stocks can be redeemed either at term or, if so desired by the holder or the issuer, at one of several intermediate dates fixed at the time of issue (after seven, ten or fourteen years for these stocks which generally have an eighteen-year term). A fall in interest rates gives holders a capital gain based on the longer maturity, and lengthens the maturity structure of an issuer's debt, while with a rise in rates the capital loss to holders is limited by the possibility of early redemption. The early redemption prices are set such that holders will exercise this option only if there is a significant increase in rates, and such that issuers will exercise their corresponding option only if there is a large fall in rates.

The third innovation in fixed-rate stocks is the issue since 1981, by the public Caisse Nationale des Télécommunications and then by the banks, of stocks with warrants attached: they carry an interest rate below the market rate but include instead a right to subscribe to additional securities at predetermined dates and conditions. If interest rates fall, holders benefit from an increased appreciation of these bonds due to the existence of such rights. However this form of stock has naturally lost much of its popularity since the appearance of interest rate futures in 1986.

Variable-rate stocks

The second area of innovation, and the most important in this period, is that of variable-interest rate stocks. The development of such instruments was assisted by the unfavourable new regulation of bank bills and term deposits introduced in 1981: these measures gave birth to the short-term SICAV and short-term FCP, and at the same time enabled a temporary compression of the monetary aggregate M2 and the fulfilment of the monetary target set for it.[12] The variable rates were initially (from 1976) based on a 'monetary' index – the money market interest rate – but from 1980 they were frequently based on a bond market index, which is an original feature of the French bond market. This formula was inaugurated with the bonds issued in compensation for the nationalization of 1981–2.

The first wave of bonds at 'monetary indexed' variable rates had coupons which depended on the average over the month of the overnight rate in the money market (referred to as T4M) or the six-month rate (T6M). The former have the disadvantage that in times of high interest rates, for technical reasons, they include a large positive margin above the rate on an equivalent fixed-rate stock, which can pose a heavy burden on the issuer if there is a significant fall in rates. Stocks indexed on the annual interest rate TAM, which corresponds to the monthly capitalization of the T4M over twelve months, do not have this disadvantage.

The second category of variable-rate stocks, which use a bond market index, have coupons calculated on the basis of the average bond yield. There are several reference rates, the most common being that of public sector non-indexed stocks on the date of subscription, TMO. For the 1981–2 nationalization compensation bonds only the TME was used: this is the average coupon rate on government bonds of more than seven years on the secondary market. These stocks are in heavy demand from the short-term SICAV and the short-term FCP, since they carry long-term interest rates without the long-term risk. Nevertheless some discounts or premia relative to the par value have been observed.

The third category is that of 'adjustable' stocks, whose rates are fixed but adjusted on the basis of the last one or two monthly TMO figures at intervals of one year (TRA stocks) or three years (TRO). TRO stocks were first issued by Renault in March 1981, and then taken up by financial institutions. They are relatively short-dated (usually nine years) compared to TMO stocks (fifteen to thirty years). The interest rates can also be 'floating', which means that the reference period for the calculation of the coupon ends only just before it is detached. With 'adjustable' rates on the other hand the coupon is known before the previous period coupon is detached.

New government debt instruments and techniques

The third area of innovation is that of new instruments for government borrowing. With a view to increasing the amount of its borrowing, improving the management of the national debt and widening the field of innovation, the government introduced in 1983 two new instruments: renewable Treasury bonds (ORT) and convertible stocks. The technique of placing government bonds was also modified in 1985.

ORT bonds replaced in June 1983 the Treasury bills *sur formules* issued to individuals. They have a term of five to eight years, they are quoted on the Bourse and they can be exchanged at the end of three years for new ORTs. All the interest is paid *in fine* (at the end of three years or at the normal term, as appropriate), which allows holders temporarily to avoid income tax. ORTs are attractive to companies because of these fiscal advantages and because they are more liquid than conventional bonds. Issues of ORTs were, however, suspended in June 1985. Mention should also be made of the new facility by which the Treasury issues additional tranches of existing bonds (*obligations assimilables du Trésor* – OAT bonds), using the new placing technique of *adjudication* which is discussed below. The issue of OAT bonds each month guarantees to the Treasury continuous (rather than 'discrete') access to the capital market and allows it to take full advantage of the development of conditions in the terms on market (the successive tranches can be adjusted). In 1987 gross issues of OATs by *adjudication* represented nearly 95 per cent of the Treasury's drawings on the capital market (the rest being secured through the traditional technique of *prise ferme* – placing bonds through sydicates which purchase the bonds themselves in the first instance).

Convertible stocks offer the option of an exchange each year (starting from the end of the second year) for a 'bond-indexed' variable-rate stock. Thus the investor is protected against capital losses from interest rate rises but can make a capital gain from interest rate falls.

The technique by which government bonds are placed was modified in 1985 in response to the recommendations of the Tricot Commission (see Section V below), so as to increase the degree of competition between the banks involved in placing and to make the market more transparent. The technique of *adjudication* (auction), used for Treasury bills on the money market since 1964, is now used for bond issues on the primary capital market: auctions of OATs are held monthly. A network of financial institutions responsible for new issues of government securities and for making a secondary market in them (comparable to 'primary dealers' in the USA) has been set up at the initiative of the Treasury: the so-called *spécialistes en valeurs du Trésor* (SVT). The role of the SVT, who numbered thirteen in December 1986, is to improve the placing of Treasury securities and to increase the liquidity of the market for them. In particular they are required continuously to quote bid and offer prices for the main securities (marketable Treasury bills, bonds which are deliverable on the MATIF, and bonds at adjustable rates) and to participate in the *adjudications* and in the placing of Treasury securities.

V

In the French case the authorities have not been forced to respond to autonomous financial innovations. On the contrary, official policies have created the innovations in the expectation of certain consequences, particularly for economic policy; even though some developments have been difficult to foresee and control.

In 1985 the Tricot Report on the cost of financial intermediation analysed the effects of the transformation of the bond market and identified certain rules and practices as unsuitable. In particular it recommended a reduction of the banks' commission (because of the growth of institutional saving), the officialization of the 'grey market', the modernization of placing techniques and experimentation with auctions *à la hollandaise* in which all allotments are made at the rate (price) offered, rather than at the highest accepted rate (minimum accepted price) – the traditional system for Treasury bills – and the diversification of syndicate leaders (with the emergence of primary dealers). The banks felt that the reduction in their commissions should be accompanied by the free negotiation of all the conditions which affect the placing of new issues; the shift from underwriting to auctions was a step in this direction.[13]

All these reforms and the preceding innovations have a number of implications both generally and for economic policy. First the emergence of variable and adjustable rate stocks discussed in Section IV offers greater security to investors against capital losses, an advantage well appreciated by both individual and institutional investors. These stocks are also very convenient for banks which employ funds in forms on which the return varies with yields on the capital market. More generally, variable-rate stocks tend to make the market more flexible and dampen upward movements in long rates. More specifically, 'monetary-indexed' variable-rate stocks increased the communication between the money market and the capital market at a time when such communication was still limited in France, while 'bond-indexed' variable-rate stocks have facilitated the growth of long-dated stocks in response to demand.

On the other hand, the rather anarchic development of these new types of stock may have confused non-professional investors and hindered the interest rate normalization desired by the Treasury. Variable rates provide less of a disincentive to borrowers than fixed rates in times of high interest rates, and thus may reduce the effectiveness of monetary policy. And the lack of an interest rate ceiling, together with the presence of an interest rate floor, also constitutes a risk for borrowers.

In any case it is unlikely that these stocks will replace fixed-rate stocks which are better suited to tranquil conditions. Up to 1984 the proportion of the latter was declining but in 1985 it rose a little as Table 4.5 shows. This tendency is even more marked for 1986 and 1987 when issues of Treasury bills are taken into account, as in Table 4.6.

Table 4.5 Structure of new government bond issues (in percentages)

	1979	*1984*	*1985*
Fixed-rate stocks	97.2	48.0	49.0
Variable/adjustable rate stocks	2.8	52.0	51.0

Source: *Les Notes Bleues*, no. 400, 5.9.88

Table 4.6 Structure of outstanding government debt (in percentages)

	1984	*1985*	*1986*	*1987*
Bonds:				
Fixed rate	91.0	84.3	89.3	88.3
Variable rate stocks	9.0	15.7	10.7	11.7
Marketable Treasury bills:				
Fixed rate	35.7	39.9	65.6	85.6
Variable rate	64.3	60.1	34.4	14.4
Total:				
Fixed rate	61.6	63.0	79.0	87.1
Variable rate	38.4	37.0	21.0	12.9

Source: *Les Notes Bleues*, no. 400, 5.9.88

Second, the widening of the range of government debt instruments (ORT, OAT, convertible stocks) at a time when the Treasury became the main borrower on the market (with between 35 per cent and 40 per cent of new issues) allowed the deficit to be financed more easily than expected after the very sharp rise in rates at the beginning of the 1980s. Together with the good performance of the bond market, largely due to the saving policy pursued from 1978, the new debt management policy pursued since 1983 seems to be such as to limit the possibility of financial crowding out by offering attractive financial products which are acceptable substitutes for monetary assets. In fact since 1983 there has been a sizeable reduction in the monetary assets of non-financial agents as a proportion of their financial wealth.[14] At the same time agents' financial wealth is rising regularly as a proportion of their total wealth, which is a new phenomenon for France. In these conditions it is not impossible that the financing of budget deficits might have a 'crowding-in' effect favourable to saving and investment (Friedman 1978).

The counterpart to this trend has been the fact that the explosive growth of the OPCVM (which tends, as in other countries, to raise the velocity of M1) has not provided a source of long-term funds for industry. On the contrary, the short-term SICAV and FCP, which hold more than half of the securities of the OPCVM as a whole, have been particularly successful in obtaining very short term funds from companies. This development has therefore left untouched the problem of industrial finance, while increasing significantly the volatility of the secondary bond market.[15] Moreover, there is a risk of financial crisis here because these institutions are engaged in a process of maturity transformation, but they do not have access to the facilities for rediscount or refinancing which the banks can use.

Finally the economic policy implications of the recent changes are important. As regards debt policy, the various innovations should (other things being equal) lower the costs of finance while providing investors with a proper return. Moreover, the French Treasury is now obliged to operate a continuous policy of refinancing and consolidating the national debt. The latter is now very large and the authorities cannot rely on inflation to reduce it. Every year an important (and growing) part will have to be refinanced,[16] and the lengthening of the maturity structure of the debt is now a priority, to be achieved without disturbing the capital market. It is for this reason that the authorities decided to tap a new section of the market by holding an auction in February 1987 of twenty-five-year OAT, a risky operation since it occurred at a time of monetary tension and sharp rises in interest rates. In the event the Treasury allotted FFr3.1 billion of these bonds (roughly half of the amount applied for) at a price below par giving a yield of 9.38 per cent as against the coupon rate of 8.50 per cent; thus the operation confirmed the rise in interest rates, and showed the Treasury unequivocally accepting the going market price.

In general a more active policy of debt management has now become necessary, but also possible, due to the development of the secondary market in government securities. The latter allows the Treasury to smooth out in time the redemption of its debt, and to take advantage of opportunities in the market to reduce the overall cost of debt service (if, for example, one stock stands at a discount compared to another, or if there is a possibility of making profitable switches between stocks). For this purpose the Treasury reactivated the Fonds de soutien des rentes ('fund for the support of yields', established in 1937) and set up in 1987 a Caisse d'amortissement de la dette publique ('office for the redemption of the national debt'). It also intervened directly in the market twice in 1987, to undertake switches of stock.

The Fonds de soutien des rentes (funded by the Caisse des Dépôts et Consignations) is primarily responsible for optimizing the structure of the debt (switches between fixed and variable rate stocks, etc.). The Caisse d'amortissement, originally entrusted with the allocation of the proceeds of privatizations to the reduction of the national debt, now has the role of reducing the debt and smoothing out the process of redemption.

The Treasury, for its part, intervened in February 1987 to exchange 'Giscard' bonds (the 7 per cent 1973 stock) for OAT bonds; these operations made it possible to stagger the redemption of the 'Giscard' stock and to reduce significantly the amount due at the final maturity date of January 1988.

Some of these operations, such as switches between fixed rate and variable rate stocks, have encountered difficulties: bondholders accept the Treasury's offers only if they anticipate a favourable movement in interest rates, which results in uneven, 'all or nothing', results.

At the same time a convergence between monetary policy and debt policy has become possible. The new interconnectedness of the capital markets and the reforms of government debt instruments now allow the Banque de France to intervene with open market operations on all sections of the market and particularly on the larger secondary markets for Treasury Bills and long-term government securities. The final disappearance in January 1987 of the *encadrement du crédit* (direct credit controls) after a transitional phase of two years may also encourage the banks to acquire government bonds. The *encadrement* had discouraged this because bond holdings were counted in the banks' lending that was subject to control.[17] The acquisition of government securities by the banks will further facilitate open market operations by the Banque de France and will enable it to influence the interest rate on the capital market directly and to control more precisely the structure of interest rates if it wishes.

Nevertheless situations of conflict between the Treasury and the Banque de France are not entirely excluded. The managers of the national debt now have at their disposal a battery of widely-held, marketable securities, which enables them to influence conditions throughout the capital market. It is necessary to avoid situations in which the Treasury acts for its own account and induces in the market developments of interest rates which the central bank would be led to correct. Such a 'double determination' of interest rates would be both expensive and inefficient.[18] At the same time it is necessary to avoid the Treasury acting too strongly on the liquidity of the economy, for example by its operations in international capital markets. Thus debt management policy and monetary policy need to be co-ordinated, and there needs to be some limit on the budget deficit. However a rigid formula of the MTFS type seems to have been excluded by the authorities.

VI

The modernization of the management of the national debt in France therefore forms part of a profound restructuring not just of the bond market but of the whole of the monetary and financial system. Markets which were narrow, segmented, administratively regulated and non-competitive are being replaced by markets which are much deeper and more inter-dependent, which allow private agents to undertake all sorts of arbitrages, which are regulated less by administrative intervention and more by competition between financial intermediaries. The Treasury itself is submitting to the laws of the market and the monopolies of the various financial intermediaries are disappearing as the markets become more closely interconnected.

There are still elements of uncertainty, independent of the changes of structure: for example, if interest rates were to rise again this would cause problems for the policy of consolidating the national debt just as it would reduce the dynamism of the bond market and the financial futures market (MATIF). However, even if the changes are not completed (further changes in the Bourse are on the way[19] and financial futures are still in the process of developing) it is clear that an important step has been taken in a very short time, though the *dirigiste* nature of much of the innovation may be surprising to Anglo-Saxon observers: the French capital market is much better adapted to the needs of the French economy in 1988 than it was three or four years before.

NOTES

1 The OPCVM should be distinguished from 'institutional investors' such as insurance companies, pension funds and the Caisse des Dépôts et Consignations. The former are 'transparent' and 'open-ended' institutions which (like unit trusts) in effect manage portfolios directly for their clients rather than on their own account. The latter receive funds under certain

arrangements and invest them on their own account; they are generally *obliged* to hold certain proportions of their funds in particular kinds of assets.

2 See De Boissieu (1982) for discussion of these terms.

3 The *établissements non bancaires admis sur le marché monétaire* (ENBAMM) – mainly institutional investors, together with stockbrokers, the SICAV and the institutions of the Treasury's monetary circuit.

4 Treasury bills in the form of notes, as opposed to those *en comptes courants* (in current accounts) which take the form of entries in the ledgers of the Banque de France.

5 Semi-compulsory and compulsory loans levied in 1976 and 1983, which matured in 1981–2 and 1986 respectively.

6 Since 1984, however, the short-term SICAV have been able to hold Treasury bills in current accounts more freely. In so far as these institutions are 'transparent', non-financial agents have enjoyed a larger indirect access to these bills. This is shown in the rise in the 'current account bills held by non-financial agents' category of the national debt.

7 The best known and most controversial of these was the exemption of the Pinay stock of 1952–8 from death duties, which resulted in substantial tax avoidance.

8 *Société interprofessionelle pour la compensation des valeurs mobilières*: a centralized clearing house which holds securities on deposit, operates accounts for the owners of securities and implements transactions between its clients.

9 It should also be noted, with regard to the Treasury's short-term borrowing which has not been considered here, that between 1967 and 1974 Treasury bills *sur formules* became less differentiated and more homogeneous; and that instead of the banks being required to hold some minimum level, Treasury bills in current accounts were from 1963–4 sold by auction on the money market. However the Caisse des Dépôts et Consignations continued in the 1970s and 1980s to buy large amounts of special bills in a semi-automatic way, although that is not in principle its accepted role.

10 See, for example, Naouri *et al.* (1986).

11 We do not consider here the important financial innovation of the creation in 1986 of the financial futures market (MATIF), which is outside the scope of the traditional bond market.

12 Cf. the effect of Regulation Q in the USA in encouraging the growth of money market funds.

13 In addition the Minister of Finance has since the end of 1985 authorized the free negotiation of commissions on public sector issues in the primary market.

14 The ratio fell from 61.5 per cent in 1981 to 51.8 per cent in 1985 for households, and from 25.4 per cent to 14.7 per cent over the same period for companies (*Bulletin Trimestriel de la Banque de France*, juin 1986, pp. 49, 52); and the trend has continued since then.

15 See the conclusions of the Conseil National du Crédit working group on saving instruments (Conseil National du Crédit, 1986).

16 The average term of government long-term debt in the form of fixed rate borrowings (which amounted to some FFr464 billion at the end of 1987)

was about seven years, and that for variable rate borrowings (FFr61 billion) was about eleven years.

17 Hence the banks held almost no bonds at all: in 1985, for example, institutional investors and OPCVM held 63 per cent of the total value of bonds outstanding, persons held 31 per cent, companies and financial institutions 5 per cent and the overseas sector 1 per cent. In 1986 the holdings of both banks and OPCVM increased, while the direct holdings of households declined.

18 See Serre and Jaillet (1989).

19 For example, the 'Big Bang' announced on 10 March 1987 by the then Minister of Finance, Edouard Balladur.

REFERENCES

Beaufils, B., Guimbert, J-P., Py, G., Richard, B., and Thiry, B. (1986) *La banque et les nouveaux instruments financiers*, Paris: Revue Banque Editeur.

Boissieu, C. De (1982) 'Innovation financière et contrôle monétaire', *Banque*, janvier.

Chatillon (Comité) (1971) *Rapport du comité du financement du 6ᵉ plan*, annexe 6, Paris: Documentation française.

Choisnel, A. and Rouyer, G. (1986) *Le marché financier, structures et acteurs*, Paris: Revue Banque Editeur.

Conseil National du Crédit (1986) *Les instruments d'épargne*, Paris: Documentation française.

Dautresme, D. (Rapport) (1982) *Le développement et la protection de l'épargne*, Paris: Documentation française.

Delessy, H. and Pescheux, J-M. (1986) 'La dette publique française', *Revue de l'IPECODE*, mars.

Eck, F. (1982) *Le Trésor*, Paris: PUF.

Friedman, B. (1978) 'Crowding in or crowding out?', *Brookings Papers on Economic Activity* 1978: 3.

Jaffre, P. (1986) 'L'unification du marché des capitaux', *Banque*, avril.

Klein, C. (1985) 'Les innovations sur le marché obligataire en France', *Eurépargne*, no. 5.

Leca (Comité) (1967) *Rapport sur la réforme du marché obligataire*, Paris: commissioned by the Minister of Finance.

Lorain (Comité) (1963) *Rapport sur le financement des investissements*, Paris: Documentation française.

Meyer, H. (1985) 'L'évolution récente du marché obligataire en France', *Eurépargne*, no. 1.

Naouri, J-C., *et al.* (1986) *Livre blanc sur la réforme du financement de l'économie*, Paris: Documentation française.

OCDE (OECD) (1982) *La gestion de la dette publique*, vol. I, Paris.

Plescoff (Comité) (1980) *Rapport du comité du financement du 8ᵉ plan*, Paris: Documentation française.

Prissert, P. (1985) *Economie monétaire et bancaire*, Paris: Revue Banque Editeur.

Serre, J-M. and Jaillet, P. (1989) 'Gestion de la dette publique et politique monétaire', forthcoming.

Tricot, B. (Rapport) (1985) *Le coût de l'intermédiation financière*, Paris: Documentation française.

5 Debt management in the United Kingdom and the London gilt-edged market

David Gowland

INTRODUCTION

Marketable bonds issued by the UK government are usually called gilt-edged or gilts because the certificates issued to the purchasers of these securities used to be edged with gold (gilt) – unfortunately these have now been replaced by a much more prosaic statement of the owner's asset. These securities have been actively traded in London for about 300 years. For much of this period the market gradually evolved with few major changes, but in the last twenty years it has had to adjust to a series of shocks (in the economists' sense) administered by the authorities and to the technological change and globalization which have affected all financial markets. The London gilt-edged market has, however, been more affected than almost any other. It is the object of this chapter to describe and analyse this series of officially-wrought revolutionary changes.[1]

In the 1950s and 1960s the Bank of England pursued a policy of 'leaning into the wind', that is of supporting the price by repurchasing stock when market pressure would otherwise have caused a fall in bond prices (rise in interest rates) and vice-versa. This was similar in effect but not in rationale (see p. 4) to the interest-rate pegging policies then in vogue in most countries. In 1971 'leaning into the wind' was abandoned as part of the 'new approach' to competition and credit control. In principle the authorities forswore any active debt management policy. In early 1974 they had once more to adopt an active, indeed aggressive policy, in the market, motivated both by a desire to control the money supply and by a need to finance a chronic budget deficit; the Public Sector Borrowing Requirement (PSBR) was 10 per cent of GDP in 1975–6).[2] The authorities' policy was usually called the 'Duke of York' strategy because it involved an initial increase in interest rates followed by a subsequent reduction so producing a pattern in interest rates reminiscent of the nursery rhyme.[3] During this period the authorities proved innovative in their marketing strategy, the most notable features of this being the initial experiments with auctions, convertible stock and indexation, that is linking the interest payments on and the repayment of principal of some government securities to the retail price index.

Despite the radical changes in monetary policy in 1979–80 after the election of Mrs Thatcher, there was considerable continuity in debt management policy until November 1985, although the 'Duke of York' tactic was quietly abandoned. In November 1985 Chancellor Nigel Lawson introduced a policy of exact funding, that is of selling just enough gilts to ensure that the public sector's contribution to monetary growth was zero. In other words government abandoned an important instrument of economic management: the possibility of using debt management, open market operations, to offset swings in private sector behaviour. By then the Bank of England had already started planning its new American-style gilts' market which was introduced on 26 October 1986, the date of 'Big Bang' on the Stock Exchange. Although contemporaneous with this liberalization of the Stock Exchange (free entry, abolition of minimum commission and single capacity), plans for the new gilts' market were initially independent of the stock exchange reforms and indeed probably preceded them in conception. By then another new feature of government policy was on the horizon: the swing of the public sector into a substantial financial surplus. Throughout the period from 1974, the Bank of England showed acute strategic awareness and considerable tactical skill in achieving their long-term objectives as well as in satisfying short-run macro-economic exigencies. Of particular interest was their efforts, culminating on the 1986 reform, to ensure that the market remained under their suzerainty yet was both technically efficient and open to foreign competition. The example of the West German government bond market revealed the dangers. By the late-1980s virtually all dealings in West German government bonds took place in Luxemburg or London. In consequence the market was indistinguishable from the Eurobond market. Both *amour propre* and a wish to retain extra leverage for reasons of economic policy made this unattractive to the Bank. The Bank wished to retain a distinct separate market but not at the price of dirigiste controls which would probably have been unenforceable anyway. The Bank devised a careful mixture of sticks and carrots so as to succeed: a feat of considerable skill and ingenuity.

TYPES OF SECURITY

At end-March 1989, gilts held by the market amounted to £135 billion (nominal value) and £143 billion (market value) – market holdings are the total issue less the holdings of central government bodies, the Bank of England, etc., but including holdings of local authorities, public corporations and the overseas sector. Gilts accounted for 75 per cent of all government debt. These gilts included £300 billion of perpetual stock and £15 billion of index-linked securities, two specialities of the UK government discussed below. The average term to maturity of gilts was 9.3 years, excluding the index-linked securities, or 10.6 including them. This represented a very slight reduction compared to the average in earlier years.

Treasury bills

These amounted to only £2.8 billion, about 1.6 per cent of national debt. Treasury bills are issued in the UK by means of a weekly tender. The Bank of England announces that, say, £100 million of Treasury bills will be issued. Bids are received and the bills allotted to the highest bidders who then arrange for the maturities, denominations, etc. of their bills. Bidders have to pay the price they bid not the allotment price. Hence the Bank is that very rare creature of the economics textbook, a perfectly discriminating monopolist who creams off the whole of consumers' surplus. Until 1971, the Treasury bill tender was covered by the discount houses who put in a syndicated bid for the whole amount offered at a common price. Effectively this determined the allotment price and 'outside bidders' determined the quantity the discount houses received. In practice prior discussion between the Governor of the Bank and the Chairman of the London Discount House Market Association (LDMA) ensured the Bank determined the rate. After 1971, the LDMA continued to cover the tender but not a common price. However, backstage manoeuvring continued and was especially relevant in the period 1972–8 when the Bank's Minimum Lending Rate (equivalent to its rediscount rate) was normally linked to the Treasury bill tender rate, although the Bank could override the formula. In general, from the early 1970s onwards Treasury bills became gradually less important as a short-term money market instrument to both the Bank and the market and commercial bills of increasing importance. An interesting development in the Treasury bill market since October 1988 has been the issue of Treasury bills denominated in ECUs (European Currency Units). This is one of the few areas where the UK has been a pioneer in moves towards European integration.

Certificates of tax deposit

Although roughly equal in size to Treasury bills, another category of public-sector debt – certificates of tax deposit – are of even less importance. They are the latest in a long line of securities whose raison d'etre is to enable the corporate sector to plan for future tax liabilities by purchasing short-term public sector debt. Given the very long lag traditional in the UK between profits being earned and taxes becoming payable, the securities enabled both parties to anticipate tax payments in all senses of that term. However, the efficiency of financial markets generally in the UK meant that they always played a small role in both public sector finance and private sector financial planning.

National Savings

Of far greater importance was National Savings. In mid-March 1989 they amounted to £26 billion, approximately 16 per cent of the national Debt. National Savings consist of a variety of non-marketable instruments, including contractual savings schemes, and National Savings Bank deposits. Typically, however, they have consisted of illiquid instruments with heavy penalties for early encashment and bonuses for long-term holdings (normally five years). They have appealed to both those who pay no tax at all, because interest on some securities is paid without any withholding tax, and to those who pay high marginal rates, because the return on some instruments is free of any tax liability. However, at least in the post-war period they have been dwarfed as a savings vehicle for standard or basic rate tax payers by building societies. The origins of National Saving lies in Nineteenth-century attempts to boost working-class thrift and to provide those of low income with safe homes for their saving. Gladstone founded the Post Office Savings Bank for this reason in 1861, for example. During both world wars, considerable publicity was given to the National Savings Movement, a large voluntary organization in schools, factories, etc. National Savings were encouraged for reasons of morale, to encourage savers to 'do their bit' for the war effort as well as to reduce consumption. Thereafter National Savings were regarded as unimportant until the late 1970s. For example the Page Report (1973) rather pompously termed them as a social service rather than a weapon of economic policy. Ironically it was only when they were used for the latter purpose that this fulfilled the former adequately; of offering the young, the poor and the old a means of saving. Until then rates of return on national savings were always low and in the inflation of the 1970s at confiscatory levels. In part this reflected an appeasement of the mortgage lobby by vote-conscious politicians anxious to avoid competition for building society funds which might force up interest rates on mortgages. Around about 1978 this attitude changed as Denis Healey revived national savings as a weapon of economic policy. Net national savings contributed only £128 million to the finance of the public sector in 1974–75 (and gilts £2.29 billion). In 1977–78, net national savings were £1.09 billion and gilts £4.91 billion. By 1981–82 national savings were £4.22 billion and gilts £7.1 billion. This reflected a conscious policy of Healey and his successor, Sir Geoffrey Howe, of relying on national savings as a weapon of monetary policy. Sir Geoffrey Howe took the process to its logical culmination by introducing explicit targets for sales of national savings from 1981–82. These were achieved with rare precision including an out-turn of £2.97 billion against a target of £3 billion. The new policy involved the invention of new instruments, including indexation, designed to be more attractive and to tap niches in the market ignored by the private sector. Of equal significance was the vigorous marketing, especially by television advertising, of both new and existing securities. In the mid-1980s the fall in personal sector saving and the down grading of debt-management meant that much less attention was paid to national savings. National savings levels fell dramatically and in 1988–89 repayments exceeded purchases and deposits. In late 1988 Lawson sought to revive national savings as part of his deflationary switch and once again new securities (such as the capital bond) were devised and extra advertising of old ones commissioned.[4] There were some oddities about this in combination with 'exact funding', discussed below.

Direct borrowing

The final major category of public debt is direct borrowing by local authorities and public corporations from financial markets, that is rather than borrowing from central government through the National Loan Fund. Throughout the 1980s, it was official policy to induce the rest of the public sector to borrow from central government rather than directly. In 1980, local authority direct borrowing amounted to £18 billion out of a total indebtedness of £34 billion. By 1988, it was only £8 billion out of £48 billion. This was the latest in a long series of changes in official attitudes, dating back to the Nineteenth century. At some periods (for example 1871–91, the 1950s) the authorities sought to channel all public-sector borrowing through central government. At other times the central government preferred to force the rest of the public sector to borrow directly. Borrowing from central government had advantages for both parties, but especially the central authorities. It increased the amount of effective control they had of the finances and so the activities of local authorities and public corporations. Moreover, these bodies often borrowed at inconvenient times or in inconvenient forms. Local authorities in the 1950s, for example, issued short-term paper on an enormous scale at a time when the government was seeking to reduce liquidity. On the other when central government borrowed on behalf of the rest of the public sector it reduced the range of public-sector securities while increasing the amount of gilts the Bank of England had to issue. In the 1970s the authorities regarded direct borrowing by local authorities as another method of increasing non-bank private-sector lending to the public sector and so of reducing the money supply. Hence the swings in official attitudes and no doubt these will continue.

HISTORY

Trading in public-sector debt in England goes back at least to medieval times when 'tallies' were bought and sold at a discount. In this context a tally was an acknowledgement by the government that it owed money to the bearer (a tally was a stick upon which the amount was marked with a knife using a conventional code and the stick then cleft in two so that each party to a transaction had a copy). Tallies were frequently sold by those who supplied goods to the government when they had cash-flow problems. More conventional sovereign debt was not without its problems. The Bardi, the largest banking house in Europe, were driven into bankruptcy by a default by Edward III in 1341, who owed them more than he wished to repay. English kings continued to default until 1672 – Charles II's famous 'stop on the Exchequer'. In between there were occasional periods of honest and intelligent debt management – notably by Sir Thomas Gresham, Elizabeth I's agent. In addition to his law, Sir Thomas discovered the connection between exchange rates and domestic monetary policy. Indeed, even after 400 years, there is little to add to his adage 'the way to raise the exchange for England is to make money scant in Lombard Street'. The modern history of the national debt starts, however, with the foundation of the Bank of England in 1694. Its purpose was to 'fund' part of William III's short-term indebtedness: to 'fund' then meant to convert short-term debt to a perpetual or long-term basis. Indeed 'funding' was the main aim of the Bank of England until the 1950s, when 'funding', 'funds' and 'fundholder' coincidentally ceased to be common cant to describe the policy, the consequent asset and the holder thereof. The Bank of England was a creation of Whig financiers and was intensely controversial for at least fifty years. For example, it was censured by the (Tory) House of Commons in 1702 for illicit intervention in a general election. Swift excoriated it as a device to transfer power, money and influence from the (Tory) tax-paying landed Squirearchy to Whig 'fund lords' via extravagant spending on unnecessary wars; The Bank was opposed by various largely Tory financial groups – goldsmiths, various land banks and the South Sea Company. In this period a wide range of securities were issued including lotteries and tontines. A lottery paid interest in the form of lottery tickets – rather akin to the premium bonds introduced by Harold Macmillan in 1956. In a tontine, each investor nominates a person (including himself). Interest payments are then divided among the holders of securities whose nominee is still alive. They combined a gamble with a means of providing for elderly or other dependants (who would not need an income after death). However late in the Eighteenth century gilts ceased to be a political football and under Pitt, Peel and Gladstone many of the foundations of debt management policy until 1947 were laid down. Policy was to fund as much as possible of the national debt at as low an interest rate as possible and, so far as possible, to reduce the total of debt.

Funding was largely accomplished by issuing perpetual debt, known as Consolidated Fund Stock or Consols. Later other perpetuals were issued – currently there are seven in existence.[5] The government normally retained the option of redeeming these stocks so it sought to have its cake and eat it – infinitely-dated debt unless interest rates fell when it could repay the stock at will. The authorities sought to manage the market to facilitate conversion operations – reissuing perpetuals at lower rates, as in 1891 (when Consols were converted from 3 to 2½ per cent, in stages) and 1931, when allegedly-scandalous pressure was put on clearing banks to help the government's operations.[6] In 1947 Hugh Dalton's departure as Chancellor brought cheap money to an end and thereafter debt management was subordinate to monetary policy. Sometimes the authorities sought to fund – to reduce money, credit or some vague concept of liquidity and so deflate the economy. However they were aware that higher interest rates were also a deflationary weapon – and more important would protect the exchange rate (then quasi-fixed under the Bretton Woods system). At other times they wished to pursue an expansionary policy to reduce unemployment – this was the 'stop-go' era when demand management policy changed from expansion to deflation or vice versa roughly every two years. There would have been no inconsistency between quantity targets and price ones if the authorities had accepted the so-called economists' theory that the way to sell more of their debt (fund) was to offer a higher interest rate. However they rejected this in favour of the 'cashier's theory'. This (almost certainly correctly) argued:

(a) Holders of gilts sought to maximize short-term gains. This seems to have been true on both logical and factual grounds. As John Flemming once pointed out, any other assumption would assure irrationality on the part of bond holders since maximizing short-term gains in a securities market is necessary to maximize long-term ones as well. Moreover, the average holding period was less than one year.
(b) Because of (a) the capital gains or loss on a bond dominated any interest payment. Hence bonds would only be bought by those expecting bond prices to rise, that is interest rates to fall. Everyone accepts this but the efficient market hypothesis (EMH) holds that these expectations determine price such that the only possible price is the one where (adjusted for wealth) as many people expect a rise as a fall in price. In this case demand for bonds equals the quantity in existence. However, the cashier's theory denied the validity of the EMH.
(c) Instead the Bank assumed that holders held extrapolative expectations – if bond prices rose, this would generate expectations of a further rise and vice-versa. Hence it would only be possible for the authorities to sell bonds when rates were falling so the market expected a further fall. This was not inconsistent with the economist's theory since the two together suggested that funding would be maximized by high but falling rates. However, the Bank denied any relevance to the level of rates.

Faced with the implications of its theory and of relatively a very high national debt, the Bank's scope for manoeuvre was limited.[7] It sought to square the circle by 'leaning into the wind', that is sell when the market was rising to slow down the rise and vice-versa. Effectively the Bank accepted that, if left to itself, the market would follow the path now called a 'speculative bubble': boom and bust. It thus sought to manage these cycles. Moreover it believed it could manage them so as to sell debt when it chose. Say the Bank wished to fund. It would *buy* gilts and so generate a price rise. This would generate market demand, hence the Bank could initiate a 'selling season' during which it sold gilts. This selling season would last until there was a sterling crisis – a frequent event in the 1950s and 1960s. Once this changed expectations the Bank would support the market and so on.

This policy was abandoned in 1971 because of its clear defects. One was described by the Chief Cashier 'as making the speculative management of portfolios altogether too easy'.[8] In a speculative bubble market the problem, of course, is to sell before the bubble bursts. The Bank's policy in effect removed this problem. Holders of gilts knew that the Bank policy of 'leaning into the wind' guaranteed that they could sell at a price close to the top of the market. The other argument was that gilts had been made into such a liquid asset that there was no macro-economic point in selling them. Liquidity is a measure of the ease of conversion into purchasing power as measured by time, cost, certainty and collateral value. In the 1950s gilts could be converted overnight into cash at a very low cost with little short-term price risk. In effect they were as liquid as Treasury bills. Hence in 1971, 'leaning into the wind' was abandoned. Until early 1974 the Bank overtly abandoned any active policy on the gilts' market. It merely bought gilts with less than one year to mature when occasion arose to smooth the cash flow effect of repayment and was prepared to supply gilts when market conditions were suitable (Bank 1971). In other words, the proclaimed policy was totally passive. Central banks, like leopards, do not change their spots overnight and the leopard of Threadneedle Street may not have abandoned support operations. Indeed, some 'leaning into the wind' would have been consistent with Barberism – rapid monetary and fiscal expansion and acceptance of a sliding exchange rate (eventually Barberism led to 25 per cent inflation, a balance of payments deficit of 4 per cent of GDP a change of government and a new Tory leader – Mrs Thatcher).

In the UK, the emphasis was on the sale of gilts to the non-bank private sector. This became evident in 1968 after an IMF loan agreement introduced Domestic Credit Expansion (DCE) to the UK. Sales of gilts to banks, the rest of the public sector or the overseas sector do not reduce DCE. Emphasis on control of broad monetary aggregates like M_3 and £M_3 through supply-side counterparts had similar consequences after 1975 (Gowland 1991) since sales of gilts other than to the non-bank private sector have no primary effect in reducing the money supply. After the collapse of Barberism and the adoption of the new approach (end-1973–early-1974) the authorities needed a new active debt management policy. In early 1974 the Bank did devise a new active gilts strategy – the 'Duke of York'. This was based in a new theory of the demand for gilts by the market which combined the cashiers and economists theory so that the government would maximize sales when interest rates were high but falling, as above. In addition a third argument in the demand function was thought to be the yield gap – longs' (gilts) yields less short-term rates (those on other assets), or in some versions the change in the yield gap.

Again this is both logical, indeed a consequence of rationality, and seemingly in accord with casual empiricism about how UK insurance company and pension fund managers operate. This enabled the authorities to manipulate rates as follows (see Figure 1.5):

(a) The authorities raise both long and short rates.
(b) They lower short-term rates. At this stage, long rates are high and the yield gap large and rising. Thus two of the three elements in the demand function favour increased demand for gilts.
(c) This generates a rise in gilts' prices and so a fall in long-term rates. Hence all three elements of the demand function are favourable to gilt sales by the authorities and a selling season on a rising market follows as with 'leaning into the wind'. The difference is that with the Duke of York, the initial fall in rates is achieved without any repurchase of gilts by the Bank. Instead use is made of market manipulation of a sort that made the Kennedy family fortune but is illegal in both the UK and USA.

The problem with the Duke of York is that its repeated use (nine times 1974–9) was inconsistent with market rationality. Gilts were sold when prices were rising on expectations of further future price rises. These expectations were falsified and the profits already made wiped out by the next round of the Duke of York – when long rates rise and gilts' prices fall. Why did the market allow itself to be tricked so often? The issue is discussed in Gowland (1982: 148–52). The likeliest explanations seem to be either that everyone believed they were cleverer than everyone else and could sell before the crash occurred or some defect in the reward structure of fund managers. Fund managers are not penalized for wrong decisions if everyone else makes the same mistake, and not rewarded for passive but profitable actions (like not buying gilts whose price subsequently falls). Hence when the 'Duke of York' was executed, a pension fund manager had to decide whether to buy gilts even though he knew it was likely (but not certain) to be a mistake. If other fund managers were likely to buy gilts, it was in his interests to do likewise. If other managers were wrong, he would not

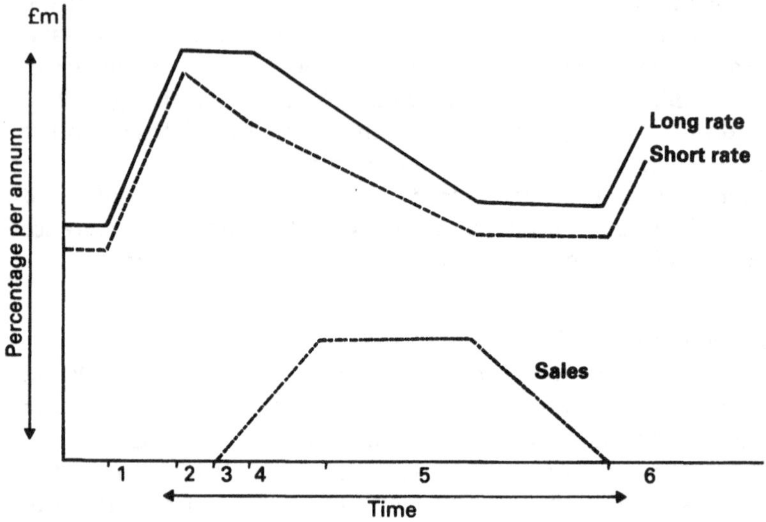

Figure 5.1 Duke of York strategy

be rewarded if he did not follow them and would not be penalized if he did. On the other hand, if they were right he would be penalized if he had not joined the bull market. Hence every fund manager should follow the herd even if he thinks it is mistaken. Hence a herd develops, none of whose members believe in its policy – each joins for fear that others will join. While the 'Duke of York' provided fascinating insights into how markets work, it is now only of historical interest since the policy has not been used since 1980.

Even before the abandonment of the Duke of York strategy, the authorities tried to sell more gilts by innovative marketing: new types of security and new methods of issuing old types. These tactics, however, became much more important after 1979. Nevertheless this was only a change in emphasis: there was no discontinuity in policy. The most important innovation – indexation – is discussed on pp. 122–4. The first innovation was the introduction of variable-rate securities (in 1975). These were a long-dated security on which the coupon rate of interest varied with short-term rates; the Treasury bill rate. The objective was to sell gilts when expectations were that interest rates would rise – that is when the Duke of York method could not work. More generally the aim was to be able to sell gilts when prospects looked worst and so the need for monetary discipline was greatest. Against this, it can be argued that the effect on monetary data was largely cosmetic as the securities were far more liquid than conventional gilts. Either realization of this or lack of market interest meant that few issues were made and the experiment was not a success. Its main relevance is as evidence of the official state of mind. In 1976 some fairly short-term Euro-deposits had interest rates linked to very short-term rates but the great explosion of floating rate notes etc. was still to come. The Bank could fairly claim to be an innovator in this area. Some government bonds were issued in convertible form, that is the holder buys a specific, usually short-dated security, but has the option to convert to a longer-term one if he so chooses. In two cases the holder had a further choice of security when he converted. This means that the purchaser is protected against a rise in long-term interest rates which would otherwise reduce the capital value of a long-term bond, but can still exploit the capital gain if interest rates fall. Convertibles were again a method of making gilts more liquid and so reduced the benefits of the authorities' sales. However, the typical convertible was a five-year stock convertible into a fifteen-year one, so the criticism had much less force. In all, between 1976 and 1985 £12 billion of convertibles were issued.

In March 1977 the authorities realized that the need for gilt-sales would be much greater after 5 April 1977, when a new financial year and monetary target commenced. On the other hand, conditions were optimal for sales at the time so the authorities wished to sell now but receive the proceeds later. Hence they invented part-paid issues, which were used on a substantial scale thereafter. On these the purchaser does not have to put up the full price of the bond when he buys it. Instead he puts up only a portion of the full amount and pays the rest in one or more instalments. This enables the government to sell bonds at one time but defer the receipts to another. 'Selling seasons' tend to produce uneven monetary growth so the device enabled a smoother pattern of growth to be achieved. It also increases the total amount of purchases, if someone, such as a pension fund, chooses to buy bonds but has not got sufficient cash at present but expects to receive some in the near future. Moreover, part-paid issues have advantages as a speculative instrument since the gain (or loss) on the whole value of a gilt, say £100, can be secured by a part payment of £15. Thus the margins or leverage on a part-paid issue is enormous. This became of less significance in the 1980s as LIFFE offered a wider range of speculative instruments in gilts with similar or smaller effective margin requirements (options, warrants, etc.). The Bank also once issued a low coupon deep-discount bond, designed to appeal to high-rate taxpayers. In the UK, capital gains on gilts have been free of all tax (or offsetability) since 1968. Hence a low-coupon bond appeals to those with high-marginal rates and a stock standing above par to those with no tax liability (principally pension funds). In many ways this was an act of desperation and was not repeated.

Traditionally the authorities sold gilts by the 'tap' system. A new issue was made at a fixed price. The authorities supplied the market with the quantity it wanted (so long as this was less than the total offered). Almost always, and by design, such demand was for only a low percentage of the stock offered. The Bank then held the rest as a tap stock.[9] This was a stock which the Bank had available to sell when it chose – when it 'turned the tap' on to increase supply. This meant that the authorities controlled price but the market controlled quantity in the short term, in contrast to the US auction system where the authorities knew the quantity they would sell but not necessarily the price. The UK authorities further restricted their options by a self-denying ordinance not to reduce the price of bonds unilaterally but to wait for the market to take the first step. To do the former seemed somehow unpatriotic, or as it was often put, 'spitting on the flag'. The authorities dropped this taboo in the early 1980s. The unmodified tap system was dropped after the 'battle of Threadneedle Street' in 1979. The price of gilts rose after a new issue prospectus appeared such that demand far exceeded supply. Stockholders and other would be applicants literally fought with each other in a mad scramble to put applications in – hence the ephitet, 'battle of Threadneedle Street'. In response the Bank experimented with tenders – that is, applicants bid at a price of their choice but, unlike a pure auction, the Bank fixed the price which would normally leave either excess demand or excess supply, which would be rationed or taken up by the Bank's public sector bidders. In effect the Bank could behave like a textbook monopolist under conditions of perfect certainty. In 1987 the Bank experimented with uninhibited auctions on the US style, although this was apparently unpopular with the market.[10] Before it had to decide finally on this old chestnut, tap or tender, the swing in public-sector finance meant that the issue was moot. Instead the Bank instituted reverse auctions in 1988, when it invited the market to offer bonds for repurchase ahead of maturity. In practice the maturity of the reverse-auctioned bond was unusually close. However, (by 29 September 1989) it involved offers of 9 per cent Exchequer Stock 2002. The final marketing innovation was 'tranchettes'. With tap stocks there had been only one or two stocks issued at once ('long', 'medium' and

and 'short' taps, but all three rarely existed let alone were issued simultaneously). With tranchettes, five stocks might be issued simultaneously – £100 million of each of five stocks instead of £500 million of a single stock. A wide range of products is an obvious marketing ploy. In practice, the reason may have been that greater sophistication in fund management meant that, say, a 1998 and a 1999 stock were no longer viewed as such good substitutes as equivalents twenty years earlier.

THE OPERATION OF THE MARKET

Prior to 27 October 1986, the UK gilt-edged market, like the London Stock Exchange, was based upon a system of brokers and jobbers. Financial institutions and private individuals alike had to buy gilts through a broker (or the national Savings Bank Register).[11] The broker had to be an individual or in partnership and could not be owned by a bank or indeed any outside body. Moreover, the broker was supposed not to take a position but merely to execute his client's order. Of course he could speculate 'on his own account'. He could not, however, supply stock he owned to a client nor buy stock a client offered. He obtained stock from a jobber, who acted as a wholesaler but could not deal directly with investors. Jobbers could take positions and, for example, 'go short' by supplying stock they did not possess in the hope of obtaining it later at a lower cost. This system was known as 'single capacity' because the broking role was separate from the wholesale or market making role. The Bank of England offered stock for sale to the investors and dealers through public offerings (see p. 118). Most securities were, however, sold by the authorities through the government broker who operated on the Bank's behalf in the market and either bought or sold stock as ordered. By long tradition, this post was filled by the senior partner of Mullens. After the reforms of 27 October 1986, the then incumbent Lord Cromwell became a Bank employee. His successor, Tunstall, retired in September 1989 and the post was abolished.

As already referred to, the marker was reformed on 27 October 1986. This was deliberately contemporaneous with 'Big Bang' on the stock exchange although the origins of the reform were independent of 'Big Bang'. The Bank's aims were both macro-economic and micro-economic. The macro-economic objective was to maintain a separate market in London in gilts under its aegis which would be a suitable theatre for official operations. For reasons of maximizing official discretion (and *amour propre*) it did not want to see gilts traded as part of the Eurobond market in, say, Luxemburg. Moreover it felt that it was neither practicable nor desirable to attain this by *dirigiste* means. Hence, to achieve its macro-economic objective, the Bank had to achieve its micro-economic one: an efficient gilts' market with low transaction costs and constant liquidity. The Bank had always wanted holders of gilts to be able to sell at any time irrespective of the amount they wanted to sell – one reason for the Bank's ill-fated strategy of 'leaning into the wind', above. The Bank therefore had to devise a package of sticks and carrots such that those trading in gilts (including international securities houses) wished to trade in them as part of the Bank's market in London. Goldman Sachs, say, could easily have added UK gilts to the stocks traded by its Eurobond wing as it did German securities. The Bank had to ensure that any calculation of costs and benefits made it preferable not to do so. In many ways the reform of the gilts' market was a defensive act by the Bank. It, rightly or wrongly, saw dangers in the status quo and felt it had to act to reserve the essential features of the old system.

Given these strategic goals, the Bank prepared and inaugurated its plan. The new scheme was based on dual capacity – brokers now called agency brokers could now take positions as well as execute client's orders. They, moreover, could now be part of a bank or other group. The crucial players in the new scheme, however, were the Gilt-Edged Market Makers, GEMMs. GEMMs were based upon primary dealers in the USA (see p. 20) and are sometimes referred to as such, although there are important differences. A GEMM had a number of obligations. Principally it had to maintain a market – that is be willing to buy or sell any quantity of any gilt at any time. In practice it has been argued by newspaper commentators that not all of the smaller GEMMs actually do this, although the Bank claims they do (Bank 1989: 53). Second, a GEMM had to be maintained as an independent autonomous body within a firm, with its own dedicated capital, that is, capital tied up in the GEMM which cannot be withdrawn from it. This was crucial to the Bank. It did not want firms or their capital to be in the market in good times and absent in bad. In contrast such behaviour is viewed as highly desirable in the context of Baumol's contestable markets theory (Gowland 1990: 28). The dedicated capital requirement together with the increase in the number of GEMMs compared to jobbers increased market capitalization from £100 million to £595 million as of Big Bang and about £400 million at end-1989. GEMMs have been given a number of privileges – some tax concessions, special access to the Bank and a facility to swap stock. This means that if a GEMM has, say, Exchequer Stock 1997 on its books but a client wants Treasury Stock 1996, the Bank will exchange the one for the other even if it has to create the stock to do so. GEMMs are able to go short when they choose and, given next day settlement, need to be able to borrow the securities to meet their obligations. This is provided by ten stock exchange money brokers, who borrow and lend gilts. The apparent profitability of this activity is revealed by the fact that it is the only area of the gilts' market where these have been net new entrants since Big Bang. GEMMs, it is argued, might be inhibited by fear that the other GEMMs might gang up on a GEMM who buys or sells a large line of a particular stock. Say it is known that GEMM A has just bought £100 million of gilt x from a bank. The other GEMMs known that it will wish to sell this and so will reduce their buying price. Hence GEMMs are enabled to offer and buy stock anonymously to and from each other via four Inter Dealer Brokers. In addition they are allowed to conceal their trade for twenty-four hours (unlike equity market makers who have to reveal it at once). This privilege has been the subject of some debate amongst economists (Roell 1989). The Bank hoped that GEMMs would play a special role in the issue of stock without the privileges their US opposite numbers have. In fact, the swing in public-sector finance meant this was never operational.

GEMMs provide 90 per cent of broking services as well as their market making role – agency brokers account for 10 per cent. The Bank has allowed conditional free entry. Hence there were twenty-seven GEMMs at the time of Big Bang. (Nine) have since withdrawn but there are two mighty newcomers: Nomura and Daiwa. This illustrates nicely the Bank's attitude to internationalization and securities houses. It welcomes everyone to its club so long as they abide by the rules. The Bank has provided a further inducement to be a GEMM by establishing a model settlements system (Bank 1987). The efficiency, speed and certainty of payment of this Central Gilts Office system do not seem to have been matched elsewhere.[12]

The performance of the market is impressive (Bank 1989). Turnover has risen from £1.25 billion per day pre-Big Bang to £4.25 billion, of which £2 billion represents trading among GEMMs. In addition there are trades in gilt futures on LIFFE amounting to an equivalent of £1.2 billion per day. As the number of bargains has fallen by about 20 per cent, the average size of bargain has more than doubled. Spreads, already low, have fallen by about half. Total dealing costs on a transaction of £1 million (commission plus spread) is about £300–£600. The market has remained highly competitive and unconcentrated: the biggest six firms account for less than half of dealings. It is possible to go on listing market achievements. It is undoubtedly in one sense a great success story. In another it is like a production of *Hamlet* from which the Prince withdrew before Act I. One objective of the market was to enable the Bank to sell gilts to finance a budget deficit and to control the money supply. 'Exact funding' and a budget surplus have removed both reasons for selling gilts. Hence the special role of GEMMs as wholesalers who would feed gilts into the market has disappeared. Moreover as a further consequence there is chronic excess capacity. The GEMMs collectively lost £190 million between Big Bang and the end of 1988: one-third of their initial capital in twenty-three months. Some have tried to substitute other types of business, such as local authority securities. However the paradox remains. The Bank created an instrument which was perfect for the purposes of the period prior to that in which it introduced it.

ISSUES IN DEBT MANAGEMENT

Indexation

The UK is not the only country to have issued index-linked securities, those on which principal and interest payments rise with a general price index. Brazil, Finland (at one time) and Israel are other well-known examples. Even among major OECD countries, France issued a large number of bonds in the 1950s linked to various specific price indices (such as railway fares and electricity) as well as the general price level. The UK is, however, unique in doing so as part of a successful anti-inflation policy and with a falling open economy. The UK government is still committed to maximizing sales of index-linked gilts and seeks to raise substantially the proportion of the national debt that is index-linked from its present level of about 10 per cent. Economists are in (very rare) almost total agreement that indexation of bonds is desirable. Friedman, for one, put it as follows:

> I know of no other (expedient) . . . that holds as much promise of both reducing the harm done by inflation and facilitating the ending of inflation . . . (it is necessary) to end inflation before inflation ends not only the conventional wisdom but perhaps also the free society. (Friedman 1978).

Even economists who are usually Friedman's bitter rivals – such as Tobin – share his enthusiasm for index-linking of public-sector debt. It is worth, therefore, examining why this is so. An important reason is that it seems to economists the only just solution. Any change in the price level arbitrarily redistributes income and wealth, usually, from creditor to debtor. The unfairness of this is reinforced by the fact that the biggest debtor is government. It seems wrong that governments should both create inflation and benefit from it. The only means open to creditors to protect themselves is through higher nominal rates. Indeed a relationship between nominal interest rates and inflation, the so-called Fisher effect, has passed from economic theory to conventional wisdom. Nevertheless, as Fisher himself pointed out, the protection is incomplete since nominal rates rarely if ever adjust fully to expected inflation. Any unexpected inflation will, of course, continue to have the unjust effects highlighted by Keynes (1923). Even if interest rates do adjust fully to expected inflation, the two underlying problems remain. The first is that inflation creates double uncertainty since both borrower and lender are interested in real magnitudes. Uncertainty about how the actual level will turn out relative to its expected level means that both parties to the contract are uncertain about their real liability or real income. In this sense indexation acts as an insurance policy to both sides. The provision of index-linked securities by the public sector enables the private sector to plan its saving and consumption over time knowing the real cost of present consumption in terms of present consumption. Moreover, the second problem is that high nominal rates and high inflation may lead to a contract that is unsatisfactory to both sides. In part this is because the tax system never discriminates between interest payments necessary to maintain the real value of capital and genuine income. Hence the government is likely to gain at the lender's expense. More basically, high nominal rates create a cash flow problem for the borrower who has to pay the interest in cash even if the real value of his obligation is falling. The latter may not offset the former. If inflation is zero and interest rates 2 per cent, a ten-year loan involves a maximum annual payment of £12, even if the loan is paid off by equal instalments, more usually either repayment is delayed until the end of the loan or the interest and capital repaid by equal instalments. If inflation rose to 20 per cent and nominal rates to 15 per cent, the lender is clearly worse off: he is losing 5 per cent per year. This real interest rate of – 5 per cent may not satisfy the borrower who has to pay £25 (instead of £12) and may not regard a fall in the real value of his debt as compensation for this onerous requirement. To summarize, indexation offers a means of removing some of the inequity, inefficiency and inconvenience of inflation. There are two counter-arguments. The first is that indexation amounts to a recognition of inflation and so is undesirable. This is a silly argument: by the same token unemployment pay is a recognition of unemployment. To try to reduce the ill-effects of something is more likely to go hand-in-hand with eliminating it than to be licence. This proposition is reinforced when as in this case indexation besides reducing the bad consequences of inflation reduces its benefits to government. The other argument is more plausible. Indexation of loans is, it is argued, desirable but other indexation – especially of wages – is of questionable value. However, indexation of the one may lead to indexation of the other – the argument for Finland abandoning indexation in 1968. Nevertheless the theoretical case for indexation is overwhelming (see Dornbusch and Simonsen 1983).

The UK authorities may or may not have been interested in the theoretical arguments for indexation, although giving the personal sector the ability to plan for the future was probably an influence. The practical benefits of indexation were, however, probably more influential. The fact was the beneficial effect on government cash flow and debt management of paying only 2½ per cent interest (and writing up the capital value of the debt without needing to sell any securities). Given the refinance problems faced by the US authorities in part because of inflation-driven high nominal rates, the gain is clear. If the government succeeds in conquering inflation, this cash flow bonus is a permanent gain – or, in general, if inflation is in the event less than the market's expectation. Indexed debt is attractive to the market when inflationary expectations are rising. This is precisely when the authorities have the greatest need to sell public-sector debt to reduce monetary growth but also precisely when non-indexed debt is least attractive. The UK authorities chose to introduce indexed debt in stages between 1975 and 1982.[13] This 'creeping indexation' produced an extra benefit for the authorities. Whenever monetary growth seemed excessive they could increase the offset from debt sales by creeping a bit further: introducing new types of indexed security or permitting new categories of holder to hold existing types of security. Creeping indexation, moreover, was probably one reason why both indexed and non-indexed gilts remained in existence. This surprised many economists, who had perhaps over-estimated the appeal of indexed securities. They had assumed that once indexed securities were available then all lenders in all markets would insist on indexation. This was contrary to Brazilian experience but could have happened in the UK. Creeping indexation was probably one reason why it did not.

Exact funding and crowding out

In his Mansion House speech of October 1985, Lawson announced a new policy: exact funding. This meant that the Bank of England was henceforth directed to sell only enough gilts to ensure that the public-sector borrowing requirement adjusted for transactions with the overseas sector less any any net purchases of national savings etc. At first sight this seemed a strange policy. The government was deliberately abandoning an instrument of economic policy. Private-sector borrowing from banks was and continued to grow rapidly. Hence monetary growth was 15–20 per cent per annum, depending on which measure was used. Debt sales seemed to everyone but Lawson the most obvious way of curbing monetary expansion. It is therefore necessary to examine why the government chose to introduce exact funding.

The first reason was Lawson's apparent preference for some sort of automatic quasi-Gladstonian policy including an exchange rate target to mirror the gold standard – at the same time Lawson introduced shadow membership of the European Monetary System (EMS), with a rate of £1 to 3 DM. Exact funding was a first step to the budget surplus he later achieved. In other words Lawson was abandoning both the Keynesianism of the 1960s and the quasi-monetarism of Healey and Howe of the 1970s and 1980s in favour of a passive policy as a deliberate choice. However, practical considerations were no doubt also relevant. In the early 1980s large-scale debt sales had led to the 'commercial bill mountain'. Normally debt sales lead to the following process. A buys a government security for £1 million. He pays with a cheque drawn on a commercial bank, so his account is debited by £1 million and bank liabilities fall by £1 million. The counterpart fall in bank assets is a fall in its deposit with the central bank. The commercial bank then replenishes its central bank account by selling a Treasury bill to the central bank. In effect, therefore, the non-bank purchase of a gilt repays part of government obligations to the commercial bank, the Treasury bill. However, what happens if the commercial bank has not enough Treasury bills to sell to replenish its account? It will instead be forced to sell private-sector securities (commercial bills) to the government so as to replenish its central bank account. From 1980 onwards this happened. In 1981–2 'over funding' was £4 billion – that is the negative impact on the money supply of gilt sales in excess of what would have been required by exact funding. At the time bank holdings of Treasury bills were only £1 billion and any significant reduction would have both dislocated markets and reduced Bank of England leverage over short-term interest rates.[14] Hence in 1981–2 the Bank of England bought £87 billion of commercial bills. At its peak in 1981–2 the Bank held £8 billion of commercial bills, against a traditional level of £50 million. In later years the problem continued so the Bank's holdings of commercial bills peaked at £12 billion – the mountain. Such a large-scale holding was unwelcome to the authorities, though it is not clear whether it was a genuine problem or simply inconvenient. Exact funding got rid of commercial bill mountains.

Neither of the foregoing were the main reasons cited by the authorities for the decision to adopt exact funding. Instead they argued that it was necessary to remove a structural version of what economists call 'crowding-out'. This is when government spending or borrowing leads to an undesired fall in private spending or borrowing. There was, and is, very little evidence for the normal short-term version of this – in fact there is little evidence either way. However Lawson argued for a more subtle and persuasive form of crowding-out: the existence of large quantities of government securities (with tax advantages and low dealing costs in an efficient market) had killed off the private (corporate) sector bond market. The argument was that neither institutional nor personal sector investors wished to hold corporate fixed-interest securities, nor even variable rate ones, when government securities were available. In consequence, it was argued companies borrowed from banks instead. This both led to capital-market inefficiency and inflated monetary growth compared to companies borrowing directly from persons and institutions rather than through bank intermediaries. This may be true but it is equally likely that the absence of a UK corporate bond market reflects either inflation or the efficiency of both UK banks and the UK equity market – so companies can use other forms of finance. The corporate bond market was a casualty of inflation and consequent corporate unwillingness to borrow at high nominal rates, given the cash flow problems discussed above. In any case exact funding was only one of a number of official initiatives to induce extra non-bank debt finance for UK companies.[15] To summarize, there were reasons why exact funding seemed desirable although they do not convince the author. There was discussion of the government's decision to maximize sales of national savings within the constrained total of debt sales to the non-bank private sector. The reason was to increase personal sector savings even though service costs were higher on national savings than gilts.

Redemption of the National Debt

The switch to a budget surplus in 1987–8 (called 'Public-Sector Debt Repayment') led to discussion about the desirability of the redemption of the national debt. The old economic issue of whether a national debt was a burden was little-discussed although it had been established that it could be, see the survey in Hillier and Lunati (1990). Nor was there much discussion on the link between the type of the national debt, budget deficit and the level of interest rates on the lines of the US debate. Both issues should have been aired as well as the newer ideas about optimal relationships between stocks such as the national debt and flows such as income or government spending. Instead there was discussion of the implications for tax and expenditure levels. However the issue is examined it does not seem to be worth making redemption of the national debt an objective of government policy. What was clear was that a shrinking national debt and exact funding had led to the chronic over capacity in the gilts market discussed above. GEMMs responded by withdrawal from the market and/or product diversification into other securities. It is ironic that having created an exceptionally efficient government bond market the UK authorities no longer felt the need for it.

NOTES

1 The monetary authorities were well aware of this and sought to manage change actively. Eddie George, for several years the Bank's chief operative in the gilts market, became famous in the financial media for his adage 'one miracle at a time'. In the UK, the Bank of England, has sole responsibility for official operations in the gilts market. The Bank's Chief Executive Officer was called the Chief Cashier. A Deputy Chief Cashier (one of two) directly supervised gilts dealing etc. for much of the period under review. More recently, the relevant official has been the Assistant Director in charge of the Gilt-Edged Division.

2 Of many measures of the budget deficit the Public Sector Borrowing Requirement is usually used in the UK. It is government spending less taxes less sales of assets plus any lending to third parties. For this purpose public corporations are not counted as part of the public sector. Hence if British Rail were to borrow £1 billion on the market this would not be part of the PSBR. PSBR is a net concept, it excludes any borrowing to finance maturing debt.

3 The Grand Old Duke of York
He Had 10,000 Men
He Marched Them Up To The Top Of The Hill
And He Marched Them Down Again

A reference to George III's son's conduct of the Walcheren campaign in 1797.

4 The capital bond was so-called because interest was rolled-up and paid on the maturity of the bond.
5 War Loan 3½ per cent, 4 per cent consols, 3½ per cent Conversion Stock, 2½ per cent Annuities, 2¾ per cent Annuities, 2½ per cent consols. 2½ per cent Treasury '1975 or after'. As the latter implies the authorities could repay them if they chose.
6 For an unusually pointed version of these events see Train (1985) pp. 43–7. Train's account is plausible but he cites no sources, compared to the more guarded versions elsewhere.
7 In the 1950s the national debt was over 100 per cent of GDP compared to about 8 in West Germany and 30 in the USA and France. In the 1980s it was about 40 per cent.
8 In the Sykes lecture reprinted in Bank (1971) pp. 17–21.
9 Usually there were two or, occasionally, three taps: short, medium and long.
10 There were initially three auctions, all oversubscribed at the minimum price: May 1987, September 1987 and January 1988.
11 Legally, of course, there was no requirement to trade on an organized exchange. Anyone could sell to anyone else however they chose, so long as legal formalities were observed. In practice, it was necessary to trade on the London Stock Exchange until the 1980s when some securities houses organized a very few large block off-market trades.
12 The Bank has tried to offer this service to other markets with varying success. It latest proposal is a Central Money Office scheme introduced in September 1990.
13 The first step being an index-linked contractural savings scheme. Savings Certificates (at first limited to senior citizens: 'granny bonds') followed and finally gilts (originally restricted to pension funds). The final step removed restrictions on who held indexed-linked gilts.
14 See the discussion in Gowland (1982, second edition 1984) Chapter 11.
15 Such as a sterling commercial paper market. For a general discussion of non-bank finance of companies see Bank of England Quarterly *Bulletin* Vol. 29, No. 3 (August 1989), pp. 583–7.

REFERENCES

Bank (1989) 'The gilt-edged market since Big Bang', Bank of England Quarterly *Bulletin*, Vol. 29, No. 1 (Feb): pp. 49–58.

Bank (1971) *Competition and Credit Control*, London: Bank of England.

Dornbusch, R. and Simonsen, M.H. (eds) (1983) *Inflation, Debt and Indexation*, Cambridge, Mass.: MIT Press.

Friedman, M. (1977) *Inflation and Unemployment*, London: Institute of Economic Affairs.

Gowland, D.H. (1982, 84) *Controlling the Money Supply*, (2nd edition, 1989), Beckenham: Croom Helm.

—— (1990) *The Regulation of Financial Markets in the 1990s*, Aldershot: Edward Elgar.

—— (1991) *Monetary Control in Theory and Practice*, London: Routledge.

Hillier, B. and Lunati, M.T. (1990) 'The debt burden' in J. Creedy (ed.) *Foundations of Economic Thought*, Oxford: Blackwell.

Keynes, J.M. (1923) *A Tract On Monetary Reform* reprinted in *The Collected Writings* (Macmillan) for the RES, 1971.

Page, H. (1973) *Report of the Official Committee in National Savings*, London: HMSO, Cmnd. 5273.

Roell, A. (1989) 'Regulating information disclosure amongst stock exchange market makers', discussion paper no. 51, London: LSE Financial Markets Group.

Train, J. (1985) *Famous Financial Fiascos*, London: George Allen and Unwin.

6 The bond market in Australia

*Kevin Davis and Mervyn Lewis**

INTRODUCTION

In 1956 Australia government debt outstanding was twice as large as the debt of private-sector entities in Australia (see Table 6.1). Thirty years later that position had been nearly reversed, and private-sector debt as at June 1986 stood at $208.7 billion, while public-sector debt was $112.6 billion (n.b. '$' refers to Australian dollars throughout this chapter). In his evidence to the UK Radcliffe Committee in 1957, Governor Coombs of the Reserve Bank of Australia could record that 'in Australia . . . the yield on government securities is generally regarded as the basic rate in the general market structure of interest rates' (Coombs 1960: para 20). That is also no longer the case. Short-term money market rates, such as that on ninety day bank bills, rule the roost. Until relatively recently, net issues of Treasury Bonds and Notes were generally believed to augment the liquidity base of the banking sector and hence affect the volume of money and were thus an integral part of monetary policy outcomes. In that respect as well, matters have changed, and following the federal government's decision in 1984 to fully fund its budget deficit (surplus) over the financial year by primary issues (redemptions) of securities, there is now a separation in Australia – albeit informal – between debt management and monetary policy.

Despite these changes, the markets for government securities occupy an important place in the Australian capital market, for a number of reasons. There has never been much of a corporate bond market in Australia. During 1985–6, for example, debenture and note

* We are grateful to Ric Battellino and Malcolm Hill for valuable comments and our indebtedness to their work, that of Ian Macfarlane, and that of other anonymous Reserve Bank officials is evident from our bibliography. They should not be implicated in responsibility for any remaining errors or opinions expressed herein.

Table 6.1 Public- and private-sector debt in Australia, 1956–86

	Private-sector debt ($m)[a]			*Public-sector debt ($m)*			*Public-sector budget deficit*[b]	
As at June	*Households*	*Trading enterprises*	*Total*	*Central government*	*State and local authorities*	*Total*	*$m*	*% GDP*
1956	3,656	1,710	5,366	9,185	1,795	10,980	290	3.3
1961	5,592	3,336	8,928	9,911	2,517	12,428	275	2.1
1966	8,713	4,770	13,483	11,673	3,705	15,378	564	3.2
1971	14,608	9,100	23,708	14,432	5,450	19,882	738	2.8
1976	31,121	20,424	51,545	21,686	8,850	30,536	1,458	2.4
1981	57,732	43,516	101,248	36,573	18,249	54,822	2,494	2.5
1986	113,900	94,800	208,700	67,500	45,100	112,600	5,076	2.6

Source: Reserve Bank of Australia, *Bulletin*, February 1987 and 'Budget-Statement No 6', *Budget Paper No 1*, various issues

Notes: [a] Excludes financial institutions
[b] Average for the five years ending the year shown

raisings by listed companies in Australia amounted to about one-sixth of the loan raisings of public authorities. Financial institutions have usually been the largest issuers, in particular the finance companies, which borrow much of their funds directly from the household sector by public issues of various types of debentures, frequently soliciting funds through the branch networks of banks with which they are affiliated.

At the time of writing there are some signs that a domestic market for corporate bonds may be beginning to emerge, with increased issues by corporations and financial institutions aimed for placement with 'professional investors'. However, it is still the case that the 'bond market' in Australia is synonymous with the markets for government and semi-government securities.

Governments are perceived as prime borrowers, and default risk on other marketable securities is priced relative to yields on Treasury notes and bonds. The bond market has also been somewhat of a pace-maker in the 1980s in terms of issue procedures and methods, speeding up the process of deregulation in Australia. Finally, and in contrast to the situation in the UK, open market operations in Australia are conducted with Treasury notes and bonds, so that conditions in the bond market have significant spillovers on other sectors of the capital market.

PUBLIC SECURITIES

The market for public-sector securities is fashioned by the constitutional and economic arrangements which exist between the federal government, the state governments and the numerous local councils and shires. Australia is a federation of six states. The Commonwealth Constitution dates from 1901 and was much influenced by the US model. It gives the federal government certain specific powers over defence, external affairs, banking and currency, interstate trade and customs, but apart from these, the other functions are exercised concurrently with the states. Thus the Commonwealth and state government both have power to levy taxes, other than customs and excise duties, and to make loan raisings.

As it has in fact transpired, revenue raising is highly centralized, with the Commonwealth government collecting over three-quarters of taxes and providing funds to the other tiers of government (predominantly the states) by way of budget allocations of grants and loans.[1] This dominance of the Commonwealth extends also to the raising of loans. Under one of the few successful moves to amend the

Constitution, the Commonwealth in 1927 took on legal responsibility for state public debts. Thereafter, the Australia Loan Council was to approve and co-ordinate state and Commonwealth government, the Commonwealth and the six state premiers, with the Prime Minister as chairman.[2] The balance of power is summarized by one observer as follows: 'Any five states acting together can notionally outvote the Commonwealth, which has two votes plus a casting vote: but the Commonwealth acquired the whip hand in the 1950s when it had to top up the borrowing programs with funds drawn from its tax revenues and has never lost control since' (Walsh 1986). Nevertheless, until the introduction of the tender system in 1982, political considerations often loomed large in the setting of new issue yields which hindered the flexible use of open market operations and monetary policy.

Nowadays, the Commonwealth government has unhindered control over the new issue of government securities. These take five major forms. Treasury bonds, issued by tender since 1982, constitute over half of the total (see Table 6.2) and are issued with a fixed coupon interest, payable semi-annually, and fixed maturity date. In recent years new issues have had maturities of between three and fifteen years, although some small amount of debt with longer maturities still remain on issue. Bonds issued since 1984 are no longer available in

Table 6.2 Government securities on issue ($m)

Type	*June 1986*	*June 1987*	*June 1988*
Treasury bonds	37,880.4	39,693.5	37,520.8
Treasury notes	6,953.5	8,140.4	7,849.6
Treasury indexed bonds	331.3	634.5	836.7
Australian Savings Bonds	3,966.0	3,459.1	3,493.2
Overseas currency debt[a]	13,832.4	15,064.1	12,691.4
Other miscellaneous[b]	1,609.8	923.0	944.1
Total	64,473.4	67,914.6	63,335.8

Sources: 'Government Securities on Issue at 30 June 1986', Table 2, *1986–87 Budget Paper No 8*
'Government Securities on Issue at 30 June 1987', Table 2, *1987–88 Budget Related Paper No 1*
'Government Securities on Issue at 30 June 1988', Table 2, *1988–89 Budget Related Paper No 1*

Notes: [a] Converted into Australian dollar equivalent as at 30 June.
[b] Comprises Internal Treasury Bills, Income Equalization Deposits, Overdue Securities, Tax-free Stock, State Domestic Raisings. There were no public Treasury bills on issue.

bearer form; all bonds must be held as inscribed stock at Reserve Bank registries.

Treasury notes, issued by tender since December 1979, are thirteen- and twenty-six-week securities issued at a discount to face value. Their 1988 share of 12.4 per cent of the total is significantly increased from that of just a few years earlier – reflecting in part the major role they play in the 'new' monetary policy based upon open market operations.

The third type of security is *Treasury indexed bonds*, first issued in August 1985 and of two sorts. Capital indexed bonds (issued by tender on a real yield bid basis but available subsequently to small investors on a tap basis offer) a fixed coupon real interest rate (4 per cent on issues to 1988) on a capital value which is adjusted in line with movements in the Consumer Price Index. Interest indexed bonds, issued on a tap basis, link the nominal interest rate paid on the fixed capital value to the same index and bear a fixed real yield determined in the light of the tender outcome for capital indexed bonds. Both have been available as ten- and twenty-year maturities, but the take-up, as Table 6.2 indicates, has been very small, and there have been no new issues since February 1988. (In some early tenders the Treasurer rejected certain bids and did not allot the whole amount on offer, because of the high real interest rates implied. Real interest rates resulting from the tender process have been in the 5–6 per cent range).[3]

Standing somewhat apart from the other securities are Australian Savings Bonds (ASBs). They are 'retail' securities which were available on tap from 1976 until September 1987 (new issues were formally suspended in January 1988) at a yield fixed for the (generally) seven-year life of the security except for very premature withdrawal. Otherwise, holders were able to withdraw funds at one month's notice without penalty if, for example, a new higher yielding series of ASBs was introduced. ASB's share of total government securities on issue (25 per cent at June 1988) declined because of an unwillingness of the government to offer new series with yields matching those generally available in the market. In part, this may have reflected recognition by the authorities that, at competitive yields, ASBs offered a two-way option which could not be matched by banks and other private-sector institutions (Hill 1985). When interest rates rose, holders of ASBs could cash in and reinvest in a new series at the higher yields; when rates fell, holders could stay put and benefit from market yields for the full seven years. Poole (1981) advocated instead that ASBs be replaced by a floating rate note, allowing yields to rise and fall in line with market trends. The suspension of ASB's in 1988, apparently indefinitely, has not involved any such replacement, as the authorities have judged that the private sector now offers retail investors a much wider range of investment opportunities, and facilities have been created for retail investors who want government paper to purchase Treasury bonds direct from the Reserve Bank (in minimum amounts of $1,000).

Also shown in Table 6.2, and comprising 20 per cent of debt on issue is Overseas currency debt – securities issued and repayable in overseas currencies. Part of the increased share (from a 6.5 per cent of total outstandings ten years earlier) is the result of exchange rate depreciation,[4] but loan raisings were substantial in the mid-1980s.

Government securities on issue declined during 1987–8 as public-sector finances swung from deficit to surplus, with the larger part of the budget surplus being applied to redemptions of overseas debt. Table 6.3 gives a breakdown of the currency distribution of overseas debt in recent years.

Table 6.3 Government securities repayable in overseas currencies, 1986–8

Currency	*30 June 1986 % share*	*30 June 1987 % share*	*30 June 1988 % share*
Sterling	4.9	5.9	6.8
US Dollars	27.9	31.7	35.2
Deutsche Marks	15.3	15.2	12.0
Swiss Francs	11.8	11.3	12.3
Guilders	7.2	8.6	8.6
Yen	33.3	27.3	25.1

Sources: Table 7, Government Securities on Issue at 30 June 1986, *1986–87 Budget Paper No 8*
Table 7, Government Securities on Issue at 30 June 1987, *1987–88 Budget Related Paper No 1*
Table 8, Government Securities on Issue at 30 June 1988, *1988–89 Budget Related Paper No 1*

About four-fifths of domestic securities on issue are held outside the official sector (see Table 6.4). Trading banks are major holders and the BIS-inspired capital adequacy guidelines encourage the banks to remain so. Other non-bank financial intermediaries have supplanted savings banks as the second major group of holders. The removal of 'captive market' regulations (see pp. 148–50) applying to savings banks helps to explain that change, and the gradual erosion and ultimate removal of the tax benefits to life offices from also adhering to captive type arrangements is relevant to explaining their declining share.

Also shown in Table 6.4 is the average period to maturity (apm) of non-official holdings of government securities. A marked decline in the apm occurred until the start of 1983 (when it was fifty-two months) as new issues had been focused at the short end of the maturity spectrum. Since then, the apm has increased as new bond issues via the tender system have, after an initial market orientation period, had an average maturity of around eight years. This is one of a number of ways in which the market for government securities has been transformed by alterations to issuing methods in the primary market.

Table 6.4 The structure of domestic-currency government security holdings, at 30 June ($m)

	1976	*1981*	*1986*	*1988*
Non-official holdings				
of marketable debt				
Trading Banks	3,796	5,208	8,655	12,662
Savings Banks	2,845	3,819	5,281	8,463
Life Offices	2,054	3,012	3,076	1,909
Authorized Dealers	800	1,347	1,441	2,287
Other financial	1,671	2,629	8,067	8,514
Other	131	916	7,790	8,240
	11,297	16,931	34,310	42,075
of non-marketable debt	2,338	3,315	4,549	3,861
Official holdings				
Reserve Bank	2,739	4,779	9,690	3,683
Other	2,639	2,795	2,025	990
Total on issue	19,013	27,820	50,574	50,609
Memo item: apm of non-official holdings of marketable debt (months)	107	66	80	69

Source: Reserve Bank of Australia, *Bulletin*, Tables I10, I12, various issues

MARKETS FOR PUBLIC SECURITIES

Marked changes have occurred in the primary marketing arrangements for government securities; these in turn have led to a significant broadening of the secondary markets. The changes in issue procedures have involved both Treasury notes and Treasury bonds. Prior to

December 1979, Treasury notes were issued on a continuous 'tap' system at pre-determined yields. Since that date, notes have been sold by weekly 'tender' or auction. Before April 1980, Treasury bonds were marketed by 'cash and conversion loans'. That system was altered to a continuous 'tap' basis from April 1980 and to the current tender system in July 1982. These three systems – cash and conversion, tap and tender – are discussed below.

In the thirty-four years from July 1945 to August 1979, 113 periodic public loan raisings were made for Treasury bonds, mostly on a cash and conversion basis.[5] This description simply means that the government sought to raise 'cash' by the sale of bonds to the public, and securities could be purchased in small parcels ($100 minimum in the late 1970s). At the same time, in the conversion loan, the holders of maturing bonds were offered the opportunity to convert their existing holdings into new bonds. Coupon interest rates were set through the Loan Council arrangements, along with issue prices (usually at par). Issues remained open for one or two weeks, with the authorities selling as many bonds as the public demanded at those rates.

Any misjudgement of market yields led to considerable variability in the sales of Treasury bonds. When rates were pitched too low, few bonds were sold to the public, and the Reserve Bank and Government Trust Funds were called upon to give the issue the appearance of success. When rates were too high or the maturities on offer were shorter than those sought, sales exceeded expectations. This variability assumed importance for debt management since cash raisings were concentrated into only three or four public issues per year.

Hence the motivation for the switch to the tap system in which one or two series of securities of various maturities were made available more or less continuously. Twenty-two series were issued under this system from April 1980 until July 1982. Once issued, a loan remained open until another series was substituted in its place. One objective was to give greater continuity to the bond-selling programme. Another was to allow a 'more market-oriented approach' to bond selling,[6] despite issue yields being determined as before by the Loan Council. If sales were large, the idea was to close off the issue and reduce yields; vice-versa if sales were flagging. Indeed, it was argued that the essence was for the authorities to set the quantities and the market determine the price (Hill 1985).

In practice, the political reluctance to raise rates in the face of a flagging market continued. These institutional rigidities and the time lags involved in withdrawing existing series, re-pricing them and issuing new ones saw many series out of line with market trends.

Admittedly, it is not easy to sell bonds under any system when yields are rising, and the tap experiment coincided with such a period. Perhaps the authorities lacked an adequate bench mark for assessing market rates while trading in the secondary market remained 'thin', in one visitor's assessment,[7] and many of the buyers of securities were subject to various arrangements which made them captive holders.

Prior to switching to a tendering system for Treasury bonds, the Loan Council commissioned a report by government officials into the form which the system might take. Presumably the officials had the example of the successful tender system for Treasury notes in their mind, and not surprisingly they recommended a variant of that system. The principal features of the resulting system are:[8]

1 Tenders are spaced throughout the year with the amount allotted per tender ranging from $400 million to $1.2 billion. The number of tenders held has ranged from seven tenders to a projected three or four tenders in 1988–9 with the lowered funding requirements.
2 The amounts of bonds on offer, and their maturities and coupons, are announced on a Thursday and bids close on the following Tuesday.
3 The minimum size of 'competitive' bids is $100,000 and thereafter in multiples of $1,000, and those making tenders must register with the Reserve Bank, which continued to act as agent for the Treasury. Others may submit bids through a registered institution.
4 All bids must be accompanied by a deposit of 5 per cent of face value (unless exempted by the Bank). Final settlement is within two weeks of the announcement of successful tenders.
5 Bids are made on a yield basis, and bids are accepted and securities allotted in ascending order of yield (i.e. descending order of price).
6 The Treasurer reserves the right to refuse any bids.
7 The Reserve Bank also takes up stock, additional to the tender, in prespecified amounts, at the weighted average yield of successful bidders.

Since tenders of bonds are spread out evenly, issues of Treasury notes deal with periods of potential surplus liquidity (July to December – the first half of the financial year) due to the pattern of government budget transactions. Tenders of Treasury notes, held since December 1979, take place most weeks and the amount on offer varies with the liquidity of the system. The bidding process, allotment and arrangements for Reserve Bank take up are similar to those for bond tenders.

In broad details, the tendering system adopted in Australia follows that in use in the United States. The mixed tender/tap system then in operation in the UK found little favour amongst the investigating committee. They preferred a system to allocate winning bids at differential yields, as in the US, rather than at a uniform price corresponding to the marginal successful tender, the so-called Dutch auction system which operates in West Germany. (A system of additional non-competitive bids tried until 1985 was also borrowed from the US.) The advantage to the authorities of the present differential price system comes from the potential, with sealed bids, to practise perfect monopolistic price discrimination. By separating the bidders and allocating securities to them at yields which differ according to their respective demands, the authorities seek to capture for themselves the 'consumers' surplus' of the tender participants. As Juttner (1982) notes, this is possible only if (a) the applicants can be kept apart, and (b) so long as existing holders of Treasury bonds can be prevented from acting as competitive suppliers of securities. While there exists a secondary market for bonds, no tender applicant will bid for stocks at a yield less than that ruling for existing issues of comparable maturity, setting an effective floor upon auction bids. At the same time, the extent to which bid yields will diverge above that level clearly depends on the willingness of applicants to collude on bids. Syndicates are permitted and do occur under the present open tender arrangements. Nevertheless, with nearly 500 bidders participating, the potential for the exercise of price discrimination remains.

Proponents[9] of the uniform pricing or Dutch auction method argue that the authorities would gain additional revenue sufficiently large to compensate for the consumer rent foregone by giving up differential pricing of securities allotted and instead issuing securities at the yield which corresponds to the marginal accepted bid. One source of extra demand is from small investors, scared off from participating in a differential price auction by the fear that they will bid too much for the securities. The other is that the differential pricing auction leads to tenders being made at higher yields than in a uniform price auction as participants seek to avert the risk that they will incur an instantaneous capital loss when trading opens after the auction on the secondary market.

On the sparse evidence available in Australia and overseas, it is difficult to judge the merit of this argument, and that of another claim that revenue gains would result from having the auction underwritten by a syndicate of market institutions. This is the method which is usually followed for the issue of local and semi-government securities in Australia, through either tender panels or dealer panels (which make a secondary market in the securities underwritten). But the parallel here is not exact, since secondary markets for some local and semi-government debt are less 'broad' than those for government securities.

Although all marketable issues of Treasury bonds are quoted on the stock exchanges of the six state capital cities (Melbourne and Sydney are the major exchanges), the 'on-change' market, as it is called, is of minor importance. It exists mainly as an avenue for small investors to dispose of their holdings. 'On-change' turnover in 1979 was $100 million, in comparison with total turnover during the calendar year in the order of $150 billion.[10] Most transactions still take place 'off-change' in the professional market.

For at least thirty years, the major secondary market for government securities in Australia has been an informal telephone market conducted away from any organized exchange and has operated along much the same lines as the market for foreign exchange in most centuries. It is interesting to observe that it is only recently that markets for securities in the UK have evolved along this path.

Trading 'off-change' in Australia sometimes occurs directly between institutional holders of securities – banks and life offices – but more usually deals are arranged through specialist bond dealers or the authorized dealers in the official money market, acting either as brokers or principals. Settlement methods differ according to which of these groups is the counterparty to the transaction, and as we shall see timing differences in settlement play an important role in monetary policy procedures.

Information about prices is transmitted much as in the foreign exchange market. Dealers' quotations are displayed on monitor screens as part of Reuters and other money market services and contain firm bids and offers. Like in any market, news travels fast in a variety of other ways. In addition, average yields on transactions by the authorized money market dealers and the major bond dealers are reported directly to the Reserve Bank. They also submit returns on the quantities of stocks traded. Estimates of bond market turnover based on these figures show a large increase in trading volumes. As Table 6.5 shows, bonds now change hands on average ten times per year versus less than once a year in pre-tender days.

Some of this increased turnover is a by-product of the auction method itself. Many, perhaps most, of those participating in the tender do not intend holding for themselves the securities obtained. They bid for securities which are then on-sold and distributed to the ultimate end-acquirers. This market-making role of the tenderers finds reflection in the time profile of trading in particular series: the

Table 6.5 Bond market activity (a)

Year to June	*Total turnover ($bn)*	*Non-official transactions (b) ($bn)*	*Turnover rate (c)*
average 1975–1978	11.5	7.0	0.8
average 1979–1982	14.0	10.4	0.8
1983	24.5	22.3	1.1
1984	57.8	54.0	2.0
1985	85.1	80.2	2.4
1986	119.5	112.6	3.2
1987	201.6	193.8	5.1
1988	395.1	375.4	10.5
1989	321.2	308.1	9.5

Source: Reserve Bank of Australia, *Bulletin*, January 1987.

Notes:
(a) Annual figures based on half year to December 1986.
(b) Excludes transactions involving the Reserve Bank.
(c) Non-official transactions as a ratio of the stock of bonds outstanding at the end of the period.

typical pattern is for stock to turn over 2.5 times during the first month after issue.[11] Other factors which have contributed to the growth of trading are:

(i) a widened demand for securities from the internationalization of the bond market;
(ii) market innovations in the form of synthetic financial instruments based around government securities;
(iii) the abolition of captive market arrangements, greater variability of bond yields and thus scope for trading profits (and losses) which have followed from deregulation and the 'new' monetary policy.

These are examined in turn below.

INTERNATIONALIZATION OF THE BOND MARKET

Australian public-sector borrowing overseas began on a significant scale in the latter half of the 1970s, when the government of the time sought to push up the managed exchange rate as an anti-inflationary weapon. Federal government debt redeemable overseas increased from $1.32 billion in 1976 to $5.37 billion in 1980, and its subsequent growth is shown in Table 6.6.

Table 6.6 Public-sector debt – overseas and domestic holdings ($m)

June	*Government securities*			*Semi-government securities*		
	Redeemable overseas	*Redeemable in Australia*		*Redeemable overseas*	*Redeemable in Australia*	
		Non-residents	*Residents*		*Non-residents*	*Residents*
1980	5,396	125	27,125	1,439	—	16,315
1981	4,652	143	27,137	1,819	—	19,093
1982	5,352	316	27,756	3,072	122	22,093
1983	6,919	697	31,356	5,596	1,472	26,880
1984	7,084	1,538	38,181	8,192	1,873	31,347
1985	9,792	2,733	43,208	13,563	2,622	36,833
1986	13,832	50,641		n.a.	n.a.	n.a.
1987	15,064	52,850		n.a.	n.a.	n.a.
1988	12,686	50,644		n.a.	n.a.	n.a.

Sources: *Treasury Round-Up*, December 1985 Supplement, 'Australian Public Sector External Debt June 1980 to June 1985'
Reserve Bank Bulletin, December 1986 and December 1988
Government Securities on Issue at 30 June 1987, *1987–88 Budget Paper No 1*

Semi-government borrowings offshore began to grow after relaxation of Loan Council restrictions in 1978 and the substantial growth in the 1980s is also evident from the table. In interpreting those figures however, it should be noted that exchange rate depreciation accounted for almost $5 billion of the $16.5 billion increase in the value of total public sector debt redeemable overseas between June 1980 and June 1985. (Similar effects occurred during 1985–6.)

Foreigners have also come to be not insignificant holders of 'domestic' government debt during the 1980s (see Table 6.6), and by 1987 held nearly a quarter of Australian government bonds outstanding. Overseas institutions and investors have been attracted by the high nominal yields on Australian securities, sometimes ignoring, often to their cost, the potential for exchange rate depreciation built into the Australian interest-rate structure. Other factors encouraging foreign involvement in the Australian bond market include: the removal of exchange controls which accompanied the floating of the dollar in December 1983, the increased liquidity of the bond market, Australia's relatively high international credit rating, deregulation overseas and the greater interest and ability of Japanese investors to hold Australian securities.[12]

By far the most important developments in the integration of the Australian financial market with those overseas are the increased investment by Australian residents overseas and greater borrowing by domestic intermediaries from overseas – both in domestic and foreign currencies. (Notably, investment in Australian equities has decreased markedly in relative importance.) As a result, and specifically since the float, the covered interest differential has deviated little from zero – implying much tighter links between the bond and foreign exchange markets than before the float. The existence of such links underlay monetary policy in 1985 and 1986 when via operations in the bond market the authorities attempted to support the exchange rate by a high interest rate strategy. By 1986 it was generally believed that the authorities had abandoned the 'clean' float and were attempting to influence the exchange rate directly by conducting open market operations in the foreign exchange market as well as in the bond and money markets.

Private-sector overseas borrowings have increased much faster during the 1980s than have overseas borrowings of public sector authorities (see Table 6.7), continuing the trend of earlier years (see Table 6.1). Much of this borrowing can be seen as an indirect consequence of public-sector deficits whereby large public borrowing on domestic markets 'crowds out' private entities. Such a view is one component of the policy strategy of the past few years which has attempted to 'wind back' public-sector deficit spending. It must be admitted, though, that there has not been a large market for corporate debt in Australia. In the absence of a domestic corporate debt market, a 'surrogate or synthetic' one has been created overseas by means of cross-currency interest rate swaps. German banks and other international entities with established reputations in the Euromarkets issued fixed-rate Australian dollar Eurobonds. Australian corporate borrowers take out floating rate debt in US dollars or another major currency. By swapping their respective debt obligations, the German bank gains, say, floating rate US dollars on attractive terms while the Australian corporate borrower acquires fixed rate medium-term funding in Australian dollars.

Table 6.7 External and public-sector debt (percentage of GDP)

June	*Public-sector (a) External debt*	*Private-sector (a) External debt*	*Net External debt*
1981	4.8	6.3	6.2
1982	5.8	9.9	10.6
1983	8.3	12.6	13.6
1984	9.2	13.6	15.4
1985	14.1	17.6	23.8
1986	17.8	20.8	30.4
1987	18.4	21.7	31.4
1988	18.9	20.9	30.8

Sources: *Treasury Roundup*, September 1987
Reserve Bank of Australia, *Bulletin*, December 1988

Note:
(a) These columns represent *gross* figures and consequently their sum exceeds the total *net* debt figure.

As a consequence, Euro-$A bonds outstanding increased from zero in 1983 to $28 billion as at June 1988 (or 10 per cent of GDP). Increased familiarity with Australian dollar bonds encouraged Australian corporations with international reputations both to tap the international market for Australian dollar bonds more extensively, and to import the techniques into Australia and revive domestic issues of corporate bonds. The issues are targeted at professional investors and are not listed on the Stock Exchange. Some bonds are swapped to create debt in floating rate form. Other issues substitute for the unavailability of medium-term fixed rate from domestic financial institutions. There may also have been some 'crowding in', with the move to a surplus in the Federal government budget and redemptions of domestic along with external debt 'creating room' for private-sector issues domestically as well as internationally.

The Australian government's approach to its external debt management is outlined in McLaughlin (1985). Under the 'global limits' approach, overseas borrowings by state authorities are limited to a particular share of the total, as are those of Commonwealth authorities. Determination of those limits plus the Commonwealth's own overseas programme reflects a desire to ensure that government overseas borrowings do not come to be regarded as excessive by international capital markets. That desire has not been completely fulfilled since the expansion in Australia's total external debt (public plus private) during the 1980s led to a slight downgrading of Australia's credit rating by US rating agencies in 1986 (Australian government $A debt is rated AAA, while the foreign-exchange debt is rated AAI on Moody's scorings).

But in general terms the strategy of having private-sector borrowers undertaking the overseas borrowing must, at least at this juncture, be deemed to have been successful. Adjustment to the sharp decline in Australia's terms of trade (nearly 20 per cent in the two years to June 1987) has been smoothed without major consequences for unemployment. In the climate of the 1980s, private-sector borrowing is probably viewed more favourably overseas than greater sovereign debt. Nevertheless the demand for Australian paper at currently available terms is far from infinite, and a recognition of that fact has led the Australian government to reduce the budget deficit and slow down the growth of external borrowings.

DOMESTIC FINANCIAL INNOVATIONS

Innovation in financial markets has seen new assets forged to compete with government debt and new uses of government securities for the creation of synthetic securities. Major changes have occurred in Australia's tax system involving, *inter alia*, the introduction of a capital gains tax, abolition in 1985 and subsequent reintroduction two years later of tax benefits from negative gearing[13] of rental investment properties, less (overly) generous tax treatment of lump sum superannuation benefit payouts, and (from July 1987) the ending of the double taxation of dividend income from share holdings. Such tax changes, by affecting relative after tax rates of return on various investments, can be expected to have altered the demand for government debt although it is beyond the scope of this chapter to ascertain their net effect. We focus instead upon the new financial market environment and the novel uses made of government securities.

One feature of the bond market noted earlier is the small role played by the household sector as direct holders of government debt. Save for Australian Savings Bonds, and they have declined in relative importance, holdings of households are minuscule, although indirect holdings via the intermediation of savings banks and life offices are substantial. Part of the reason for the small value of 'retail' holdings can probably be found in the thinness of the market (although the Reserve Bank tends to make a market for small volumes on-change) and transactions costs associated with selling debt 'on-change'. Recent changes may see some growth in direct holdings by small investors. ASBs are no longer available, and a direct purchase facility is now available at the Reserve Bank for small investors. Also, the Reserve Bank now offers a repurchase facility for small parcels of debt, thus ensuring marketability.

On the other side of the ledger, there has been a large increase in the availability to households of competing retail instruments bearing wholesale-market-related interest rates. Cash Management Trusts (the Australian variant of US Money Market Mutual Funds) which commenced in 1980, and their clones at various depository institutions, are an obvious example. Semi-government paper offered by the Central Borrowing Authorities of the state governments is another competitor. Having brought under one roof the borrowings of their various instrumentalities (except some large ones) the states have achieved sufficient economies of scale to enable them to tap the retail market. While some of the states have gone in for some aggressive marketing of their debt, the federal government has largely eschewed attempting to become a large direct seller of its debt to households.

At the wholesale end of the financial markets, conventional government securities have underpinned at least two market innovations. One, bearing the unlikely acronym DINGO (for discounted investment on negotiable government obligations), involves financiers separating coupon interest payments from principal repayments on government debt and selling the two income streams separately.[14] This is just one of the many innovations in financial markets in recent years aimed at tailor-making financial securities to fit investor and borrower needs.

Futures markets play a similar role, and the Sydney Futures Exchange in December 1984 introduced a futures contract on a (theoretical) ten-year bond after an earlier unsuccessful atempt to create a market in two-year bond futures. The futures contract is for a hypothetical 12 per cent coupon bond with face value of $100,000 and the cash settlement price is determined by an arithmetic mean of a random selection of bid and offer yields from a panel of bond traders. During the year to June 1988, turnover of futures contracts averaged $1 billion per day, compared with turnover in the physical market of $1.5 billion per day. Options contracts on ten-year bonds are now also available. Consequently, bonds of around ten years maturity have become the most heavily traded of all maturities in recent years and the increased depth in this segment of the market is reflected in lower yields than on surrounding maturities.

Admittedly, the ten-year futures contract – and the latter three-year contract introduced in the middle of 1988 – were chosen because of the large amount of trading which already took place at those maturities. Once established, the existence of the contracts encourages market participants to increase trading in those maturities because of the ability to hedge exposures by means of the futures market. This is an illustration of the self-reinforcing nature of market liquidity (Lewis 1990). Considerations of liquidity have also seen both the Commonwealth and the State central borrowing authorities concentrate outstandings in a few 'hot' or benchmark bonds, chosen by market participants as preferred for trading because of the large amount on issue and desirable dates of maturity.

One further role of the bond market concerns the dynamics of short-run interest rate determination. Interest rates have become much more variable and changes in some specific rates appear to now have strong psychological effects in the markets. One such yield is the Treasury note tender yield, another the Reserve Bank's rediscount rate on Treasury notes and a third is the prime (or indicator or base) lending rate of the trading banks. These rates have assumed significance due to the different way in which monetary policy is now operated in Australia.

MONETARY POLICY

The old policy

Prior to the deregulation of the Australian financial system in the 1980s, monetary policy was conducted primarily by way of direct controls upon the banking sector.[15] Despite continuing Reserve Bank avowal of a preference for more market-oriented measures, yields on government debt were, given recent experience, remarkably stable. The ten-year bond yield, for example, remained unchanged for the seventeen months ending November 1976. Treasury note yields were unchanged between November 1977 and February 1979.

In this environment, the official view was that for banks, at least, virtually perfect substitutability existed between cash and other government securities so that growth in monetary aggregates was related to an LGS base (comprising bank holdings of government debt plus the stock of base money) rather than to base money as conventionally defined.[16] Monetary control proceeded largely by way of changes in the Statutory Reserve Deposit (SRD) ratio (a 'frozen' cash reserve ratio applied to trading bank deposits) which were seen as altering the banks' holdings of free LGS assets in excess of the conventional requirement of 18 per cent of deposits and thus influencing lending behaviour. Bank lending behaviour was also influenced by moral suasion and quantitative lending guidelines.

Here we have an illustration of the way in which a conceptual framework can condition actual behaviour. To the extent that the LGS base did in fact underpin bank deposit growth, open market operations were of limited value. While the stock of bonds in private hands could be changed, no guarantee existed that the change would be in the holdings of the non-bank private sector which was necessary if the LGS base was to be affected. Sales to the banks simply changed the composition and not the total of the LGS base. The introduction of Australian Savings Bonds in 1976, directed at the non-bank sector, reflected these concerns. With the pegged exchange rate prevailing at the time, matters were even worse. The total supply of LGS assets available to the private sector was, as a result, outside official control, being affected by swings in the balance of payments.

Visiting North American[17] and a number of Australian academics[18] remained sceptical on this point, arguing either that the composition of LGS assets between cash and government securities did matter or that it would matter if open market operations were prosecuted more vigorously and interest rates allowed to fluctuate. But demand conditions were not amenable to open market operations. Most of the non-official holdings of debt were in the hands of 'captive' institutions: trading banks, savings banks, life offices and authorized dealers in the short-term money market. To the extent that the captivity requirements were effective, forcing institutions to hold greater than desired shares of their portfolios in government debt, the demand of this group could be expected to hinge primarily upon portfolio sizes and be relatively interest-rate inelastic.

The captive market arrangements were designed partly with the objective of reducing government funding costs in mind. The data presented in Table 6.8 are consistent with the hypothesis that captive market arrangements reduced bond yields *vis-à-vis* other interest rates, but that had implications for the ability of the captives to compete with other institutions and thus ultimately their demand for government debt. In the years immediately after 1981, savings banks' portfolio restrictions were significantly relaxed, the 30/20 rule applying to life offices was abolished, and the bank portfolio constraints lightened as part of the reform of bond market arrangements.

Later developments in 1988 saw the reforms continued with the phasing out of the variable cash reserve requirement of Statutory Reserve Deposits (SRDs) and their replacement by a fixed one per cent cash ratio (along the lines of that in the UK) and the removal of the former distinctions between trading and savings banks. When the new arrangements are in place the remaining captive requirement will consist of a prime assets ratio (PAR) maintained by trading and savings banks as 10 per cent of domestic liabilities in Australian currency and held as cash and/or Commonwealth government securities. It must be doubted in the end whether captivity served even the narrow interests of debt management, and other explanations for the decline in the yield differential shown in Table 6.8, such as a higher growth rate of public sector debt, greater volatility in government yields making those assets more risky, and a decline in the relative size of the finance company sector, can be advanced.

Table 6.8 Relative interest rates: finance company debenture rate less bond rate

Period (a)	*2-year securities*	*5-year securities*
1977–81	1.28	1.28
1982–6	0.59	0.49

Source: Reserve Bank of Australia, *Bulletin* December 1986

Note:
(a) Average of interest rate differentials prevailing at end of June of years shown.

While the captive market arrangements were in place the conduct of monetary policy was adversely affected. Demand for debt from other holders was subdued, and growth in demand from the captives depended on their ability to expand balance sheets. As the captive institutions declined in relative importance, and monetary controls operated on a shrinking base, it was apparent that the wider interests of monetary policy were certainly not being well served by the controls over the bond market. A more flexible exchange rate policy was also adopted, culminating in the floating of the $A in December 1983.[19] That, together with the changed structure of the bond market, has enabled a 'new' monetary policy to be fashioned.

THE NEW MONETARY POLICY

Monetary control is based virtually entirely upon Reserve Bank open market operations in government debt – concentrated at the short end of the market. Those operations are in response to developments in a 'checklist' of indicators[20] (in contrast to the monetary targeting approach abandoned in early 1985) and appear to involve an operating target of short-term interest rates rather than, for example, a quantity variable such as base money. In fact, institutional liquidity management arrangements in Australia make base money as conventionally defined an unimportant magnitude for the operation of policy, as will become clear below.

It is helpful to keep in mind Roosa's (1956) distinction between the 'defensive' and 'dynamic' dimensions of policy when considering the present relationship between monetary policy and debt management.[21] Monetary policy (actions to influence the growth of money and credit) is now significantly disconnected from debt management (sales of non-cash securities by the government to finance its deficit and refinance maturing debt). Since 1984–5, net issues (redemptions) of government securities over the financial year have covered the Commonwealth government budget deficit (surplus). On a day-to-day basis, however, net flow of funds to and from the government accounts are substantial and these are smoothed to maintain monetary conditions on course with the broad objectives of economic management.

Thus the Reserve Bank must wear (at least) three hats: agent for government debt raisings (debt management), smoother of the flow of cash in the system (the defensive dimension of monetary management) and maker of monetary policy (the dynamic dimension). Despite the regular tender programme and the now familiar ebb and flow of government receipts and repayments, cash movements are not fully predictable: tax receipts are uneven and settlement of bond tenders can occur at any time in the month following announcement of successful applicants. As a consequence, and an addition to the Reserve Bank's defensive actions, various 'safety valves' are built into official cash arrangements in Australia.

The 'official' cash market

Banks and authorized money market dealers[22] maintain exchange settlement accounts at the Reserve Bank. Cash payments between the public and the government and the Reserve Bank pass through these accounts. But exchange settlement account balances are not the main focus of monetary and liquidity management. Loans made by banks to authorized dealers are as good as cash because withdrawals of those loans yield exchange settlement funds to the banks. Since loans to dealers bear interest, banks hold virtually no free cash reserves at the Reserve Bank. Dealers, in turn, are able to operate with virtually zero exchange settlement accounts because of the three 'safety valves' made available by the Reserve Bank. Those are: lender of last resort facilities extended to the official dealers (at penal rates); the Treasury note rediscount facility open to all holders of Notes at a published, above-market, rediscount rate; and (most importantly) the ability of the dealers to create Reserve Bank 'float'.

Float arises from the Reserve Bank practice of giving same-day credit to dealers' accounts for their deposit of cheques drawn upon banks, but not debiting banks' accounts until the next day. The dealers can thus purchase securities from the Bank even when the system has zero exchange settlement account balances by borrowing from the non-bank sector and creating Reserve Bank float. While the float position will (if nothing else changes) be restored to zero the next day, this type of action enables liquidity fluctuations to be smoothed out over a period of time. Where the liquidity constraint is intentional and a tightening of policy is pursued, the attempts by dealers to attract non-bank loans to replace bank loans to dealers (which decline as the system settles with the Reserve Bank) push up short-term interest rates. Ultimately, the portfolio readjustments set in train bring about a new equilibrium involving lower bank (and other) intermediation.[23]

Operating targets

One of the implications of these arrangements concerns the usefulness of the monetary base as an operational target for policy. Traditionally the choice for an operating target for policy is posed as one between a short-term interest rate and base money. In the Australian environment, base money is of little value in that role on a day-to-day basis. Banks and dealers hold virtually no cash reserves so that base money consists almost entirely of currency and the trading banks' required reserves in SRD accounts (equal to 7 per cent of the previous months' deposits). Consequently base money shows little responsiveness to current market operations, with float and banks' loans to dealers providing the short run adjustment. The responsiveness of base money is at best a lagged indicator of changes in financial conditions. A more appropriate quantity indicator of changes in cash market conditions would appear to be banks' loans to dealers. As noted, these effectively constitute the free cash reserves of the banking system and will vary in line with changes in the system's liquidity.

In its day-to-day operations the Reserve Bank appears to focus more upon short term interest rates – particularly commercial bill and money market rates – than upon banks' loans to dealers as an operating target. There has been very little analysis of the appropriateness of this strategy, Dotsey (1987) being the exception. He suggests that the approach of focusing upon a short-term yield is, in the Australian context, appropriate for minimizing the variability in a money stock target.

Operational procedures

For Treasury notes and for bonds of less than one year to maturity, open market operations are conducted through the official short-term money market dealers (currently nine in number) which were established in 1959 for that purpose. With dealings in longer-term bonds the Bank has found it appropriate to establish a group of reporting bond dealers (twenty-three in number at June 1988) with which it deals. Some stockbrokers are members of this group, but brokers play a much reduced role in the market than pre-1959 when they dominated trading.

Open market operations are focused at the short end of the market. There is little doubt that the various institutional changes made during the 1980s (floating, tenders of Treasury Notes and Bonds) have reduced the variability of short-term interest rates. MacFarlane (1986), for example, notes that the standard deviation of the daily change in the official cash rate[24] has fallen from 2.64 percentage points in the two years prior to the float (in December 1983) to 0.86 in the subsequent three years. Further out along the maturity spectrum, however, yields have exhibited considerable variability.

Until August 1984, market operations involved straightforward sales or purchases but since then repurchase agreements between the Bank and dealers have become significant. Repurchase agreements are equivalent to a collateralized loan and thus provide a useful way for the Bank to offset temporary swings in the system's liquidity. Being at the Bank's discretion, they are not like the 'borrowed reserves' concept of the US system and there is little if any general public knowledge about their terms and conditions.

The lack of public information about interest rates associated with dealings with the Reserve Bank is more widespread. Of the three safety valve mechanisms, only one involves the authorities in publicly quoting a rate – that being the Treasury note rediscount rate. Dealers' borrowings from the Reserve Bank are at undisclosed rates, and the cost of the use of float is reflected in the 'official' cash rate – the rate paid by dealers on borrowings from the market – and other money market rates. The rediscount rate is the only signal given by the authorities – and it is far from apparent at this stage as to what extent the authorities have led or followed the market. Generally it has been set so far above market rates as to inhibit significant recourse to discounting.

In other areas, though, the amount of information provided to financial markets has increased markedly. Daily estimates of the market's cash position, the outlook for the forthcoming week, annual projections of the pattern of government transactions, regular reviews of the Bank's operations over the previous quarter, and a higher profile education and information disseminating role by Bank officials and via the Bank's *Bulletin* are all relatively recent developments.

In implementing the new monetary policy, the authorities have had to deal simultaneously with the transition of the financial system from a regulated to deregulated environment in which traditional indicators may be of less relevance. Also, the Australian economy has been buffeted by external disturbances; specifically a 20 per cent worsening of the terms of trade in the mid-1980s, sudden recognition of a large and growing external debt position and losses of confidence in the $A as the current account of the balance of payments responded sluggishly to measures designed to rectify a massive current account deficit.

Bond rates have been sustained at historically high levels for most of the second half of the 1980s and combined with a tightening of fiscal policy and control of wages growth have brought about a slowing of domestic demand, in line with the objective of curing the current account problem. Achievement of debt management objectives as well, embracing initially large net issues and later net redemptions of securities, must be seen as a considerable plus for the new system.

Alternative institutional arrangements and operating procedures, which might have achieved the desired outcome and which might cope with future economic disturbances more efficiently, remain open for discussion. We have noted various suggestions for modifying the tender of government securities. It might be appropriate to consider conducting open market operations further out along the maturity spectrum given the increase in turnover at the ten-year mark noted earlier. Redemptions of securities and the expectation of a series of fiscal surpluses has raised questions about the liquidity of the remaining series on issue and whether open market operations will need to switch to Metzler-style purchases and sales of private bonds.[25] Monetary policy could also be implemented through the foreign exchange market in the form of unsterilized intervention (open market operations in foreign securities). Already the switch from indirect support of the exchange rate to direct intervention in the foreign exchange market begs the question of whether sterilized intervention (effectively an open market swap of domestic for foreign bonds) has a role as a useful policy tool, and whether unsterilized intervention has effects which differ from those of domestic market operations.

However, considering the extensive regulatory and institutional changes which have occurred during the 1980s, there is perhaps also something to be said for allowing participants, and especially observers, some respite from change until well into the next decade!

NOTES

1 A succinct overview of the structure of the public sector can be found in Reserve Bank of Australia (1979, 1978b) and a description of recent developments in spending, financing and taxation in INDECS (1986). It is worth noting here that the Australian financial year runs from 1 July to 30 June, hence the general use in the text below of end-June figures for stocks.
2 The history of the Australian Loan Council is examined by Boehm and Wade (1971) and Gilbert (1974). Data on public debt from the formation of the Loan Council to 1980 can be obtained from McAuley (1980).
3 Carew (1985), pp. 124–6 outlines these arrangements.
4 During 1985–86 $2.85 billion of the $4.04 billion increase in the $A value of this debt outstanding was due to exchange rate depreciation.
5 Juttner (1982).
6 M.J. Phillips (1983), p. 2.
7 Poole (1981).
8 Reserve Bank of Australia Bulletin, January 1987, p. 11.
9 Juttner (1982), Cohen and Scott-Kemmis (1982), Cohen (1983).
10 Information supplied by the Reserve Bank of Australia.
11 Reserve Bank of Australia, January 1987, pp. 13–14.
12 These factors were suggested by The Treasury (1985).
13 Negative gearing involves financing a property purchase by borrowing to

the extent that interest payments on these borrowings exceed rental income on the property. The absence of a capital gains tax made this particularly attractive as did the tax deductibility of nominal interest payments in an inflationary environment.

14 Other innovations of this genre included DIGGERS (discounted investment government guaranteed earnings return) and DRAGONS (discounted receipts of Australian government obligatory negotiable securities). A dingo is an Australian wild dog, while 'digger' is the old name for an Australian soldier (with origins in the gold rushes of the 1850s).

15 Davis and Lewis (1980) provide a survey.

16 A clear statement of this view can be found in Statement No 2, Budget Paper No 1, 1984, p. 63.

17 Dewald (1969), Purvis (1976), Poole (1981).

18 Lewis and Wallace (1973), Sharpe (1979).

19 See Polasek and Lewis (1985) and Hall (1985) for a review of these developments.

20 The use of a 'checklist' approach was first publicly articulated by the Governor of the Reserve Bank in mid-1985. The indicators checked 'include all the monetary aggregates; interest rates, the exchange rate; the external accounts; the current performance and outlook for the economy, including movements in asset prices, inflation, the outlook for inflation and market expectations about inflation' (Johnston 1985).

21 See Battellino and MacFarlane (1987) for an outline of this relationship in Australia and in a number of other countries.

22 The dealers are the conduit through which open market operations are conducted. They finance a book of short term (predominantly) government debt by loans from banks and the non-bank private sector.

23 For a fuller analysis of the process see Davis and Lewis (1987).

24 The 'cash' or 'official' rate is the rate paid by authorized dealers on client's loans outstanding.

25 These issues are discussed in Johnston (1988).

REFERENCES

Battellino, R. and MacFarlane, I.J. (1987) 'Open market operations – some international comparisons', *Reserve Bank Bulletin*, December.

Boehm, E.A. and Wade, P.B. (1971) 'The anatomy of Australia's public debt', *The Economic Record*, Vol. 47, No 119: 315–37.

Carew, E. (1985) *Fast Money 2*, Sydney: George Allen & Unwin.

Cohen, A.M. and Scott-Kemmis, L. (1981) 'Techniques for the marketing of public-sector debt instruments', *Australian Financial System Inquiry*, Part 4.

Coombs, H.C. (1960) '"Memoranda of evidence", in committee on the monetary system', in *Principal Memoranda of Evidence*, Vol. 1, London: HMSO.

Davis, K.T. and Lewis, M.K. (1980) *Monetary Policy in Australia*, Cheshire: Longman.

—— (1987) 'The development of the new monetary policy in Australia',

Conference on Pacific Basin, Monetary Policy, Federal Reserve Bank of San Francisco, September.

Dewals, W.G. (1969) 'Multiple expansion of bank deposits under Australian institutional conditions: comment', *Economic Record*, June.

Dotsey, M. (1987) 'Open market operations in Australia: a US perspective', *Reserve Bank of Australia Research Discussion Paper 8702*.

Gilbert, R.S. (1984) *The Future of the Australian Loan Council*, Research Monograph No 6, Canberra: Centre for Research on Federal Financial Relations, ANU.

Hall, M.J.B. (1985) 'Financial deregulation and monetary policy in Australia', *Banca Nazionale del Lavoro Quarterly Review*, September: 261–77.

Hill, M.R. (1981) 'Bond interest rates', in D.J.P. Juttner (ed.), *Interest Rates*, Cheshire: Longman.

—— (1985) 'Bond and money markets', in M.K. Lewis and R.H. Wallace (eds), *Australia's Financial Institutions and Markets*, Cheshire: Longman.

INDECS Economics (1986) *State of Play 4. The Australian Economy up to Date*, London: Allen & Unwin.

Johnston, R.A. (1984) 'Talk by the Governor', *Reserve Bank of Australia Bulletin*, June.

—— (1985) 'Monetary policy – the changing environment', *Reserve Bank of Australia Bulletin*, June.

—— (1988) 'Recent developments in government securities markets', *Reserve Bank of Australia Bulletin*, November.

Juttner, D.J. and Madden, G. (1982) 'Price-setting procedures for government securities-take-it-or-leave-it, auctions, tenders', *Working Paper 8205A, Centre for Studies in Money, Banking and Finance*, Macquarie University.

Lewis, M.K. and Wallace, R.H. (1973) 'Current issues of monetary policy in Australia', *The Bankers' Magazine*, October.

Lewis, M.K. (1988) 'Liquidity', Ch. II in J. Creedy (ed.), *Foundations of Economic Thought*, Oxford: Basil Blackwell.

MacFarlane, I.J. (1984) 'Methods of monetary control in Australia', *New Zealand Association of Economists Annual Conference*, August.

—— (1986) 'Open market operations since the float', *Reserve Bank of Australia Bulletin*, December.

Matthews, R.L. (ed.) (1982) *Public Sector Borrowing in Australia*, Canberra: Centre for Research on Federal Financial Relations, ANU.

McAuley, J.P. (1980) 'The structure of Australian public debt', *Research Monograph, No 34*, Canberra: Centre for Research on Federal Relations, ANU.

McLaughlin, P.A. (1985) 'Australia', in H. Mehran (ed.), *External Debt Management*, Washington: IMF.

Phillips, M.J. (1985) 'Monetary policy from the inside', *Reserve Bank of Australia Bulletin*, November.

Phillips, M.J., Carew, E. and Cohen, A. (1983) 'Papers on the treasury bond tender', *Macquarie University Centre for Studies in Money, Banking and Finance, Working Paper 83034*.

Polasek, M. and Lewis, M.K. (1985) 'Australia's transition from crawling peg to floating exchange rate', *Banca Nazionale del Lavaro Quarterly Review*, June.

Poole, W. (1981) 'Australian monetary policy: an outsider's view', *ANZAAS Congress*, Brisbane: 11–15 May.

Purvis, D.D. (1976) 'The role of the monetary base in Australia', *Australian Journal of Management*, April.

Reserve Bank of Australia (1979) 'Submission to The Committee of Inquiry into The Australian Financial System', *Occasional Paper, No 7.*

—— (1985a) 'The Reserve Bank's domestic market operations', *Reserve Bank of Australia Bulletin*, June.

—— (1985b) 'Government securities, the market for Treasury bonds', *Reserve Bank of Australia Bulletin*, February.

—— (1987a) 'Recent developments in the market for Treasury bonds', *Reserve Bank of Australia Bulletin*, January.

—— (1987b) 'Some aspects of the public sector in Australia', *Reserve Bank of Australia Bulletin*, April.

Roosa, R.V. (1956) *Federal Reserve Operations in the Money and Government Securities Markets*, Federal Reserve Bank of New York.

Sharpe, I.G. (1979) 'Australian money supply analysis – the relationship between the monetary base, secondary reserves and the money supply', *Journal of Banking and Finance*.

The Treasury (1985) 'Australia public debt sector external debt June 1980 to June 1985', *Treasury Round-Up*, December, Supplement.

Walsh, C. (1986) 'Federalism Australian-style: towards some new perspectives', *Research Paper No 86–1*, The Flinders University of S.A., forthcoming in H.G. Brennen, B. Grewel and P. Gruenewegan (eds), *Taxation and Fiscal Federalism: Essays in Honour of Russell Mathews*, Cambridge: Pergamon Press.

7 The bond market and the changing financial structure of Italy

Giuseppe Mauro

INTRODUCTION

The Italian financial system has experienced a period of significant transformation which not only reflects the changes which happened in other countries, but more importantly the peculiar characteristics of Italy's economy. These innovations have been boosted by several factors, the most important being inflation in the 1970s and the volatility of nominal rates of interest.

Another important source of innovation is related to the development of new technologies which led to a reduction in transaction costs and a weakening of official control over the lending activity of banks, a first step towards a future deregulation. This process has caused the introduction of new instruments and new intermediaries in the financial market and has influenced the demand and the supply of capital on the market, especially by enlarging the scope and nature of financial intermediation.[1] In particular, keener competition on the market for capital has had positive effects on the allocation of financial resources.

These new tendencies in the markets have led to a growth of 'securization' in the system, that is to the development of the markets for bonds and shares which, by using negotiable financial instruments, are going to receive an increasing share of savings which were previously handled by the bank system.

In Italy, the development of the monetary market can be considered as the starting point of this process of transformation. The reasons for the creation of a market for short-term financial investments are well known. The sharp increase in the budget deficit and the problems related to its coverage are the fundamental elements which explain the development of government borrowing instruments – BOT (Buoni Ordinari del Tesoro) and CCT (Certificati di Credito del Tesoro) – and to the updating of the methods of issue. These new instruments suit the preferences of the savers with respect to profitability, liquidity and risk.

This process began in the early 1970s when, due to the process of disintermediation of bank liabilities, the ownership of the BOT was no longer restricted to the Central Bank and the commercial banks, but expanded to include private investors. This has created a direct link between the Treasury and the public and has encouraged the creation of a new competitive market.

The introduction of the CCT caused a further innovation in public debt instruments, due to the new techniques of indexation, profitability and methods of issue. Because of their remarkable growth and direct allocation to the market, these instruments, along with the BOT, are the leading titles in the market and are considered to be the principal instruments for raising money by the Treasury (Ciampi 1985) and their return represents 'the rate around which clusters the returns of any other financial activity' (Gnesutta 1984).

The increase in public-sector borrowing requirements is the most important reason for the growth of longer-term bonds in recent years. Debt management has a direct influence overall on the financial market, since in Italy bonds are in practice the only kind of securities traded on the financial markets. This development, along with the creation of new intermediaries on the market, has been the watershed between the old financial structure based on a closed circle of 'intermediaries' and the new one which is 'market-oriented'.

The monetary policy pursued by Italian authorities and oriented to limit money financing of the public-sector deficit has given peculiar Italian characteristics to financial innovation, even if it has still caused the interest rates to grow in real terms in order to secure the allocation of the new bonds among the public.

This chapter is organized as follows; in the next section the evolution of the financial market in the 1970s is analysed. The laggard development of the market for capital caused the bank system to have a predominant role in the market. This peculiar structure of the financial market assists the use of a monetary policy based on the control of the CTI (Total Domestic Credit) as intermediate goal and on the imposition of administrative controls on the bank assets.

The next section highlights the implications which derive from a very high public-sector deficit and from the choices that the authorities have taken with respect to the non-money financing of the Treasury, which have meant that public expenditure was financed on conditions determined by the market.

The subsequent section explains and describes the development of the market for bonds. This has caused the market for bonds in Italy to be important only in public-sector bonds because of the size of public bonds issue. This has had important effects on the level and structure of interest rates, on the duration of loans and on the composition of the wealth of the personal sector.

The new techniques of issuing, the operational innovations and financial instruments are the other causes of the widening range of instruments in the financial market; the new structure of the market is significant both for the management of public debt and for creating a more stable equilibrium in the financial system.

Finally, the development of the markets for BOT and CCT can be viewed as an important instrument to introduce new types of bonds which have been already introduced in foreign markets. The presence of these instruments in the Italian market, though in a tentative way, is a significant index of the outgoing innovation process. This is the subject of the last section.

SOME RELEVANT ASPECTS OF THE PRE-EXISTING FINANCIAL SYSTEM

Up to the late 1970s the Italian financial structure was very simple. The shortage of institutional investors and the lack of an efficient market for capital and the insufficient number of financial instruments favoured an increasing role for intermediation. The banking system had an undisputed leadership since it was the principal channel of flow of funds from the personal sector to the firms and to the public sector.

The marked split between saving and investment had, in fact, increased the qualitative and quantitative functions of the financial intermediaries who sought to fill the gap between the requirements of the surplus units and the deficit ones.

If we look at the behaviour of the financial saving with respect to the GDP (Table 7.1) of the macrosectors of the economy, the sharp difference between the balance of the personal and the public sector one is clear. The characteristic is still important if we compare the Italian financial system with the one prevailing in the most developed countries.

The origin of intermediation by the banking system can be attributed to the high level of actual and expected inflation and to the variability of the interest rate. This factor has influenced the composition of the financial saving of the private sector, which

Table 7.1 Financial surpluses and deficits (as a percentage of GDP)

Year	*Household*	*Corporate sector*	*Public sector*	*Overseas sector*
1965	8.0	−0.6	−4.4	−3.5
1970	11.0	−5.3	−5.8	−0.8
1976	16.3	−10.1	−9.9	1.5
1977	15.4	−4.7	−8.7	−1.1
1978	16.8	−4.3	−10.2	−2.4
1979	15.7	−3.5	−10.0	−1.7
1980	13.5	−8.6	−9.8	2.4
1981	14.7	−7.0	−12.8	2.3
1982	15.7	−4.9	−14.0	1.5
1983	16.7	−4.7	−14.0	−0.2
1984	17.4	−4.7	−15.3	−0.8
1985	17.0	−5.6	−16.0	1.2

Source: Bank of Italy

largely goes into its most liquid component, the time deposit.

There are other important aspects of the system which are worth noting. The security market slumped in the 1970s due to the impact of capital losses and the behaviour of the monetary authorities who aimed at reducing the issues of short-term securities in order to achieve the desired level of aggregate demand for funds.[2] This aspect reflected the hypothesis that the lack of demand for bonds had been caused both by the decreasing rate of interest, with short-run rates greater than long-run rates, and the fact that this structure did not suit investors.

The negative return on long-term bonds had created expectations of further losses, speeding up the conversion of long-term financial assets into time deposits. Therefore the market for securities was characterized by uncertainty and variability and it was completely different from the model which prevailed in the 1960s. In that period the Central Bank had encouraged the demand for bonds by the public as a result of a stabilization policy with respect to the long-term interest rate which ensured a fixed positive return and so a reduction in the risk of capital losses, rather like 'leaning into the wind' in the UK.

The other important factor which should be taken into account was the marginal relevance of financing through share issues by firms due to the weakness of the stock market. This weakness stemmed from different factors. Investments were risky and gave poor returns due to the slump in firms' profits and to taxation. The other factor was the use of financing instruments, which were thought to be more convenient, especially given the unwillingness of existing shareholders to dilute their equity (and control) by new issues.

The possibility of having a firm grow without issuing new shares not only allowed the majority shareholders to control the firm but made irrelevant for the firm any change in the price-earnings ratio, or in Tobin's 'q'. On the other hand, the willingness of the banking system to finance firms (using their assets as a rationing criterion without bothering about liabilities) made the cost of credit to the firm independent of their liabilities-net capital ratio (Ministero del Tesoro 1982).

In short, the peculiarities of the Italian financial system before the sharp modifications occurred were:

a) absence of a direct link between personal sector and firms;
b) large liabilities of firms towards the banking system; and
c) a sharp reduction of the subscription of securities by the public which had a two-fold effect: increase in money financing by the Treasury and creation of 'double intermediation', that is the allocation of bonds through the banking system. In this circumstance the security market becomes an important link between banks and ICS (Institute for Special Credit – long-run credit) which causes an enlargement of the intermediation procedure.[3]

   personal sector → banks → ICS → firms

THE MONETARY POLICY

This peculiar configuration of the financial structure caused the monetary policy to be founded on two basic points: control of the CTI[4] as intermediate goal; and introduction of administrative controls on credit as instruments to achieve this goal.

Control of the CTI as intermediate goal

The choice of CTI as intermediate goal is justified by: uncertainty with respect to the behaviour of the economic units and the lags in the transmission of the monetary policy to the real sector of the economy (Caranza, Fazio). In this context it is worth noting the importance of the 'announcement effect' claimed by monetarists (Passacantando and Cotula 1984). They maintained that a monetary policy is more effective if it is announced before implementing it.

For Italy it is essential to control CTI as a result of the disequilibria which the Italian economy experienced after the first oil crisis when the increase of the balance of payments suggested that it was better to control CTI instead of the interest rate.

Introduction of administrative controls on credit

The control of CTI was pursued by administrative measures aiming to modify the volume and composition of the supply of bank credit. The obligation imposed on the banks to invest a proportion of their deposits in securities[5] was aimed at boosting the demand for long-run investments by the ICS when the demand for securities by the public was very low because of the volatility of interest rates and the high level of inflationary expectations.

The ceiling imposed on the expansion of credit through the banking system had an essentially selective characteristic; it was aimed at reducing the credit granted to the private sector in order to increase the supply for banking credit towards the public-sector bonds in order to limit the creation of new money and so create an artificial demand for securities, this phenomenon having the effect of lowering their rate of return.

However it is worth noting that the intermediate goal was expressed as the 'quantity of credit'.[6] The instruments usual administrative controls became ineffective when the environment for which they were designed changed and when they were applied for a long period. There is a consensus among the distortions that these mechanisms have produced (Arcelli 1983, Ciampi 1986).

First of all, the CTI is difficult to control because a large component of it is represented by the public sector borrowing requirements. This fact has meant that the goal in terms of quantity was never achieved in the years in which the control of the CTI was attempted.[7]

The restrictions imposed on the banking system[8] cause increasing costs on the distributional and operational efficiency of the banking system, because the reduction of competition among banks led to a structure of interest rates at which banks lent which does not reflect the behaviour of supply and demand.

Furthermore, the 'ceiling' favoured a higher degree of liquidity by increasing the demand for securities by the bank system, which in turn caused a higher degree of intermediation and a lower profitability of bonds. Due to the presence of BCT, the portfolio of banks was very liquid. This in turn allowed banks to cut down the primary liquidity requirements and so it augmented the bank multiplier (Camera dei Deputati 1984). The development of financial innovation in Italy is both another symptom and a cause of the decreasing effectiveness of these policies.

The limits we have mentioned above explain the modifications which have characterized Italy's financial system in recent years and the consequent modification of the monetary policy. The principal modifications are related to the use of indirect instruments of control and to the development of the market for Treasury securities. The goal in terms of growth of the monetary aggregates is pursued by the regulation of the money base and of M_2. On the other hand, changing the interest rate permitted the demand for financial assets by the public, especially public sector bonds, to satisfy Treasury funding requirements without excess liquidity.

THE EFFECTS OF PUBLIC-SECTOR DEBT ON THE RULING OF THE MONETARY POLICY

The development of the public-sector deficit in Italy dates from the 1970s and has been caused by the increase in social security payments and by the increase in other transfer payments to families and firms. These factors have widened the redistributive function of the state and represent a marked intervention in the allocation of resources which has sharply affected the growth of accumulation of the Italian economy.[9]

The increasing requirements and the increasing volume of public deficit and debt are shown in Tables 7.2 and 7.3, where the public debt/GDP ratio is represented. From this table it is possible to note how this ratio has been increasing from 1970 (44.2 per cent) to the 99.6 per cent in 1985 – a ratio which placed Italy first among the more-industrialized countries.

The deficit and the debt/GDP ratio have continued to grow since 1985. Some academic commentators see Italy in a perpetual debt trap.[10] Italy's budget deficit is incompatible with European Monetary Union. Drastic action will be necessary to eliminate it – perhaps on the lines of Poland's big bang in January 1990. This converted an even larger deficit into a surplus in not so dissimilar *economic* circumstances.

The increase in public debt in absolute value and as proportion of the GNP does not seem to be the unique cause of the hyperinflation and stagflation which characterized the Italian economy in the 1970s. A more plausible hypothesis is that Italy is facing a situation of a structural nature, that is a situation which does not depend on cyclical fluctuations of the economy but instead on 'irreversible increases in the

Table 7.2 Finance of the public sector deficit (in percentages)

	1970	*1975*	*1981*	*1982*	*1983*	*1984*	*1985*	*1986*[1]
Deficit	100.0	100.0	100.0	100.0	100.0	100.0	100.0	100.0
– of which in interest bearing form			51.3	53.5	53.4	60.4	51.9	
Composition								
– marketable securities	1.3	52.5	63.2	72.0	84.8	79.1	67.3[2]	93.2
– post office deposits and overseas holdings[3]	13.4	22.7	10.1	10.6	10.1	10.4	10.3	3.2
– money base	85.3	24.8	26.7	17.4	5.1	10.5	22.4	3.6
			As a percentage of GDP					
Deficit	5.1	13.1	13.3	15.4	16.3	15.5	17.9	
Marketable securities	—	6.9	8.5	11.1	13.9	12.3	12.1	
Post office deposits and overseas holdings	0.7	2.9	1.3	1.6	1.6	1.6	1.8	
Money base	4.4	3.3	3.5	2.7	0.8	1.6	4.0	

Source: Based on Bank of Italy data

Notes:
1 Provisional
2 Including accumulated interest
3 Including miscellaneous securities

Table 7.3 Growth of public sector debt

	1976	*1977*	*1980*	*1981*	*1982*	*1983*	*1984*	*1985*
Total debt (billion lire)	102.395	123.944	228.240	283.130	361.466	455.361	560.200	681.783
As percentage of GDP	65.4	65.2	67.4	70.5	76.8	84.4	91.1	99.6
	In percentages							
Marketable BOT	9.4	20.0	30.7	34.8	35.2	30.3	27.3	22.1
Medium- and long-term debt	16.0	20.1	21.7	19.7	22.4	32.9	37.1	43.2
Postal savings bank	15.7	15.5	14.5	12.6	10.9	9.7	8.9	8.7
State pension fund	16.5	11.5	7.7	6.5	6.5	6.4	6.8	5.3
Other internal debt	1.0	0.9	0.7	0.6	0.5	0.5	0.4	0.4
External debt	1.4	1.3	1.5	2.3	2.7	2.7	2.9	2.7
Indebtedness to Bank of Italy and official banks	40.0	30.7	23.2	23.5	21.8	17.5	16.6	17.6

Source: Bank of Italy

public expenditure/GNP ratio which found their roots a long time ago and have been increased in the recent past' (Camera dei Deputati 1984).

The need to reduce the effects of the deficit on the money base has caused the Central Bank to increase its efforts to sell public bonds (see Table 7.4). Since the late 1970s and especially in the early 1980s, the public sector borrowing requirements have been satisfied by selling bonds on the market. In the first nine months of 1986 more than 90 per cent of the public sector borrowing requirements was financed by securities sold directly on the market and only 2.6 per cent by increasing the money base.

No doubt, the shift towards financing by market-oriented means has been caused by the inadequacy of the CTI as a goal and by the inefficiency of the administrative controls when used to pursue monetary policy. More precisely, an effective monetary policy should be independent of the size of the public sector borrowing requirement and should limit its inflationary effects. There has been a long debate on the financing policies pursued by the Treasury.[12]

Some authors see in the choices adopted by the authorities the sign of a radical change in strategic behaviour, which has been pursued by the passage from money-financing to capital-market financing. In the latter case, the high level of interest rates which is necessary to increase the private demand for securities can generate two main consequences for:

a) the budget of the public sector (it can cause the deficit to grow because of the increasing service charges faced by the Treasury);
b) crowding out of firms; and
c) the personal sector.

Furthermore, in the long run, the capacity of the market to allocate new bond issues can be less effective and cause a possible instability in the financial system. Another criticism of this method of financing originates from the positive effect that this way of financing has on the General Index of Prices. In this case, however, it is worth noting that financing the deficit with money has direct consequences on inflation while financing it with bonds has only a measurement effect through interest rates (compare this with the debate about mortgage rates in the UK in 1989–90).

The increasing bond financing by the Treasury highlights the influence that the government of public debt has on the whole financial system. Data (Tables 7.4 and 7.5) show how the whole security market is dominated by the public bond market. In effect, the new

Table 7.4 Net issues of public sector securities by category (in percentages)

Borrower	*1976*	*1977*	*1978*	*1979*	*1980*	*1981*	*1982*	*1983*	*1984*	*1985*
Public sector	68.2	78.1	81.8	78.9	80.0	83.2	81.6	89.0	92.0	92.8
BOT	49.2	18.7	18.8	40.6	86.6	68.1	47.3	12.2	11.7	12.6
CCT	—	21.3	30.8	42.1	9.1	5.7	39.7	73.2	71.5	74.9
Other	19.0	38.1	32.2	−3.8	−15.7	9.4	−5.4	3.6	8.8	5.3
Special credit institutes	25.9	17.2	15.2	19.2	19.2	15.2	11.8	8.4	5.4	5.0
Public corporations	5.9	4.7	3.0	1.9	0.8	1.6	6.6	2.6	2.6	2.2
Total	100.0	100.0	100.0	100.0	100.0	100.0	100.0	100.0	100.0	100.0
As a percentage of GDP	10.2	13.5	14.1	9.0	8.7	12.3	14.6	16.9	12.9	15.3
Investor										
Domestic and foreign	15.8	16.5	29.6	48.8	48.9	61.4	35.1	59.7	82.3	53.2
Bank of Italy	52.0	−10.8	6.9	−12.7	−0.7	12.1	6.0	4.6	−2.4	16.6
Credit agencies	32.0	90.2	59.4	55.6	43.0	18.7	48.5	27.9	10.3	13.6
Other intermediaries[1]	0.2	4.1	4.1	8.3	8.8	7.8	10.4	7.8	9.8	16.6[2]

Source: Based on Bank of Italy data

Notes:
1 Special credit institute, insurance companies, pension funds.
2 Figure affected by treatment of local authority investment.

Table 7.5 Total outstanding of public sector debt by category (in percentages)

Borrower	*1976*	*1977*	*1978*	*1979*	*1980*	*1981*	*1982*	*1983*	*1984*	*1985*
Public sector	55.3	59.7	63.5	65.1	66.8	69.9	72.2	75.7	78.2	81.0
BOT	25.1	23.4	22.2	24.4	32.3	38.6	40.3	34.3	30.8	27.3
CCT	—	3.9	8.8	12.8	12.3	11.2	17.0	28.8	35.4	41.4
Other	30.2	32.4	32.5	27.9	22.2	20.1	14.9	12.6	12.0	12.3
Special credit institutes	35.0	31.7	28.8	27.8	26.9	24.9	22.3	19.4	17.3	14.9
Public corporations	9.7	8.6	7.7	7.1	6.3	5.2	5.5	4.9	4.5	4.1
Total	100.0	100.0	100.0	100.0	100.0	100.0	100.0	100.0	100.0	100.0
As a percentage of GDP	70.6	73.5	77.8	73.3	67.4	69.3	74.0	81.6	84.6	93.1
Investor										
Domestic and foreign	18.6	18.0	20.2	24.1	27.5	33.8	33.9	39.4	45.9	47.3
Bank of Italy	31.4	23.6	20.4	16.1	13.7	14.2	12.5	10.7	8.6	9.9
Credit agencies	46.0	54.3	55.4	55.3	53.6	46.4	46.7	42.8	37.8	33.4
Other intermediaries	4.0	3.2	4.0	4.5	5.2	5.6	6.9	7.1	7.7	9.4

Source: Based on Bank of Italy data

issue of public bonds are around 93 per cent of overall issues, while in terms of total number of securities there is an increase from 55 per cent in 1976 to 81 per cent in 1985. Securities issued by private companies are as before a minor part of the Italian financial markets.

The issue of bonds by private firms is limited by an unfavourable tax regime (in spite of the 1974 reform) and by the keener competition of the Treasury both with respect to interest rates and to the favourable credit conditions offered by the ICS. In short, the evolution of the structure of public debt in Italy seems to have had the following characteristics:

a) increase in the proportion of marketable securities as a proportion of the total PSBR (65.3 per cent in 1985) compared with 25.4 per cent in 1976 (Table 7.4);
b) reduction of the quantity of public debt owned by the Central Bank (from 40 per cent to 17.6 per cent);
c) the marginal importance of the debt owned by foreigners;
d) shrinking of the average maturity of the debt from 6.5 years in 1970 to 1.2 years in 1982.

Only in the last few years has a reduction in the uncertainty, along with a greater diversification of issues allowed an increase in the maturity of the newly issued securities.[15] As a result the cost of the debt is now slightly falling.

THE EVOLUTION OF THE MARKET FOR PUBLIC BONDS

The market for BOT

We have already pointed out that the bond market in Italy consists largely of public bonds and its development is based on the needs for financing and desired structure of the public debt.

The extension of the range of bonds offered on the market and the evolution of techniques of issue are not only a symptom of the period of evolution in our financial system but reflect the need to secure non-monetary financing of the Treasury and give the Central Bank greater control over the monetary base.

The first important modification in the structure of the Italian financial system was the creation of a large market in short-term bonds issued by the Treasury[17] in response to the increasing PSBR and the acceleration of inflation. The development of this new market dates back to 1975[18] when the system of auctions was reformed. The aim of the reform was to create conditions to enable the market to be competitive and so ensure that the PSBR was financed at market rates.

The new law envisaged the enlargement of the categories of operators who could take part in the bond auctions, permitting, along with the banks, institutional investors and the Central Bank to take part in the auction on a competitive basis. The Central Bank was no longer obliged to be the residual purchaser. There are other aspects which are worth mentioning: each operator was allowed to present several bids at different prices and for different quantities (along with an estimation of his 'minimum requirements').

Those innovations were aimed at widening the use of BOT as an instrument of monetary policy with this new issue market having the leading role in determining the short run interest rates (Salvemini 1975).

On the other hand, allowing the Central Bank to participate in the auction offering a predetermined price was an instrument to avoid excessive fluctuations in the BOT revenue.

Initially, the increase in the supply of BOT was taken up by the banking system. In fact, even if the public has not deserted the market, the introduction of a ceiling on the expansion of bank credit would have led the banks to invest large amounts in public bonds (Table 7.6 and 7.7). Furthermore, the development of the market in BOT led the banks to increase the liquidity of their deposits with obvious implications on the management of the monetary policy and on the reaction of banks to variations in interest rates (Cottarelli, Cotula, Pittaluga 1985).

This tendency was reversed in the subsequent years when a process of disintermediation was the result of the change of policy by the authorities. In this period the proportion of BOT bought by the personal sector and firms experienced a sharp increase and it reached about 70 per cent of the total of bonds in circulation.

This second stage determined the creation of a wide and articulated monetary market because the decrease in the hyperintermediation is accompanied by a marked rise in transactions in the respective markets. The magnitude of the differential between the return on BOT and the lending rate[19] and the high tax rate on the time-deposit interest rate are the principal determinants of the increase in private-sector preferences for short bonds. Both these factors were consequences of the goal of limiting money-financing of the PSBR. This aspect is in turn related to the desire of the Central Bank to acquire a greater autonomy in its relations with the Treasury.

The competition of public bonds could not be met by banks, given the restrictions imposed on the banking system and their liability management policy. Moreover, the tax system discriminated against

Table 7.6 Distribution of public sector debt (in percentages)

	1976	*1977*	*1978*	*1979*	*1980*	*1981*	*1982*	*1983*	*1984*	*1985*
BOT	14.4	25.4	26.1	24.0	29.9	30.9	33.5	26.6	22.6	12.9
CCT	33.5	5.8	9.8	14.3	11.2	12.0	16.7	30.2	35.7	46.6
Debt to special credit institutions	52.3	41.6	37.9	37.4	37.4	38.6	33.3	30.0	29.7	28.4
Other medium- and long-term debt	17.6	17.3	17.7	16.6	14.4	11.9	9.8	7.8	7.1	7.9
Other (see Table 7.3)	12.2	9.9	8.5	7.7	7.1	6.6	6.7	5.4	4.9	4.2
Total	100.0	100.0	100.0	100.0	100.0	100.0	100.0	100.0	100.0	100.0
Frozen BOT/Deposits	5.2	11.3	12.0	10.6	13.2	13.4	15.5	12.9	10.2	5.6

Source: Based on Bank of Italy data

Table 7.7 Interest rates on various securities (percentage value)

	1979	*1980*	*1981*	*1982*	*1983*	*1984*	*1985*
Bank deposits	10.2	11.8	13.9	15.0	14.2	12.9	11.7
BOT (6 months)	12.1	16.0	19.8	19.4	17.8	15.3	13.7
CCT	14.0	17.3	20.2	20.8	19.8	16.9	14.6
Treasury bills	13.1	15.2	19.4	20.2	18.3	15.6	13.7
Special credit institution securities	13.6	15.3	19.6	20.9	18.3	15.2	15.2
Public and private corporate bonds	14.1	16.1	20.5	20.8	18.1	15.0	13.0

Source: Bank of Italy

banks.[20] This caused an increase in the elasticity of the demand for money with respect to the interest rate paid on public bonds.[21] The turning point in the process of strengthening the monetary instruments of control was the so-called divorce between the Treasury and the Central Bank in July 1981, i.e. the abolition of the agreement by which the Central Bank was committed to buy any BOT which was not allocated by the monthly auction. In consequence, it has been possible to avoid increasing the money base to finance the Treasury requirements, despite a rising and unpredictable public deficit.[22]

The new mechanism gives a greater autonomy to the Central Bank in the control of the monetary aggregates. The Treasury was more interested in raising interest rates so as to allocate the BOT in the pursuit of its public debt policy. In this context the role for the base price and the quota of allocation were modified.[23] The base price, which was before pre-determined and rather low, is now an 'exclusion price', that is, it represents the ceiling in the Treasury debt.[24]

The 'award rates' will no longer be determined by the Central Bank offer, but will represent market demand since they will be formed by the operators who took part in the auction. However, the Bank of Italy can act indirectly on the demand for BOT in order to regulate the overall liquidity of the system. These technical modifications of the auction and in the market structure are aimed at improving the flexibility of the system.

The introduction of fortnightly (instead of monthly) auctions is designed to make the management of the public debt more flexible, because it allows a more strict and updated link between the volume of the issues and the borrowing requirements of the Treasury. In practice, using this kind of auction it is possible to avoid some of the distortions which characterized the previous systems, as well as the formation of agents' expectations which did not match the authority preferences.

The fortnightly auction allows the spreading over time of large issues. Moreover, the decision to restrict the issue of shorter-term BOT to the banks makes these securities reserves for the banks. While these innovations in financial markets helped the Bank of Italy in some ways, they also reduced the impact of open market operations and minimized the diffusion of the effects of the intervention by confining variability to short-run securities variability in revenue. They offer to the authorities a fortnightly monitoring of market opinion.

The reform in the market for BOT is completed by the introduction of the competitive auction[25] as a different method of issuing securities. In the traditional method, the so-called marginal offer method, the market clearing price was paid by all agents. In the new system each agent is allowed to submit bids at different prices but has to pay this price so long as it is consistent with the goals of the monetary policy, which are free in practice.[26] This system introduces a sort of discriminating monopoly akin to that in the UK and USA.

It has been possible to reduce the service costs to the Treasury, because the non-competitive offers will be satisfied at the weighted average mean price, augmented eventually by a spread[27] (rather than at the market clearing price). In addition the new system requires agents to be skilled and so induces an increase in market efficiency. While a minimum price is essential when the marginal method is applied, this is unnecessary when the competitive method is applied.

The lack of a minimum price causes the third positive result, that is the decrease in uncertainty, faced by the Treasury, about the result of the auctions in relation to the volume of the issue.

The last important change in the market of short bonds reflects the institution of a consortium which guarantee the allocation of BOT. It consists of the engagements of the principal banks to underwrite a predetermined quantity of securities.[28]

The implications of this agreement have a two-fold nature and deal with the need to make the demand for BOT more reliable and to favour the growth of dealers in the monetary market. In the first case the short-run control on the money supply is favoured (and the independence of the Central Bank from the Treasury increases). In the second case banks can act as intermediaries between the Treasury and the Bank of Italy improving the effectiveness of monetary policy.

Indexed securities: the CCT

The most important change in the market for securities is the introduction of 'indexation', floating-rate securities, due to the variability of interest rates caused by inflation. Floating-rate securities are the most important response to uncertainty. This method is aimed to safeguard the investor from capital losses as well as revitalizing the market for long-term funds, by equating the actual and market returns.

The theoretical reason for introducing floating-rate securities is that inflation causes an unfavourable impact on financial markets and on the mechanisms of efficient allocation of resources. Several studies on this subject[29] have pointed out that an absence of these clauses will create distortions in the process of allocation of resources from the surplus sectors to the deficit ones; the management of public debt will be more difficult; the proportion of savings going into non-productive activities will increase and the authority will have less ability to control inflation.

As concerns Italy, the need to create a policy to safeguard financial savings from inflation by using indexation has been clearly pointed out by the Baffi Commission (Ministero del Tesoro 1981).

There are four different goals that can be pursued using indexation:

a) greater equity by safeguarding social groups with less power;
b) efficient allocation of resources, induced by a decreasing propensity to short-run financial investment;
c) economic growth; and
d) decreasing the rate of inflation through increasing the commodity supply growth rate and the weaker pressure on labour costs.

Among the three different forms of indexation – financial, real and currency – the one which has been widely used in Italy has been the financial one; the securities indexed using price indices are irrelevant in practice. In financial indexation the reference parameter is represented by other nominal interest rates ruling on the market.[30] In most cases the floating rate securities which have been issued have a variable return which is determined by the rate on BOT.[31]

The CCT can be considered a further innovation in the structure of the financial system and their diffusion is aimed at achieving a funding of public debt. The finance of the PSBR by a mixture of medium- and long-run instruments can avoid neither a certain variability in the service costs to the Treasury when the variability of rates is very high, nor a decrease in the cost of the debt, but it does decrease the risks of market instability caused by the need for frequent renewal of large quantities of public debt (Cotula 1984) and so it increases the effectiveness of monetary policy by the Central Bank.

CCT were first issued in July 1987 with a two-year maturity to promote the development of the market. In this initial stage the most important purchasers were banks, which tried to safeguard themselves against increases in interest rates. Only after the substantial modifications introduced in 1981 were a significant proportion of them bought by savers.

The reasons for this increased interest in CCT can be seen in the type of indexation used, which was based on the return on six-months BCT instead of on the weighted average of three-six-twelve-months and to the introduction of a spread on this rate (which can be made variable from a minimum of 0.3 per cent to a maximum of 1 per cent in relation to the duration).

The CCT are a convenient investment since they are very liquid (because of a well-developed stock exchange), elastic and transparent (due to the term of issue) and have a favourable fiscal treatment due to reduced administrative costs and tax exemption.

Since 1985 several modifications have been introduced in the rules governing the CCT. The most important are related to:

a) Their maturity. The latest issues have a ten-year maturity with the possibility of conversion, after one year, into bonds with a fixed rate and with five years' maturity.
b) The rate of interest. The reference parameter is now represented by the return on twelve month BOT and the period for the payment of interest is annual instead of biannual.
c) The mechanism of allocation. On their introduction CCT were allocated by public subscription at a single fixed price set in the original law establishing their existence. The actual allocation was effected by varying the quantity offered in proportion to the quantity demanded. The subscribing bank was allowed to subtract one lira from the issue price as compensation for the expenses incurred in allocating bonds among the private sector.

From 1985 a system of competitive auction has been applied to the CCT issues as well. (In this case the price is determined by the marginal bid.) This rule has been introduced to limit a situation of chronic excess demand for stock, due to the increase in the average term of the bonds to be issued.

Since with this new technique the issue price is determined by the auction and not by the issuing decree, the CCT no longer have a fixed initial price as before. At these auctions only banks and Central

Institutes for Credit are allowed to attend, thus excluding all other financial intermediaries.

Through this second stage the composition of the portfolio of the private agents has changed completely, and now it shows a mix of public bonds owned. The greater revenue they offer and their characteristics of liquidity and negotiability has led the personal sector to substitute medium- and long-floating-rate bonds for BOT. These are the reasons why the CCT market is now so well-developed and efficient.[32]

As a result of this rapid evolution, their proportion of the total of financial securities owned by the private sector has grown from 2.3 per cent in 1980 to 15 per cent in 1985 (Table 7.8), and they are now preferred by savers to the time deposits. According to Bank of Italy data around two-thirds of the net issues of public bonds are purchased by savers.

Trends begun in the previous years have moved much faster in recent years when a new range of public bonds have been issued. The Treasury has in fact issued, along with BOT and CCT, other kinds of floating rate bonds indexed to the price level or foreign currency values.[33] These new instruments allow the Treasury to match the requirements of a larger number of savers concerned with the optimal mix of their financial wealth.

These innovations are the CTE – Treasury certificates in CTE and the CTR (Real Treasury Certificates). The CTE, which appeared in 1982, are bonds in ECU with a variable maturity from seven to eight years, allocated on both the internal market and on the foreign market on various occasions. The mechanisms allow for a fixed revenue, while the amount of each coupon and the capital value of the bond is indexed to the exchange rate lira in terms of ECU. This kind of indexation offers the saver a great deal of protection against capital losses and variability in the income he receives from his investment.

On the other hand, however, it should be noted that the excessive weight of weak currencies in the unit of account could make savers require a high premium in order to underwrite the bonds and could also reduce the reliability of ECU as a way of preserving the real value of financial investments (Ministero del Tesoro 1981). Of course it is very hard to predict exchange rates of European currency with the ECU and so to evaluate their expected return.

As concerns the issue techniques, the CTE are allocated 'on the spot'. A bank consortium is formed for this purpose, which foreign banks are allowed to join, and directly underwrites the whole issue at

Table 7.8 Financial data for the private sector (end-period data on a consistent basis)[1]

	1975	*1976*	*1977*	*1978*	*1979*	*1980*	*1981*	*1982*	*1983*	*1984*	*1985*
M_2	84.1	84.5	85.7	84.3	82.7	80.4	74.8	74.1	68.9	64.5	60.6
of which bank deposits	67.5	68.4	70.3	69.3	67.6	66.0	61.0	60.5	56.8	52.9	49.3
BOT	0.2	1.6	3.1	3.9	5.9	9.3	13.3	13.2	13.3	13.9	13.5
Variable-rate CCT	—	—	0.6	1.5	2.2	2.3	2.7	4.2	8.3	11.5	15.0
Other medium- and long-term debt	3.1	3.0	2.6	3.4	3.2	2.4	2.5	1.3	2.3	2.8	2.0
Local authority debt	—	—	—	—	—	—	—	—	—	0.1	2.1
Other financial securities	12.6	10.9	8.0	6.9	6.0	5.6	6.7	7.2	7.2	7.2	6.8
Total	100.0	100.0	100.0	100.0	100.0	100.0	100.0	100.0	100.0	100.0	100.0

Source: Bank of Italy

Note: [1] net of borrowing.

par price, thus offering the Treasury a total guarantee of the whole allocation of the loan.[34]

The second innovation in the public debt policy is the issue of Treasury Certificates with a real indexation. They are issued at par, can be reimbursed after ten years and have a real interest rate of 2.5 per cent. Both the capital value and income are annually revised on the basis of the implicit GNP deflator – Accounts Data. Even though the issues have been for small amounts, because of the negative attitude of the Central Bank towards real bond issues,[35] the operation is significant because it has set a precedent.

The arguments in favour of introducing this innovation are mainly related to the need for diversification in financial savings, since this instrument safeguards the real purchasing power of invested capital, as well as because of the implications for monetary policy managements.

The last point is very important: the crucial point of the debate is related to an attempt to disrupt the vicious circle of the increase in the budget deficit caused by the payment of interest on the pre-existing debt. This result can clearly be achieved when there is a slowdown in inflation; in the opposite case there will still be a delay in the payment of the financial charges correlated with the debt.

Another positive aspect of these new types of bond is that the introduction of real floating-rate bonds can increase the demand for securities by foreigners so the inflow of capital from other countries can help finance the balance of payments.

THE OTHER SECURITIES

Along with public bonds,[36] the market for bonds in Italy consists of securities issued by firms and by the institutes for special credit even if, as we have previously highlighted, the extraordinary development of the market for public bonds has not been followed by a parallel development in the market for private bonds.

However, the innovations introduced by the Treasury have stimulated analogous initiatives by private agents, allowing the introduction of new instruments of great interest which have enlarged the range of securities on the market. It is possible, in principle to distinguish between four different types of securities: ordinary securities, floating rates securities, securities with special mechanisms, and convertible securities.

The market for fixed-rate securities has become less and less important with a sharp reduction in new issues during the years of inflation, but the other kind of securities have increased, though in a modest way.

The behaviour of ICS is worth mentioning in this context. Those intermediaries after the administrative commitments on the bank system were largely abolished, have been compelled to go on the market to raise the funds they need and so they have to face the competition of other issuing agents, especially the Treasury.

This fact has made vital the introduction of new instruments with special characteristics as regards their maturity and interest rates so as to suit the demand of savers in periods of greater economic and financial instability by safeguarding them from the risk of capital losses.

The direct allocation of new securities has reduced 'double intermediation'. In recent years the private funds have been more important than those from banks among the ICS' liabilities.

The market has been characterized by financial indexation (related, for example, to the prime rate or to the BOT revenue, and to the rate served on interbank deposits). The currency and real securities have had a marginal relevance, the reason probably being the complex mechanism which is difficult for the public to understand.

The development of such loans can be attributed to the parallel requirements of investors and issuing agents in response to the variability in the interest rates. From 1981 onwards, these securities have offered an actual return which was greater than on 'real' bonds; this effect being the result of the interest rate policy pursued by the monetary authority.

The other important innovations are concerned with the development of convertible securities and with the introduction of new instruments, such as the warrants, zero-coupon bonds, deep-discount bonds and drop-lock. The convertible securities are a hybrid instrument between securities and stocks where the holder is allowed to convert his securities into shares of the issuing firms or of other predetermined firms. Without examining the minutiae it is possible to point out that this instrument is extremely flexible and so offers great advantages both to the issuing firms and to the owner. The issuing firm can reduce the cost of capital while the owner can experience capital gains by converting the securities when the value of shares increases; when the value of shares is stable or decreasing, the security offers a fixed interest rate and the repayment of capital at maturity if the owner does not take advantage of the conversion. This security allows the owner to wait and see what happens on the market before converting the securities and allows him to convert his securities at the most favourable conditions.

In 1983 security warrants were introduced on the Italian financial market. In Italian experience warrants have taken various forms, from the possibility to buy shares issued by the borrowing company to the option of buying different types of securities, either issued or owned by the society. The buyer has the advantage of having different options open to him during the life of his securities. The advantage of the different alternatives will be determined by the ruling market conditions. The issuing firm has the advantage of raising cheaper funds and of enlarging its equity in the future.[37]

The other innovations copying the Eurobonds and North America markets are deep-discount securities, including those which do not pay any interest until maturity, called zero-coupon bonds. Those securities have two great advantages compared with the traditional ones: a limited tax liability when they are bought and a certainty of return. Since they are in practice fixed-rate securities because the difference between the issue price and the reimbursement price is just the revenue on the investment, these zero-coupon bonds are particularly useful when the interest rates are decreasing. Moreover, by using the coupon-stripping technique it is possible to separate the coupon from the security and negotiate the two parts separately.[38]

The drop-lock represents a sophisticated method of indexation. Drop-locks are securities with a variable interest rate which are convertible into securities serving a fixed rate of interest by using an automatic conversion clause. The conversion occurs when the index parameter falls below the trigger rate. These securities offer a form of guarantee against the variability of the interest rates.

Those innovations have made the security market thicker and more articulated, allowing some intermediaries to attract longer-term savings. However, the market is still in evolution and, being experimental, is still small. The same considerations apply to the so-called cash-back and purchase-fund clauses.

Table 7.9 offers a synthetic, though clear representation of the fact that the bond market is still dominated by public sector securities.

CONCLUSIONS

The management of public debt and the evolution of the security market are related phenomena. The financing requirements of the public sector are the dominant feature of the security market, which has acquired a greater articulation and thickness as a consequence of the innovations introduced by the Treasury to raise the money it has needed.

Table 7.9 Monetary and financial markets[1]

Instruments	*Issuers*					
			Financial intermediaries			
	Central and Local Government	*Non-financial firms*	*Banks*	*CCI*	*Others*	*Total*
Short and medium-term bills:						
– BOT	28.9	—	—	—	—	28.9
	(19.9)					(19.9)
– Bankers' acceptance	—	0.1	—	—	—	0.1
– CDs	—	—	1.4	4.2	—	5.6
				(4.2)		(4.2)
Fixed rate bonds	10.6	1.5	—	11.1	—	23.3
	(30.5)	(9.9)		(34.6)		(75.0)
Bonds with financial indexation:						
– CCT	33.0	—	—	—	—	33.0
– others	—	2.7	—	4.7	—	7.4
		(0.9)				(0.9)
Bonds with new features:						
– drop lock and deep discount bonds	—	—	—	0.1	—	0.1
– in ECU	0.7	—	—	—	—	0.7
– real indexation	0.2	—	—	—	—	0.2
– with warrant[2]	—	—	—	0.1	—	0.1
– others[3]	—	—	—	0.2	—	0.2

Unregulated debentures and investment funds	—	—	—	—	0.4	0.4
Total	73.4 (50.3)	4.3 (10.9)	1.4 —	20.5 (38.8)	0.4 —	100.0 (100.0)

Source: Caranza, C. and Cottarelli, C. (1986) 'Financial innovation in Italy: a lopsided process' (Temi di discussione) *Servizio studi della Banca d'Italia*, No 64, May

Notes:

1 Data refer to percentage shares over total debentures in circulation at the end of 1984; data ralative to 1975 are reported in brackets.

2 Warrant for the purchase of a fixed rate bond.

3 Drop lock, cash-back, mixed fixed and variable coupon, with advanced repayment clause etc.

The 1975 reform of the rules in the BOT auction was the first step towards the creation of a wider and more efficient market. Their characteristics of liquidity and short-run investment, along with increasing returns, have given public bonds an extraordinarily wide diffusion. This has helped to reduce the oligopolistic power of banks and so has created a new and more efficient financial market.

The new policy is pursued by introducing new types of loans, sometimes financially-indexed, like the CCT. The indexation mechanisms have been introduced to pursue two different goals:

a) as an incentive towards the investment in long-run bonds by the public; and
b) to increase the average life of public bonds in order to avoid the instability created by frequent issues of large amount of debt.

The development of the market for public bonds and the decrease in bank intermediation have induced the monetary authorities to impose less strict controls on the bank system, by gradually reducing the administrative restraint imposed on the system, and to pursue instead a policy of indirect controls. The abolition of the Central Bank engagement to buy unwanted securities issued by the Treasury and the modifications imposed on the issuing techniques are important contributions towards a more effective monetary policy. However, the market financing of public debt and the use of interest rates have caused a sharp increase in real interest rates, which in turn has increased the burden of the public debt (because of its increasing size and as a consequence of the introduction of variable interest securities).

Another important aspect to be taken into account is related to the problem of international transactions. As a consequence of the deregulation and the globalization of international transactions, capital is more mobile and more sensitive to the differential in the interest rate and to the exchange rates. The appealing revenue offered by securities has induced foreign investors to enter the Italian market, albeit in a most tentative way and with marginal relevance. This behaviour has been determined by a sort of financial protection in Italy which has made the inflow of foreign capitals very difficult if not impossible.

Three conclusions can be drawn:

a) first of all, the formation of a wide and articulated security market has been increased by the public sector intervention;
b) The innovations introduced by this sector have been copied by

other financial intermediaries and, in a less important measure, by the private firms; and

c) the public sector debt is the fundamental factor of destabilization, not only for its wide dimensions but also because the need to finance it does not allow a complete liberalization of the financial markets.

NOTES

1 On this subject, and more precisely on the possibility of modelling the financial innovation as a reaction to the public controls see Kane (1981: 135ff.). For a complete analysis of the financial innovation see the recent work by Podolski (1986).

2 This policy was suspended at the beginning of the 1970s since the differential between the domestic and the foreign rates favoured the outflow of capitals abroad.

3 The purchase of ICS liabilities by the bank system can be fully understood by considering the following data: in 1973–76 period the raising of funds by the ICS was assured by banks for 96 per cent of the total.

4 The definition of CTI is similar to the credit proxy in the USA.

5 The portfolio constraint had been introduced in 1973 and the ceiling on the growth of bank credit in 1974. The same instrument operated for almost ten years until July 1973 except for a short break from March to November 1975. In the recent past it has operated only for six months from January to June 1986.

6 The two-stage procedure has been criticized by several authors for theoretical reasons. See Friedman (1974, 1984) and Arcelli (1978) in this respect.

7 For the price/quantity debate see Poole (1970).

8 The administrative commitments create a hidden tax as has been evidenced and discussed by Bruni Monti Porta (1980) and by the Monti Commission (1982).

9 The system of regulation along with the capital flow controlling mechanism implements the theoretical model described in McKinnon and Mathieson (1981). This particular situation is called 'financial repression'.

10 Estimates, assuming invariant monetary and fiscal policies, have been made by Morcaldo–Salvemini (1984).

11 See Smith (1982) for this problem.

12 An example in this field is Valiani (1985).

13 See Spaventa (1984) and the Report to the Commission No. 5 (1984).

14 In the same line of thought are the works by Montesano (1981) and Franco–Mengarelli (1981).

15 The average public bonds life in 1985 was 3.5 years.

16 The problem has already been evidenced by Baffi, in 1974.

17 This aspect was highlighted by B.I.S. (1983). It is worth noting that the distinction between the capital and the monetary market in Italy is not very sharp. This is due to the fact that BOT, which are typical instruments of the money market, are used to accomplish public-sector borrowing

requirements and that the revenue on medium- and long-run bonds is linked to the revenue on BOT by their indexation. BOT have an implicit interest rate represented by the discount on the nominal price.

18 The issue procedures have been affected by several changes in the last period. Until 1962 the 'rubinetto' system was adopted. This system consists of fixing the price of issue of the titles and leaving the quantity floating, that is by issuing the exact quantity of titles needed by the market. This procedure controls the interest rate while the quantity is free to float.

The system of allocation through bid was introduced in 1962 in order to allow the Treasury to control the quantity of bonds issued. The bid is of a mixed type because while the minimum bid price is fixed and the quantity to allocate is fixed as well the award is effected at the highest rate offered by the participants to the auction. Furthermore the separation between the BOT suitable for legal bank reserve and for free investment was introduced.

19 This hypothesis has been confirmed by econometric estimates. See Zautzik in this respect.

20 This aspect was more important when the BOT were tax-free. Now this is no longer true since a decree has introduced 6.25 per cent taxation on revenue from interest on all bonds issued after September 1986. The rate was increased to 12.5 per cent in October 1987.

21 A more complete analysis of this phenomenon has been developed by Vaciago–Verga (1982). There are other studies which try to correlate the disintermediation with the problem of controlling the money base; thus the primary cause for disintermediation is seen to be the monetary policy (Bruni 1982). In the outgoing phase the decrease in the growth rate of bank deposits should also be attributed to the financial innovation process and thus to the introduction of new instruments and new intermediaries on the market. But the primary cause is still the monetary policy pursued.

22 'The public receipts–expenditure disequilibrium influences the money base creation because Bank of Italy underwrite bonds or purchase the residual quantity that the market does not demand. Any other intervention after this purchase is able only to partially reabsorb the liquidity excedence of the system. When the Treasury expenditure is concentrated in a limited time lapse, the short period control of bank reserves is very difficult' (Ciampi 1980).

23 The possibility of relying upon the interest rates variations 'does not mean that Bank of Italy accepts completely the monetarist view, by trying to control the money basis at any price in terms of interest variations on the market. There is still a conscious attention to the interest rate structure but the Bank of Italy renounces any aim to control the rate of interest at a price of not being able to control the money base' (Arcelli 1982).

24 After that the issues have been extended to the ICS and the central bank.

25 The competitive bid was introduced in May 1983 for three months BOT and was later extended to six months BOT as well.

26 For a deeper study on this subject see Monti–Onado (1984).

27 'The introduction of the competitive bid will allow an average issue rate less than the marginal issue rate in any circumstance; the cost for the Treasury will thus be decreasing, especially when there are important movements in the demands and in the offer' (Bank of Italy 1982).

28 The titles to be underwritten are related to the share that each bank

possesses on the deposit and BOT market with an underwriting equal to 100 per cent of this share.

29 Among the various authors who have studied the problem of indexation, it is worth noting the works by Friedman (1974) and Modigliani (1976).

30 The first indexed securities were issued by the ENEL in 1973.

31 This is against the guidelines expressed by the Baffi Commission. The advice was considered and extended by the Monti Commission (1982).

32 It is worth noting that the future demand of CCT will be completely satisfied, that is the Treasury has decided to match whatever demand there is for CCT. This mechanism would avoid the creation of sham demand for bonds in order to avoid rationing. In this last case each agent is compelled to exactly formulate his demand given the ruling issue conditions and the price.

33 In March 1987 the Treasury introduced on the market a new financial product called CTS (Discounted Treasury Certificates). The CTS are halfway between a floating rate security (indexed with half the interest rate on twelve months BOT) and a fixed revenue bond (with a discount on the price). These new titles have seven years maturity and have been created with the two-fold goal of reducing the interest rate and to decrease the cost of the debt borne by the Treasury in decreasing interest-rate periods.

34 Interest on CTE is served on an annual basis.

35 'We think that the indexation of public debt should not be pursued even if we think that the equity objective in respect to investors is very important. But this equity should be granted by stopping the waste of savings and not by promising revenues which will never mature on the dead plant of a chronic public deficit' (Bank of Italy 1983).

36 The range of bonds offered by the public sector is completed by the BTP (multiannual Treasury Bonds). Those are titles with a medium-long-term (two to nine years' maturity) and a fixed interest rate. Their importance among public bonds was marginal but now is going to increase. The revitalization of the long-run market allows economists to rely on the revenue curve, while the previous period was characterized by short-run securities. The recent development of the market for fixed securities can thus be considered an important signal of the modifications of the Italian financial system.

37 The first warrant bonds have been issued by the IMI. They entitle the owner to purchase fixed-interest securities previously issued by the same institute. In the recent past they have been issued by IRI. In this case the owner is allowed to buy shares of societies belonging to the group. The warrant system has also been applied to the CCT market. In this case the owner is entitled to buy different bonds at a fixed price and by paying a fixed premium.

38 The issue of these bonds have been marginal up to now and have been effected by the ICS's. Their diffusion is limited among the institutional investors.

39 Only in May 1987 the 15 per cent non-interest-bearing deposit on the purchase of foreign bonds was abolished. It discriminated against the purchase of foreign bonds by national investors. Commitment of deposit of these bonds in the banks is still in force, thus causing foreign bonds to be nominative.

REFERENCES

Arcelli, M. (1978) 'Obiettivi finali e obiettivi intermedi della politica monetaria', *Banche e Banchieri*, September. 1978.

—— (1982) 'Problemi monetari e creditizi', *Relazione al convegno: Politiche monetarie e creditizie, crescita del reddito nazionale e livelli di occupazione*, Trento: Cassa di Risparmio di Trento e Rovereto, pp. 25–37.

—— (1983) 'E' ancora attuale l'obiettivo intermedio del credito totale interno?', *Economia italiana*, No 3.

Baffi, P. (1974) 'Il risparmio in Italia, oggi', *Bancaria*, No 2, February.

Banca di Italia (1982) *Relazione annuale*, Roma, pp. 227–8.

—— (1983) *Relazione annuale*, Roma.

—— (1986) *Relazione annuale*, Roma.

B.I.S. (1983) *Relazione annuale*, Basilea, p. 62.

—— (1984) *Financial Innovation and Monetary Policy*, Basilea.

Bruni, F. (1982) 'La disintermediazione delle aziende di credito: una analisi macroeconomica di alcune sue cause', *Bancaria*, No 3, March.

Bruni, F., Monti, M. and Porta, A. (1980) 'Bank lending to the public sector: determinants, implications and outlook', *Giornale degli economisti e Annali de economia*, November–December.

Camera dei Deputati (1984) *L'indebitamento pubblico in Italia: evoluzione prospettive e problemi*, rapporto alla V Commissione, September.

Caranza, C. and Fazio, A. (1983) 'Methods of monetary control in Italy, 1974–1983', in D.R. Hogman (ed.) *The Political Economy of Monetary Policy: National and International Aspects*, Federal Reserve of Boston, Conference series No 26, pp. 1228–9.

Castellino, O. (1975) 'Crisi del reddito fisso ed emissione di titoli indicizzati', *Banche e Banchieri.*

Ciampi, C.A. (1980) 'Tra mercato e controlli: aspetti operativi della politica monetaria', *Bancaria*, No 12, December.

—— (1985) 'La politica creditizia e l'innovazione finanziaria', *Bollettino economico*, No 5, Roma: Banca d'Italia.

—— (1986) 'Rientro dell'inflazione e politica monetaria: l'esperienza italiana 1979–1985, *Bollettino economico* No 6, Roma: Banca d'Italia.

Cottarelli, C. and Cotula, F.G. (1985) 'Differenziazione dei tassi sui depositi: effetti sulla politica monetaria e sulla gestione delle banche', *Bancaria*, No 5, May.

Cotula, F. (1984) 'Innovazione finanziaria e controllo monetario', *Moneta e credito*, March, p. 5.

Franco, G. and Mengarelli, G.C. (1981) 'Debito pubblico, base monetaria e inflazione', *Bancaria*, No 11, November.

Friedman, B. (1977) 'The inefficiency of short-run monetary targets for monetary policy', *Brookings Paper on Economic Activity*, No 2.

—— (1984) 'The value of intermediate targets in implementing monetary policy', *Working Paper Series*, No 1487, November.

Friedman, M. (1974) 'Monetary correction. A proposal for escalator clauses to reduce the costs of ending inflation', *Occasional Papers No 41*, London: The Institute of Economic Affairs.

Gnesutta, C. (1984) ' "Divorzio" e "Merchant Banking": alla ricerca di una nuova struttura creditizia; Moneta e Economia nazionale', *Piemonte vivo ricerche.*

Gowland, D.H. (1986) 'Monetary policy in an age of structural change: the United Kingdom 1985–1986', *Quaderni dell'Istituto di Scienze Economiche dell'Universita G. D'Annunzio*, No 4.

Kane, E.J. (1981) 'Accelerating inflation, technological innovation and the decreasing effectiveness of banking regulation', *Journal of Finance*, May, p. 135.

McKinnon, R.I. and Mathieson, D.J. (1981) 'How to manage a repressed economy', *International Finance*, No. 39, December.

Ministero del Tesoro (1981) *La difesa del risparmio finanziario dall'inflazione*, Roma: Istituto Poligrafico e Zecca dello Stato.

—— (1982) *Il sistema creditizio e finanziario italiano*, Relazione della Commisione di studio istituita dal Ministero del Tesoro, Roma: Istituto Poligrafico e Zecca dello Stato.

Modigliani, F. (1976) 'Alcune implicazioni economiche dell'indicazzione delle attivita finanziarie con particolare riguardo ai mutui ipotecari', *Giornale degli economisti e Annali di Economia*, January–February.

Montesano, A. (1981) 'Inflazione e financiamento del deficit pubblico', *Bancaria*, No 11, November.

Monti, E. and Onado, M. (1984) *Il mercato monetario e finanziario in Italia*, Bologna: Il Mulino.

Morcaldo, G. and Salvemini, G. (1984) 'Il bilancio pubblico per il quinquennio 1984–1988: alcune simulazioni', *Temi di discussione*, No 30, July, Roma: Servizi Studi della Banca d'Italia.

Passacantando, F. (1981) 'Obiettivi, strumenti e indicatori della politica monetaria', in G. Vaciago (ed.) *Congiuntura e politica monetaria in Italia*, Bologna: Il Mulino.

Podolski, T.M. (1986) *Financial Innovation and the Money Supply*, Oxford: Blackwell.

Poole, W. (1970) 'Optimal choice of monetary policy instruments in a simple stochastic macromodel', *Quarterly Journal of Economics*, May.

Salvemini, M.T. (1975) 'Osservazioni sul mercato dei Buoni del Tesoro ordinari', *Moneta e Credito*, No 11, pp. 389–92.

Sarcinelli, M. (1981) 'Stagflation and financial structures in the seventies: the case of Italy', *Quaderni di Ricerche*, No 17, Roma: Ente Luigi Enaudi.

Smith, G. (1982) 'Monetarism, bondism and inflation', *Journal of Money, Credit and Banking*, vol. 14, No 2, May.

Spaventa, L. (1984) 'La crescita del debito pubblico in Italia: evoluzione, prospettive e problemi di politica economica', *Moneta e Credito*, No 147, September.

Vaciago, G. and Verga, G. (1982) 'Domanda di moneta e disintermediazione delle Banche', *Moneta e Credito*, No 137, March.

Valiani, R. (1985) 'Quali soluzioni al problema dell'accumulo del debito publico?', *Economia italiana*, No 1.

Zautzik, E.A. (1984) 'La domanda di BOT da parte del pubblico', *Temi di dicussione*, No 28, April, Roma: servizio studi della Banca d'italia.

Index

For Product Safety Concerns and Information please contact our EU representative GPSR@taylorandfrancis.com
Taylor & Francis Verlag GmbH, Kaufingerstraße 24, 80331 München, Germany

www.ingramcontent.com/pod-product-compliance
Lightning Source LLC
LaVergne TN
LVHW011131300926
849160LV00008B/598

* 9 7 8 0 4 1 5 8 5 4 8 7 0 *